About This Book

Why is this topic important?

The Internet, now ubiquitously present in our lives, gives us all access to a major part of human knowledge. With a simple click of a mouse we can obtain materials from libraries, museums, newspapers, television and radio programs, and universities and schools located all around the world. Formal e-learning is quickly becoming popular and thousands of courses offering instruction at many levels and in many areas are now available on the Internet. This book describes new techniques for distance learning, or e-learning, and for constructing knowledge from remote information sources.

What can you achieve with this book?

The main thesis of this book is that instructional design, or *instructional engineering*, particularly in an e-learning context, must be based on knowledge engineering and is most effective when it employs graphic models representing the knowledge and competencies learners are to acquire. Furthermore, this book demonstrates why instructional engineering needs to move beyond information management to become knowledge management. This book will revolutionize your thinking, showing you effective new approaches to e-learning methodologies.

How is this book organized?

The eight chapters in this book take you from theory to practice. Chapter One defines the forthcoming context in which all training will take place, the knowledge society and economy. Chapter Two describes the virtual learning center and the instructional engineering questions that occur in this environment. Chapter Three discusses the foundations of instructional engineering in scientific instructional design, software engineering, and knowledge engineering. Chapter Four introduces a specific instructional engineering method based on knowledge representation, and Chapter Five introduces a Web-based support system for that method. Chapters Six, Seven, and Eight present case studies that illustrate how my colleagues and I used the instructional engineering theories and methods presented in this book to construct e-learning courses for three diverse groups of learners: university students, professionals seeking continuing education, and corporate employees requiring highly specific training. Finally, the Conclusion offers the reader insights into the challenges that await instructional engineering in our rapidly evolving knowledge society.

About Pfeiffer

Pfeiffer serves the professional development and hands-on resource needs of training and human resource practitioners and gives them products to do their jobs better. We deliver proven ideas and solutions from experts in HR development and HR management, and we offer effective and customizable tools to improve workplace performance. From novice to seasoned professional, Pfeiffer is the source you can trust to make yourself and your organization more successful.

Essential Knowledge Pfeiffer produces insightful, practical, and comprehensive materials on topics that matter the most to training and HR professionals. Our Essential Knowledge resources translate the expertise of seasoned professionals into practical, how-to guidance on critical workplace issues and problems. These resources are supported by case studies, worksheets, and job aids and are frequently supplemented with CD-ROMs, websites, and other means of making the content easier to read, understand, and use.

Essential Tools Pfeiffer's Essential Tools resources save time and expense by offering proven, ready-to-use materials—including exercises, activities, games, instruments, and assessments—for use during a training or team-learning event. These resources are frequently offered in looseleaf or CD-ROM format to facilitate copying and customization of the material.

Pfeiffer also recognizes the remarkable power of new technologies in expanding the reach and effectiveness of training. While e-hype has often created whizbang solutions in search of a problem, we are dedicated to bringing convenience and enhancements to proven training solutions. All our e-tools comply with rigorous functionality standards. The most appropriate technology wrapped around essential content yields the perfect solution for today's on-the-go trainers and human resource professionals.

Pfeiffer
www.pfeiffer.com   *Essential resources for training and HR professionals*

ABOUT THE INSTRUCTIONAL TECHNOLOGY AND TRAINING SERIES

This comprehensive series responds to the rapidly changing training field by focusing on all forms of instructional and training technology—from the well-known to the emerging and state-of-the-art approaches. These books take a broad view of technology, which is viewed as systematized, practical knowledge that improves productivity. For many, such knowledge is typically equated with computer applications; however, we see it as also encompassing other nonmechanical strategies such as systematic design processes or new tactics for working with individuals and groups of learners.

The series is also based upon a recognition that the people working in the training community are a diverse group. They have a wide range of professional experience, expertise, and interests. Consequently, this series is dedicated to two distinct goals: helping those new to technology and training become familiar with basic principles and techniques, and helping those seasoned in the training field become familiar with cutting-edge practices. The books for both groups are rooted in solid research, but are still designed to help readers readily apply what they learn.

The Instructional Technology and Training Series is directed to persons working in many roles, including trainers and training managers, business leaders, instructional designers, instructional facilitators, and consultants. These books are also geared for practitioners who want to know how to apply technology to training and learning in practical, results-driven ways. Experts and leaders in the field who need to explore the more advanced, high-level practices that respond to the growing pressures and complexities of today's training environment will find indispensable tools and techniques in this groundbreaking series of books.

Rita C. Richey   Kent L. Gustafson
William J. Rothwell   M. David Merrill
Timothy W. Spannaus   Allison Rossett

Series Editors   *Advisory Board*

OTHER INSTRUCTIONAL TECHNOLOGY AND TRAINING SERIES TITLES

Confirmative Evaluation:
Practical Strategies for Valuing Continuous Improvement
 Joan Conway Dessinger and James L. Moseley

Learning to Solve Problems:
An Instructional Design Guide
 David H. Jonassen

Instructional Engineering in Networked Environments

GILBERT PAQUETTE

Pfeiffer

A Wiley Imprint
www.pfeiffer.com

Published by Pfeiffer
An Imprint of Wiley
989 Market Street, San Francisco, CA 94103-1741   www.pfeiffer.com

For additional copies/bulk purchases of this book in the U.S. please contact 800-274-4434.

Pfeiffer books and products are available through most bookstores. To contact Pfeiffer directly call our
Customer Care Department within the U.S. at 800-274-4434, outside the U.S. at 317-572-3985,
fax 317-572-4002, or on-line at www.pfeiffer.com.

Pfeiffer also publishes its books in a variety of electronic formats. Some content that appears in print
may not be available in electronic books.

ISBN: 0-7879-6466-2

Library of Congress Cataloging-in-Publication Data

Paquette, Gilbert 1942-
Instructional engineering in networked environments / Gilbert
Paquette.
     p. cm.
Includes bibliographical references and index.
   ISBN 0-7879-6466-2
   1. Internet in education. 2. Education—Computer network resources.
3. Computer-assisted instruction. I. Title.
   TK5105.875.I57P33 2003
   371.33'4—dc22
2003018770

Acquiring Editor: Matthew Davis	Manufacturing Supervisor: Bill Matherly
Director of Development: Kathleen Dolan Davies	Editorial Assistant: Laura Reizman
Production Editor: Nina Kreiden	Illustrations: Lotus Art
Editor: Elspeth MacHattie	

Printed in the United States of America

Printing   10 9 8 7 6 5 4 3 2 1

To the memory of **ERIC BLEICHER**

CONTENTS

LIST OF FIGURES AND TABLES

Figures

Tables

FOR THE PAST SEVERAL DECADES instructors in the field of educational technology have focused on training instructional designers. A quick survey of graduate programs in this area indicates that the majority of the classes are geared toward instructional design from the viewpoint of learning psychology or from the viewpoint of using multimedia tools for the latest technological advances. Courses have emphasized a systematic approach to the development of instructional products usually consisting of various approaches to analysis, design, development, implementation, and evaluation. The assumption, especially at the master's degree level, is that the graduates of these programs will find jobs that require these newly acquired skills in developing instructional products.

The reality is that most instructional designers are not trained while enrolled in graduate programs labeled with some flavor of instructional technology. Many are instructional designers-by-assignment; meaning, they were recently recruited from among the professionals in a given field to develop a course. Some of these designers-by-assignment will complete short workshops in instructional design or technology tools. They are then considered prepared to develop instructional products.

Technology tools for putting information on the Internet or for developing other technology-based instructional products are getting easier and easier to use. Although graduates from instructional technology academic programs or workshops once had an edge because of their technical skills, they now possess technical skills that are becoming less and less important in creating some form of technology-based training. Too often the resulting instructional products teach very poorly or do not teach at all.

To date, most of these technology development tools have focused on the technical skills required to implement a given technology, for example, to create a Web site. Very few of these tools have focused on selecting what to teach, structuring the subject matter content, sequencing the subject matter content, presenting the content, or providing practice in skills related to the content. Because these technology-facilitating tools are available, almost everyone nowadays considers him- or herself an instructional designer. Educational technologists are in the same position that computer scientists found themselves a couple of decades ago. As computer application programs become easier and easier to use, the need for formal courses to teach these skills became less and less important. In the same way that applications to create technology-based training become easier and easier to use, formal training in the use of these applications is becoming less and less important.

Those in the field of computer science recognized early on that their role was not to teach computer literacy but to study the nature of computation. They focused their attention on the underlying principles that comprise a computation machine. In a like manner, teachers of instructional technology will eventually abandon the role of training instructional designers to use instructional applications and turn their attention to the underlying principles of instruction. They will begin to focus on how these underlying principles affect instruction and how they should affect learning. They will began to develop tools, not just for making the development of a particular technology easier, but more important how to determine the knowledge and skill to be taught, how to structure the knowledge and skill to be taught, and how to effectively and efficiently represent this knowledge and skill in databases that can be effectively used by computational devices for the purposes of instruction. They will develop instructional algorithms that can be represented in computer programs and used over and over again like the programs underlying word processors, spreadsheets, and graphic applications.

Instructional Engineering in Networked Environments represents an important contribution to this new role for instructional technology. Dr. Paquette and his associates have diligently studied the complex issues surrounding knowledge acquisition, knowledge structure, and knowledge representation. Their work is an outstanding example of the kind of thoughtful principles and resulting tools that are required for the next generation of instructional technologists.

This work is not just another tool for developing some form of technology. Rather, it is a carefully researched set of principles for knowledge acquisition, structure, and representation. These principles have been captured in a wonderful conceptual tool that enables the new breed of instructional technologists (telelearning systems engineers) to efficiently and effectively develop instructional products that are founded in solid principles of instruction.

In this book Professor Paquette provides one of the most sophisticated tools yet developed for a true technology of instructional engineering. All serious instructional designers will find that this work significantly improves the efficiency and effectiveness of their instructional product development efforts. Future instructional engineers will find that the principles taught and the tools described will provide a foundation for future developments in instructional engineering.

October 2003   *M. David Merrill*
                                                 Professor of Instructional Technology
                                                 Utah State University

ACKNOWLEDGMENTS

THE AUTHOR would like to thank the various teams of the LICEF Research Center of Télé-université who contributed to the emergence and the consolidation of the ideas presented throughout this book.

More particularly, I wish to acknowledge the contributions of Claire Aubin, who was the first to suggest the creation of an instructional engineering workbench and who, with Françoise Crevier, has contributed to several concepts important to the instructional engineering method discussed here; of Eric Bleicher, who is the main designer of the MOT and MOT+, tools, which produced an enormous step forward in building the method; and of Ioan Rosca, who is the main architect of the ADISA support system for MISA and who coordinated most of its data-processing development.

I also wish to acknowledge the support I received at the onset of this project from Jacqueline Bourdeau, Diane Ruelland, Chantal Paquin, and Michel Léonard. Michel provided constant support from the beginning and continues to do so. He is also responsible for most of the training sessions offered on the instructional engineering method. Ileana de la Teja, Andrée Longpré, Karen Lundgren, and Ioan Rosca have made contributions to the most recent versions of the method. Josiane Basque, Sylvie Doré, and Lise Damphousse have produced a master's-level course at Télé-université using one of the versions of the method.

Finally, I wish to acknowledge the support of the organizations who financed various versions of the method and its tools: the *DMR Group* and the *Centre de recherche informatique de Montréal* (CRIM), the *Fonds de développement technologique du Québec* (FDT), the *Fonds de l'autoroute de l'information* (FAI), the *Social Sciences and Humanities Research Council* (SSHRC), the *Telelearning Network of Centers of Excellence* (TL-NCE), the Canadian *Defense Industrial Research Program* (DIRP), and the *Research Chair for Cognitive Telelearning Engineering,* to which I have recently been appointed.

INTRODUCTION

L IKE OUR OWN EPOCH, the century of Pericles, the Renaissance, and the Age of Enlightenment were marked by significant cultural and scientific revivals. However, the creativity and discoveries of these past ages affected only a small proportion of the world's population. The effects were nothing like the massive changes we are currently experiencing. Owing to the technological advances that have greatly increased our ability to communicate with and learn from each other, we are now witnessing a true cultural revolution that is sewing together the social fabrics of the many cultures on this planet. Governments are establishing technology policies for distance education, or *e-learning* (*electronic learning*), corporations are acting on the recognition that knowledge is their main capital, and individuals, informed by the mass media about the technological innovations succeeding one another at an accelerating pace, are hastening to acquire the information-processing tools considered essential to acquire knowledge.

The vast, irreversible movement leading us toward a knowledge society gives new importance to human learning. Learning is the process by which information, scattered or structured in various domains, becomes knowledge and skills, integrated into the intellect of an individual and allowing him or her to acquire and use new competencies. In e-learning and network distributed learning an individual builds knowledge from remote information sources. And this method of learning raises multiple instructional, technological, and economic issues.

The Internet brings much of the human knowledge contained as information in libraries, museums, newspapers, television and radio programming, research facilities, and universities and schools directly to us wherever we are. With all this information readily accessible and easily sortable into manageable Web documents and graphics, e-learning is becoming increasingly attractive to both instructors and learners, and thousands of courses are now available via the Internet. This book describes new techniques for designing e-learning and for building knowledge from remote information sources. I call the methodology that manages all these techniques *instructional engineering*.

The Value of Instructional Engineering

Instructional engineering is a means for going beyond information management to knowledge management. It is an essential support for our transition from an information society to a knowledge society. The ultimate goal of instructional engineering is to empower people with new competencies. The development of competencies, that is to say of the generic skills that people can apply to knowledge, constitutes the main goal of learning. Individuals' competencies, their capacities to acquire, process, and communicate their knowledge, constitute the most important assets of both the individuals themselves and their organizations.

The main thesis of this book, then, is that instructional engineering, particularly in a e-learning context, must be based on knowledge engineering and that graphic models of the processes involved in translating information to knowledge are an essential tool for instructional engineering. This book will open your thinking to new approaches to using e-learning methodologies.

The Contents of This Book

The eight chapters of *Instructional Engineering in Networked Environments* address, first, basic principles; second, a specific methodology; and third, a series of case studies. Chapter One presents a synthesis of the topics covered in the book. I define the context that the evolving knowledge society and economy present, I review the various technological models for e-learning to illustrate the diversity among the approaches, and I present the processes and tools used to build an e-learning environment, emphasizing the challenges offered by the interoperability of learning objects.

Chapter Two discusses virtual learning centers and the main instructional engineering questions that occur in such environments. A virtual learning center allows e-learning designers to integrate e-learning roles, operations, and resources. This chapter suggests the dimensions of the role of the instructional engineer.

Chapter Three presents the bases of instructional engineering, which I locate at the crossroads of scientific instructional design, software engineering, and knowledge engineering. It also introduces an approach to knowledge representation and the idea of target competencies for learners.

Chapter Four offers the main concepts, processes, and operational principles of an *instructional engineering method,* MISA, that employs graphic representations of knowledge.

Chapter Five is devoted to the functions of an instructional engineering support system accessible on the Web. This workbench supports design teams as they use MISA and create learning events and build virtual learning centers.

Chapters Six, Seven, and Eight present practical instructional engineering case studies. These applications of instructional engineering involving MISA and the virtual learning center concept were carried out between 1999 and 2001 in three distance training contexts: a university course, the continuing education of members of three corporations of professionals, and a training session in a corporation.

The final section of this book encourages the reader to evaluate the challenges that e-learning designers will encounter as the knowledge society becomes our everyday reality.

The Audience for This Book

This book is addressed mainly to training experts and to those who wish to better understand the challenges of technology-based learning so they can maker fuller use of the new technologies for training and teaching. In writing this book, I wanted to fill the gap that exists between the traditional methods of instructional design and the new possibilities offered by the new, extremely powerful training tools we now have at our disposal. We can, obviously, mimic the classroom environment by simply placing class materials (information) on a Web site, but to fully use the potential of information and communication technology (ICT), we must consider the myriad choices it opens to us for pedagogical strategies, media, communication resources, and delivery models. Up until now e-learning has been perceived as particular training contexts. In the future, due to the enormous training needs entailed by the knowledge society, the reverse seems likely to occur. The distributed classroom, connected to a network, will become a particular e-learning mode integrated, often in the same course, with various delivery models such as self-training on the Web, on-line teaching, communities of practices, and electronic performance support systems in the workplace.

Instructional engineering can enhance the quality of the courses, the programs, and the learning events we create now and in the rapidly approaching future. It can intervene at various levels for an entire organization or several similar organizations, for training programs, or for a single course or training session. The series of principles, procedures, and tasks it offers allows designers and teachers to make a structured identification of the knowledge and competencies to be learned, to produce instructional scenarios describing learning activities, to define the context of use and the structure of the training materials, and finally, to define the infrastructures, resources, and services necessary to deliver the course (or series of courses) and maintain its quality over time.

A failure to take this larger view before tackling the design of individual elements (the micro-design) can affect more than quality. For example, a study carried out by University of Ottawa researchers showed that the preparation of a four-hour e-learning course for the technicians of a large company required 1,156 hours of multimedia self-training development. That is, each hour of the finished course took 250 hours to prepare. This 1:250 ratio is recognized as the norm in the industry for sophisticated multimedia simulations. However, according to the same study, a course of the same duration for the same type of learners that had few multimedia sources of information but instead featured continuous interactions between the learner and the trainer on the Internet required 144 hours of preparation, a 1:30 ratio.[1] This comparison shows that time and effort can be considerably reduced and that a stronger pedagogical model may be produced as a result of a simple analysis of the possible delivery alternatives.

Preparing for the Future

In 1993, Kent Gustafson remarked that "while there have been moderate additions to the tool set and some changing of perspective from a behaviorist to a cognitive psychological orientation, to date they do not represent a fundamental change in the tool set. . . . The instructional design methodology is simply just too incomplete and too inadequate to tackle many of the challenges of the next decade and the next millennium."[2]

In the ten years since then, much effort has been devoted to micro-design and developing prototypes for computerized materials. This is certainly a necessary part of the response but it does not solve the more general problems of e-learning systems engineering. In addition, the actual e-learning authoring tools on the market rely on traditional methodology. Even when well adapted and useful in certain cases, these tools cannot cope with all the dimensions of developing and implementing e-learning environments.

The answer my colleagues and I have offered to the kinds of concerns expressed by Gustafson has been to develop the methodology presented here as an example of instructional engineering and its potential. I am convinced that e-learning and its engineering are the future of education. I also believe that knowledge modeling is the future of instructional engineering.

I hope the reader will gain from this book, regardless of the methods or tools he or she adopts thereafter, a deeper understanding of the concepts, processes, and principles that underlie the use of knowledge modeling in the field of e-learning systems engineering. I especially hope that this book will contribute to better use of the extraordinary means now at our disposal to learn, to help to learn, and to design new ways of learning. I wish you a fruitful reading and invite you to send your comments to my Web site, at www.licef.teluq.uquebec.ca/gp.

October 2003   Gilbert Paquette
Montreal, Quebec

Instructional Engineering in Networked Environments

1

The E-Learning Challenge

AT THE ONSET of this new millennium, in the advanced societies now called *postindustrial* societies, most employees are *knowledge professionals.* This fact tells us that the information available to us will grow exponentially in the future. This imminent growth will also be fueled by the 200 million Internet users who spend a substantial part of their time researching and producing new information on electronic networks; communicating and sharing without borders; and exchanging data, texts, pictures, and sounds ever more rapidly.

Given this massive flow of new information—a fruitful source for new knowledge—and the activities of knowledge workers that are modifying the very nature of work and creating an enormous need for information and for highly effective methods for turning that information into knowledge, we need to ask how long traditional training and educational models can continue to prevail.

To answer that question, this chapter discusses the developing knowledge society and the rapid increase of Internet technologies and considers the impact of these changes on training needs. It then presents an overview of

1

technology-driven, pedagogical (*techno-pedagogical*) models for e-learning, the processes that govern the development and management of an e-learning system, and the system actors and the technological resources that support them. The chapter concludes with a survey of the e-learning delivery tools and systems current at the time this book was written.

The Knowledge Society

A striking phenomenon associated with the development of the knowledge society is the shift that is occurring in the traditional education paradigm, as illustrated in Figure 1-1. The tradition in most educational institutions and in workplace training is that learning originates from a trainer or a professor who is the learner's main source of information and expertise. The professor or trainer prepares the course, selects the instructional materials and activities, and lectures and coaches the learners, who in turn solve problems and complete exercises, assignments, and projects.

Figure 1-1. An Education Paradigm Shift.

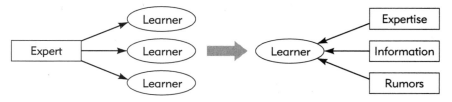

We are now witnessing a radical shift of this traditional paradigm. It began four decades ago with the ubiquitous arrival of television. Today, owing to the exponential growth of information and its availability to anyone anywhere on communication networks, everyone is becoming a lifelong learner.

Learners with easy access to what others know are exposed to many sources of information and expertise. They are also exposed to rumors and unreliable information. This means they must be able to select and integrate information from various sources in order to compose a coherent and useful synthesis for their work or social activities. In short, today's learners have to develop, with minimal help, abilities and knowledge superior to those of the past. They must select, process, and use the right information to communicate. Are we aware of the complexity of this task? Not only are learners faced with a rapidly increasing quantity of information and knowledge but they are also required to differentiate what is useful and valid from the not useful and inaccurate in that mass of available information. Traditional education does not train us to accomplish these tasks. Instead, as the Québec Council for Higher Education has recently stated (in light of the discussions held at many international conferences on education and learning since the beginning of the 1980s[1]): "Special attention must be given to superior cognitive capacities (aptitudes, action planning, reasoning and problem solving) and social abilities (autonomy, communication and collaboration capacities). These abilities are those sought by employers to take [into] account the impact of ICT [information and communication technologies] on the employment market."[2]

What we actually have today is not yet a knowledge society but an information society. We hope that it will become a real knowledge society. This can happen only if our education and training emphasizes the abilities that allow us to process intelligently the facts, data, and information we encounter both at work and in our daily lives. From a more general perspective, important social contradictions are developing: the globalization of the economy tends to reduce national, linguistic, and cultural diversity while centralizing power among large, private corporations; the gap continues to widen between the rich and the poor, between the educated and the uneducated, between those who master the new means of communication and those who do not have access to them. These complex problems offer major challenges. Learning models, methods, and tools must be improved. Before we can have a knowledge society we must have a knowledge revolution that results in the intelligent use and the mastery of learning technologies by the largest possible number of people.

Knowledge Management

Knowledge directly affects the competitiveness of corporations. It is not surprising that corporate managers are receptive when theoreticians stress the importance of managing their companies' knowledge. For example, a full decade ago Peter Drucker suggested that the future belongs to corporations who know how to strategically exploit their knowledge, claiming: "knowledge is now the decisive production factor."[3] This type of discourse has been rapidly embraced. A Delphi Group knowledge management study involving 500 organizations found that the percentage of these corporations that had started initiatives to manage knowledge within their organizations grew from 28 percent in 1997 to 51 percent in 1998, that is, in only one year.[4]

Figure 1-2 illustrates the knowledge management process in a corporation. Beyond the information cycle present in every organization, more and more often management has an increased interest in developing new processes that facilitate the transformation of information into knowledge. The new knowledge, skills, and competencies acquired by the staff allow the organiza-

---

Figure 1-2. The Knowledge Management Process.

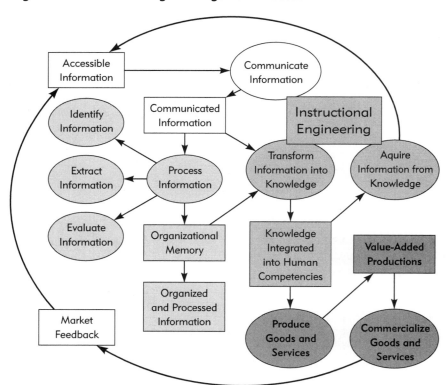

tion to improve the quality of its products and services, thus securing an advantageous position in a competitive market.

These new processes go well beyond the computer management of data or documents. They aim to secure the knowledge held by the organization's experts. The experts' knowledge is then documented, pooled, and reused by the other organization personnel through information, training, and performance support systems. Although such processes have always been informally present in organizations, the new awareness of their importance is leading organizations to reengineer their work processes using new technological tools. The result is improved, formal development of new knowledge, principles, methods, models, and strategies to deal with the competitive market. This new phenomenon, in contrast to the simple consultation of information in databases, puts much more emphasis on employee knowledge and competencies, because higher-level knowledge requires acquisition and maintenance processes that can be learned only through informal and formal training activities that are continuous, accessible, and effective.

Instructional engineering plays a crucial role in designing and delivering education and training that meets learners' new needs whether these learners are in school, a corporation, a department, or some other kind of organizational entity. Instructional engineering plays a crucial role. Instructional engineering is what designers do as they build and maintain global learning systems that focus on engaging learners in two main processes:

1. *Knowledge extraction,* the process of transforming the knowledge of an expert in a given field into structured information, which is subsequently made available to the whole organization

2. *Knowledge dissemination,* the process of transforming information into knowledge that is internalized by the learner as new competencies, typically ones useful to the learner's organization

Pedagogy and Technology

The use of new learning technologies such as educational software, multimedia, and the Internet is growing rapidly in both North America and Europe and even in developing countries.

Since the Internet and the new training technologies became widely available in the middle of the 1990s, e-learning has been growing rapidly. Network (Internet and intranet) and CD-ROM technologies are increasingly replacing more traditional training methods. In addition, most observers recognize that Internet and intranet training is tending to supplant multimedia education provided on CDs.

The world market for workplace e-learning was evaluated by many studies as being only $US 2 billion in 1999. According to Deloitte Consulting[5] and W. R. Hambrecht[6] independent studies, companies in all countries expect to increase their e-learning expenses from $US 3 billion in 2000 to $US 12.5 billion in 2003. This total could increase to $US 18 billion in 2005, according to the most recent estimate by IDC.[7] These estimates from various sources converge. The trends are constant, leading to a situation where e-learning would account for more than half of all kinds of workplace training.

In the public education sector, in universities and colleges as well as K-12, the same enormous growth is noted, as shown in Table 1-1.

Table 1-1. World Trends in E-Learning, by Sectors, in $US Billions.

	2001	*2003*	*2005*
Enterprises	3.5	7.0	21.0
Colleges and universities	2.0	7.0	15.0
K-12	1.5	6.0	12.0

Source: Giga Information Group (http://www.gigaweb.com/).

In the area of public education, where until recently instructional engineering and technological course delivery systems were seldom perceived as significant, universities are directing some energy toward e-learning and the new training technologies. In the United States, a recently published survey indicates that in 2000–01 over half of the postsecondary institutions offered distance courses.[8] From 1995 to 1998, the number of distance courses doubled in the United States, totaling 52,270 courses offered to 1.6 million students. On the international level the number of Internet courses offered is growing rapidly as well, creating new needs for design and delivery tools and methods in both public and private educational environments.

This new pattern recognizes the vital importance of training and also that today's training must do more than traditional training, as is suggested by several experts on organizational practice. For example, in his book *The Knowledge-Enabled Organization,* Daniel Tobin claims that the majority of current organizational training does not lead to measurable improvements. Rather than use traditional approaches centered on the transmission of information in a classroom, he recommends employing a new paradigm of continuous construction of knowledge and competencies.[9]

We must recognize the revolutionary potential of new educational technologies. In the past, education was centered on the expert, the master, sharing his or her knowledge or know-how with a great number of students. In contrast, newly implemented interactive resources place the learner at the center of the educational environment and greatly reduce the time devoted to lecturing activities. This invites the trainer to change roles, defining himself or herself as an instructional designer and, more generally, as a facilitator, a motivator, and a coach.

Through e-learning, educators and trainers are beginning to mobilize technologies for knowledge and higher-level skill acquisition—and not mainly for entertainment, as has become largely the case with television. We may yet hope that the interactive communication fostered by the Internet will be in contrast to the passivity fostered by television. In much e-learning, learning events centered on competencies to be acquired can be available at any time and at any place. Through these learning events individuals can immerse themselves in learning activities and even select personalized scenarios, thus developing their aptitudes to *learn how to learn.*

All this potential can be mastered and channeled only through the implementation of instructional principles that although well represented in theoretical writings have not been effectively available for educational practitioners until recently. Now the advantage of allowing the learner to construct knowledge is no longer a theory but a fact experienced by an increasingly large number of Internet users. With the ability to access and use multiple sources of information and expertise at any time and any place through television technology, CDs or DVDs, and Internet networks, the learner acquires knowledge in many ways. The educational potential of these multimedia technologies lies not only in the multisensory integration and interactivity they offer, but first and foremost in the education paradigm shift they represent, from the transfer of information by the instructor to the construction of knowledge by the learner.

The shift from traditional lectures to e-learning using the new training technologies requires a transition strategy, one that gives people and organizations time to adapt to the new methods and training tools. The best training is that which meets the knowledge management needs of the organization and of the learners. Here again instructional engineering techniques are essential, defining the most adequate technological models and the bridges that need to be built between the training of today and that of the future.

Network-Based Learning Models

The world of education is bubbling with techno-pedagogical ideas. With the extremely rapid growth in multimedia telecommunications, e-learning models are proliferating, as are development tools and delivery platforms.

The term *e-learning,* or *distance education,* now covers several very different techno-pedagogical realities, ranging from simple multimedia integrated into a traditional classroom to complex, interactive multimedia models that make learning available at any time and in any place. I have classified these teaching models under six paradigms: the high-tech classroom, the distributed classroom, hypermedia self-training, on-line training, the community of practice, and the performance support system. The following sections analyze their potentials and limits, examining a series of qualities every e-learning system should possess. I focus here on the "pure" models. The integration of these models into a more complex architecture is discussed in the following chapter.

High-Tech Classroom

The *high-tech classroom* is simply a traditional classroom where a number of technologies are permanently installed and used. These include sophisticated multimedia equipment, computers linked to a local or wide area network, and an electronic projector for presentations or Internet demonstrations. A videoconference system may be installed on classroom workstations. A bidirectional link may be provided so classroom presentations can be accessed by individuals outside the classroom (remotely located). In other words, the classroom is open to external information, but classroom offerings and that information are not necessarily distributed in several places.

These classrooms are often called *multimedia laboratories.* Now, as high-tech equipment spreads to many classrooms and other training locations, the term *electronic campus* is coming into vogue.

At some schools and institutes of higher education, advantageous financing plans encourage students to purchase notebook computers they can use in these classrooms, thus benefiting from the broadband networks and other equipment installed on the premises. Moreover, they can also use these computers as training tools outside the classroom.

Distributed Classroom

The *distributed classroom* is a virtual high-tech classroom, one spread over several distant locations.[10] These locations are equipped with a videoconferencing system and a variety of peripheral equipment connected to a computer: cameras, voice sensitive microphones, videocassette players, and CD or DVD readers. The learning events are presented live by a professor or trainer, who delivers a lecture using a variety of instruments. In this model the students and the instructor are all present at the same time in their different rooms, linked through telecommunications. The communication is mainly one-way, from the instructor to the learners, although the learners have access to ways to ask questions and communicate with others in other rooms. Also, if all the rooms are identically equipped, the learners may use the system for seminars in which they are invited to present to each other work they have produced for the course.

There are several varieties of distributed systems. For example, some deliver the presentations to each student's workstation rather than to a single screen viewed by all the participants present in the room, thus enhancing the interaction possibilities. Several universities and companies now use a distributed classroom system to deliver training off campus and in company offices spread throughout several countries.

Hypermedia Self-Training

Hypermedia self-training[11] favors individual learning. The term *hypermedia* refers to the hyperlinks that allow the learner to browse in a network of pages and other external resources viewable on the computer screen. The learner, working alone, accesses this network as prepared multimedia documents on the Internet, or on CD or DVD for audiovisual materials that require too much bandwidth to be viewed efficiently. The instructional material can then be entirely local (on a CD or downloaded on the workstation), on-line with audio or video streaming via the Internet, or a hybrid, part local and part on-line. Although some hypermedia material can be viewed only from one page to the next, the learner's progression through the contents of this network is typically not linear. Thus the student not only can progress at his or her own pace but also can follow a flexible course plan, using the hyperlinks that appear most relevant considering his or her current or target knowledge. Self-training entails the complete absence of tutoring by a trainer. Also, there is no imposed collaboration between learners. Hence there are no place or time constraints imposed by the training model.

Since the arrival of the Internet, thousands of hypermedia courses have been published on the Web, and this number continues to increase daily. The training portals maintained by educational organizations grant access to series of such courses and programs and also various support services that constitute the basic elements of a virtual campus (this topic is discussed in more detail in Chapter Two).

On-Line Training

On-line training[12] also uses the Internet, multiple media, and hyperlinks but in an extremely different way. It is managed by a trainer delivering presentations to a dispersed group of learners and coordinating their remote interactions, mostly in an asynchronous mode; that is, the participants are not expected to be present simultaneously. The learners can thus progress at their own pace, interact between themselves, and use the instructional materials between the stages defined by the instructor. During each stage, the pace of the activities and most of the content of the exchanges are managed by the instructor. He or she will allocate, for example, three weeks for a module, launch a discussion, suggest work to be done, and then act as an adviser and content expert until the following module.

In this model the main technological tools are those that can be used in an asynchronous mode: newsgroups, e-mail (for private communication between the learner and the professor, tutor, or trainer), and file transfers (for exchanging documents and evaluating assignments). This model has been used for at least fifteen years in such distance or open universities as the Télé-université du Québec and the British Open University and is increasingly being employed on university campuses all over the world, where it becomes a practical alternative to classroom education.

Community of Practice

Communities of practice[13] may use the same asynchronous communication tools as those used in the on-line teaching model and may also at times use tools for real-time communication, such as audio- or videoconferencing on a workstation or in a classroom. The main characteristic of this model is communication and discussion among the members of a group of specialists centered on a common task—for example, learning how to use training technologies or solve specific medical problems. There is no trainer as such but rather a facilitator. As a general rule, unlike the professor or trainer the facilitator has less information than the participants, but he or she has mastered techniques for managing fruitful exchanges between the participants. The participants learn by exchanging information (some of which they may not have had at the beginning of their work together), and they compare various practices through case studies. A document server allows them to enrich their common knowledge base. Using these tools, they can solve problems in teams or carry out projects through which they will acquire new knowledge or skills.

This model is particularly well adapted to continuing vocational education; it has been used, for example, by teachers, physicians, and engineers to increase their knowledge and improve their practice. This model has also been used in university distance learning programs in which, for example, a course module is presented as a workshop organized around a task to achieve or a practice to reinforce.

Performance Support System

Just like the community of practice, the electronic performance support system (EPSS)[14] is centered on a professional task. However, in this case the training is mainly individual. It occurs in close connection with professional activities: during the activity when the learner needs training to progress in the task, after the activity when the learner wants to delve deeper into questions generated by the task, or even before the activity if the learner foresees the need for additional training before starting a task. An EPSS is closely integrated with the computer system used on the premises of the organization offering this support to its people, and in particular with institutional databases. A manager or a content expert, and sometimes on-line computerized advisers, maintain various training modules and provide task assistance. The user can thus obtain just-in-time information about the tasks to be achieved. Training in this model is seen as information processing. These features make the EPSS a dynamic training environment that is increasingly popular in collaborative learning at workplaces and in knowledge management activities.

Summary of the Models

The six e-learning models may be summed up as follows:

Three models are trainer centered: the high-tech classroom, the distributed classroom, and on-line training. The remaining three models are mainly learner centered.

Two models, the high-tech and the distributed classrooms, are synchronous, requiring the simultaneous presence of the learner and the trainer in designated locations. The four other models are mainly asynchronous: the actors communicate between themselves or with the resources at the moment that is appropriate for them and from the location they select.

Two models, the hypermedia self-training and the performance support system, favor autonomous learning. The other models opt for communication and sometimes collaboration between learners.

Two models, the community of practice and the performance support system, are centered on the practice of a work task, or inspired by it. The other models tend to enable the processing of more general information.

Analysis of the Models

These models can be compared to each other in terms of the desirable characteristics suggested by the analysis of the new training contexts earlier in this chapter. Some of these characteristics pertain to flexibility, aiming to free learners (and trainers) from location and time constraints and also giving them more freedom in their use of instructional resources and their progression through the instructional activities. Other characteristics focus on the accessibility of local or global information, collaboration between learners, assistance from training agents, and the usability and ergonomics of the technological environment. Finally, some characteristics concern economics. They relate to the integration of work and training, the reusability of facilities, the maintenance or evolution of training environments, and finally, the relationship between training time and knowledge retention, to maximize training effectiveness.

Table 1-2 summarizes the characteristics associated with each model. A plus sign (+) indicates that a model is strong in a particular characteristic, and a minus sign (−) indicates a deficiency. These evaluations are more or less subjective; hence I invite you to perform your own evaluations after considering mine.

Table 1-2. Characteristics Analysis of Six Techno-Pedagogical Models.

Characteristics	*1*	*2*	*3*	*4*	*5*	*6*
			Model			
Frees users from location constraints	–	–	+	+	+	
Frees users from time constraints	–	–	+	+	+	+
Favors personalized learning	–	–	+		+	+
Access to local or global information	–	–	+	+	+	
Favors interactions between learners	–	–	–	+	+	
Offers training assistance	+	+	–	+	–	
Integrates user-friendly technologies	+	+				–
Favors work-training integration	–	–			+	+
Facilitates reengineering and reuse	+	+	–			–
Maximizes learning efficiency	–	–	+	+	+	+

Note: 1 = high-tech classroom, 2 = distributed classroom, 3 = hypermedia self-training, 4 = on-line training, 5 = community of practice, 6 = performance support system.

Processes and Development Tools

Figure 1-3 presents the main processes in an e-learning system, the actors involved, and the resources the actors use. *Resources* are any documents, software tools, and telecommunication or direct services used to input or process an activity managed by an actor. There are four main processes in the system's life cycle, going from a creation phase to a production phase to a delivery phase and finally to a maintenance and revision phase, where deficiencies revealed by the delivery of the learning system (LS) are detected and improvements are made to close up the loop and start a new cycle.

Together, these processes allow more interaction between the actors than traditional instruction does. The phases of creation, production, delivery, and maintenance and revision are enacted in a less sequential way. Although the

Figure 1-3. E-Learning Processes, Tools, and Actors.

Note: In diagrams such as this one, the tasks are framed by ovals, the resources or productions by rectangles, and the actors by hexagons. An R-link means that an actor "governs," or is responsible for, the task. A C-link means "is composed of," and an I/P-link means that the resource is an input or product of the task. (Links are discussed further in Chapter Three.)

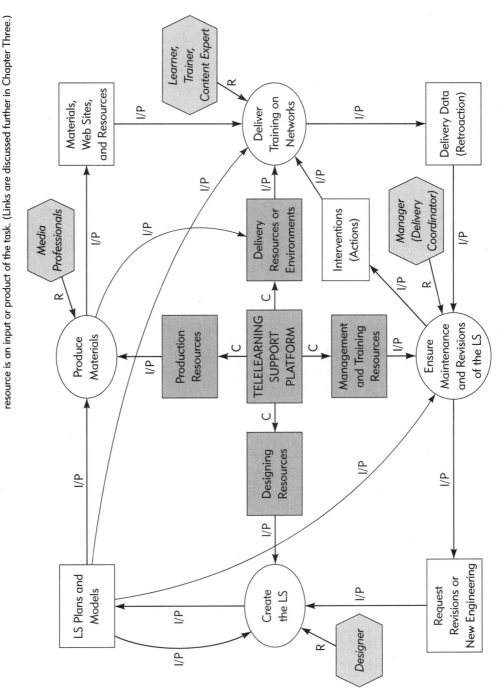

processes can be discussed as occurring in a logical iteration, to understand their practical application it is best to think of them as operating more or less in parallel, with information continually shared between them. Let us look as these processes in more detail.

Designing the Learning System

The starting point for a learning system is a problem analysis performed by an educational organization: a university, college, corporate institute, department of human resources, or community educational group. Once an educational problem is defined, we can decide to start the production of a new learning system or to review an existing learning system. The first scenario is referred to as *instructional engineering* and the second as *reengineering*.

A learning system is a structured collection of materials, resources, environments, services, and human or technological infrastructures that support learning. Such a system can be described in terms of four models: a *knowledge model* describing the contents and the current and target competencies; an *instructional model* defining the course structure, learning activities, instruments, and other resources necessary to the learners and the human resources; *a media model* establishing the design of the Web site(s) or other resources and the design of each material used in the course, regardless of its format; and finally, a *delivery model* describing the roles of the actors at the time of delivery, the tools and channels of communication, the environment and services used, and the plan for the implementation, management, and maintenance of the learning system. As shown in Figure 1-3, the creation process produces inputs (models) for the three other processes and also for itself, for continuous reengineering.

There are two categories of e-learning system creation tools: specialized creation tools or job aids and integrated or nonintegrated design tools. Specialized creation tools (*job aids*) are used, for example, to analyze tasks and needs, to select the media, or to produce questionnaires or quizzes used to assess knowledge acquisition. There are also tools that permit the production of conceptual maps or knowledge models. The MOT software that produced the model shown in Figure 1-4 is one such tool (and it is discussed in some detail in Chapter Three).

Figure 1-4. Sample Screen for MOT: A Specialized Design Tool.

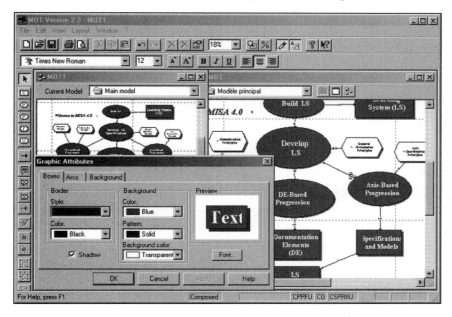

Designers may also use two other types of creation tools—integrated or nonintegrated—for courseware design. The use of nonintegrated tools makes it difficult to maintain the coherence of an e-learning system. Moreover, data transfer from one tool to another is a fastidious task that often causes errors and reduces the design team's productivity. Finally, such a solution does not allow the full operational use of instructional engineering principles and therefore does not adequately support the work of the design team.

Using integrated tools such as Designer's Edge or ADISA (discussed in Chapter Five) for courseware design ensures the coherence of the models. Such macro-design support tools, often called *front-end* tools, are used primarily to prepare work for another tool that will be used in the actual production of instructional materials for the learning system.

Producing Instructional Materials

Regardless of the courseware tools used, once the total design, or *macro-design,* is completed or sufficiently advanced, work can be started on the design of individual materials, the *micro-design*. Then these materials can be produced, following the requirements of the media model produced at the macro-design stage. These materials will generally be integrated into (or linked to) a Web site that becomes the environment for the network of materials, activities, and services that constitute the "physical" e-learning system.

The type of development represented by these designing and production steps mobilizes important principles, methods, and tools and requires a solid methodology. It is easy to understand why many companies offer custom content authoring software targeted to e-learning content creators who have little time and few means. In 1997, I counted almost 400 multimedia courseware production tools available in the United States. Most of the tools offered have production functions for the Web, and new tools are being produced specifically for Internet delivery. Using these custom authoring tools, organizational content experts and trainers can produce their own computerized materials. However, multimedia development still requires the production of the basic media elements: graphics, sound and video sequences, and so forth. This need can be filled by contracting with media professionals or by using prefabricated content from media element banks. However, this latter option may generate some monotony and infringe on copyright laws.

Most important, a content expert who develops material with a custom tool does not generally master basic educational and media competencies, sometimes producing courseware whose quality is disappointing. Moreover, acquiring proficiency in these custom tools requires a rather long learning curve, with the risk that the expert or trainer may spend more time handling the tool than carrying out his or her primary role of designing instructional content and activities. Many educational organizations use custom authoring tools for the production of simple and time-limited training. An interesting solution to some of the problems presented by the use of these tools is to integrate small training products (less than one hour long) produced this way into a larger and more diversified training environment, which then offers learners more global and collaborative training activities. To create more elaborate productions, training organizations hire specialized firms while preserving their right to control the design and delivery of these materials on their internal networks or on the Internet.

Delivering Training on Networks

Once the materials have been validated and revised, the delivery model produced in the macro-design, or creation, phase is used to guide the way they are assembled with other resources and to build the actor's environment that will be implemented at delivery time. These resources are documents, tools, and e-services that users can employ to obtain information, produce assignments, collaborate with others, receive assistance in various situations, and finally, self-manage their own activities.

Many asynchronous delivery tools and services may be used in the actual transmission of the learning system to the user, such as forums, e-mail, file transfers, and bulletin boards. Synchronous delivery tools include chat rooms, audio or video streaming, bipoint or multipoint audio- or videoconferencing, whiteboards, screen sharing, and real-time e-presentations.

Maintaining and Reviewing the Learning System

As learning system delivery begins, maintenance and review activities also begin. If the system is, say, a specific university course, the responsible professor and his or her team will train the trainers, tutors, and supervising managers. The course groups are then created, trainers are assigned to groups, and the course starts. The evaluation results are sent to the registrar's office by the trainers or tutors, coordinated by the supervising managers. The managers organize the delivery of the learning events that are their responsibility and supervise the delivery by collecting data on-line from feedback questionnaires completed by the learners and trainers, from messages exchanged by learners and trainers in forums or by e-mail, or from learners' evaluations. The results of these analyses are transmitted back to the design team in the form of requests for changes that will improve the system.

Platforms and Portals

An e-learning platform is a software system that contains the tools and resources necessary to support the learning system actors—learners, trainers, content experts, and managers—at delivery time.[15] A platform normally offers functions that allow

> A *teacher-designer* to create standard courses grouping learning activities, instructional multimedia resources, and self-monitoring tools for students' activities
>
> A *learner* to consult recommended instructional materials and resources on-line or to download those materials, to self-manage these materials and resources by observing his or her own learning evolution, to produce exercise or problem solutions, and to conduct self-assessment or to transmit productions or exams for evaluation by a teacher-trainer
>
> *Learners and facilitators* (tutors, content experts, animators, managers, and so forth) to communicate, to suggest discussion topics, and to collaborate on common productions
>
> A *platform administrator* to install the learning system and ensure its maintenance, to manage users' access rights, and to create links to external information systems

There are currently more than 300 distance delivery platforms available throughout the world, most of them obeying this definition. A number of comparative studies have analyzed these systems.[16] The majority of the platforms are based on a *Web hypermedia courseware* approach, integrated to various degrees with communication tools. Thus they favor certain techno-pedagogical models such as hypermedia self-training and asynchronous on-line teaching over others such as communities of practice and performance support systems. They also assume that each Web course is conceived independently from other courses and that the functions at the institutional level are in general limited to managing training operations.

The recent evolution from platforms toward *learning portals* is bringing a paradigm shift in this area, if not in practice at least in long-term objectives, because "portals carry a different training perspective rather than simply generalizing access to a predefined, preformed, even predigested content."[17] E-learning portals are organized as integrated Web environments where the processes and services offered are more important than the platforms. These environments can be structured for one or many organizations, offering interfaces granting access to courses or instructional resources produced by various editors, on-line tutorial services, participation in professional communities, and links with performance support tools.

Perhaps increased use of learning portals can counteract the trend reflected in the finding reported by *Training* magazine that in all the training offered on the Internet in 1999, only 36 percent allowed interaction between people, a 14 percent decline from the interaction available in 1998.[18] These figures show that we still have a way to go before we make the best use of the true power of the Internet, which lies more in its capacity to create learning communities based on individuals' interactions than in its ability to provide more and more information.

Learning portals have great potential for increasing learners' access to formal and informal training, for facilitating communication and idea exchanges within the communities of practice, for integrating various functions while proposing an organic vision of learning, and for ensuring continuity between work and training while supporting competency and knowledge management in an organization. However, this enormous potential is far from being fully exploited today.

Even if they are increasingly evolving toward openness and diversity, the most popular platforms today are limited to a variety of weak of instructional strategies, providing in proprietary formats stereotyped steps or templates that facilitate the instructional task for trainers who are new to e-learning. Although some offer tools to import materials produced outside the platform, they remain relatively closed to the integration of external instructional materials. This means that course creators face problems when they wish to reuse learning system components and when they need interoperability of resources and instructional materials.

Several international groups are tackling the problems found with current platforms by developing technical specifications standards for instructional materials. The IMS Global Learning Consortium[19] is an international organization whose objective is to define the global architecture specifications for on-line learning. Its members include such major manufacturers of authoring and training management tools as Allen Communications, Microsoft, PeopleSoft, Oracle, Saba, Sybase, IBM Education, Lotus, and Macromedia. Among the other organizations contributing to this standardization effort are the Aviation Industry CBT Committee[20] (AICC), the IEEE, ARIADNE, and the Advanced Distributed Learning Initiative. This last organization has produced the Sharable Courseware Object Reference Model (SCORM), a first definition of a reference model for computerized instructional objects that can be shared by a large variety of authoring tools and learning management systems.

Table 1-3 presents a summary of the five processes just discussed and their associated tools.

SUMMARY

In this chapter I have highlighted the main trends marking our progress toward becoming a knowledge society. Under the impact of the Internet and multimedia technologies, work and life in our societies are undergoing significant changes. Knowledge acquisition, and therefore learning and training, is now a prominent preoccupation of people, organizations, and governments.

In this vast societal movement, e-learning has become a major trend that we can no longer ignore. Most employees are now knowledge professionals. Thus it has become necessary not only to remove location and time constraints from information access but also to empower learners with the means to involve themselves, individually and in learning communities, in knowledge construction processes through which they will be able to develop the higher-level competencies they need to continuously adapt to the fast pace of knowledge evolution. Needless to say, this is an ambitious objective but one that we must achieve to ensure that wider distribution of technologies will lead to wider democratization of knowledge. Knowledge must be available through a variety of models, approaches, and tools so it can be adapted to users' diversified needs.

This chapter presented six techno-pedagogical training models. Two of them, the high-tech classroom and the distributed classroom, were very

Table 1-3. Synthesis of Instructional Engineering and Delivery Tools.

Tool Group	Relevant Processes	Tool Examples	Comments
1. Creation and instructional engineering	Design the models of LS: knowledge, instructional, media, delivery	ADISA/MOT Designer's Edge	There are few macro-design, or front-end, systems. Most of them cover only some of the tasks. The designers use various specialized tools such as graphic model makers or software packages. The ADISA workbench is a new support system for the main creation tasks of an e-learning environment.
2. Materials production	Produce materials and media elements	Authorware Director Dreamweaver FrameMaker PhotoShop Toolbook	The custom authoring tools allow the fast development of multi-media products. If the production is somewhat complex, the instructional system software developers will use a variety of media production and programming tools.
3. Delivery tools and services	Deliver the information; support communication	Outlook NetMeeting MediaPlayer Multimedia One	Various commercial tools offer synchronous or asynchronous communication services. Other tools and services created for instructional purposes are used for collaboration, follow-ups, and remote tutoring.
4. Training management systems	Manage the events and the students' files; maintain and revise the LS	PeopleSoft SAP SIGAL TopClass Training Office	SIGAL is an example of a competency management system for an organization. The general management systems such as SAP offer a training module. Management tools are also offered in integrated systems, or integrators. No system covers all of the required functions, particularly regarding the management of training quality.
5. Platforms or integrative systems	Produce materials; deliver training on the Internet; manage training	Explor@ Learning Space Librarian Virtual U Web CT	These systems aim to integrate delivery tools or services with materials. Certain systems integrate the materials in a proprietary format. Other systems facilitate the integration of the materials and resources produced outside the tool.

popular at the end of the 1990s. They have the advantage of feeling familiar to educators and trainers accustomed to traditional classroom settings, but they require expensive videoconferencing equipment and the simultaneous presence of learners and instructors. Although extremely useful in certain contexts, these models are probably not fulfilling the needs of the present and will fall further behind in the future, when mobile, busy people will need to develop and use high-level intellectual skills in a socioeconomic context that requires continuous and lifelong learning. New techno-pedagogical models such as hypermedia self-training, on-line training, communities of practice, and performance support systems are better adapted to fulfilling the needs of the knowledge society.

Taking into account the colossal energies currently devoted to this field, significant technical progress is expected in the areas of general Internet standards and specific standards for network-based learning, platform interoperability, and new generation authoring and delivery systems. However, the most important evolution must take place elsewhere. The following chapters go beyond technological innovation questions and address the more profound pedagogical issues that must come to shape our instructional engineering methods and principles.

2

Virtual Learning Centers

THE PREVIOUS CHAPTER surveyed the rapid development of e-learning technologies and uncovered some of their current limitations in an environment where information and knowledge are increasing at an exponential rate. In such an environment it is no longer acceptable to build each course or learning event with components limited to those offered by a proprietary platform, no matter how good of its kind. More fundamentally, learning events need to become more open, to offer a variety of adaptable possible paths, and to support emerging learning-community processes.

In this chapter I present an open delivery architecture for a virtual learning center. This e-learning center efficiently implements learning portals that offer not only a variety of resources and pedagogical material but also a variety of activities, scenarios, and techno-pedagogical models. Evolution to this level of instructional design seems necessary to meet the challenges of the knowledge society, which are to manage an exponentially increasing mass of information and knowledge and to acquire skills and competencies of a higher level than ever before.

The Concept of a Learning System

The first important concept for understanding the virtual learning center is that of the learning system, which I suggest as an alternative to the traditional course concept. When we think of Web-based e-learning, we cannot be satisfied with a course implicitly defined as a set of Web pages offering hyperlinked information, exercises, and texts to which are added some communication tools. This limited notion does not provide for the integrated use of the wide variety of pedagogical and delivery models discussed in the previous chapter, nor does it allow the integration and reuse of a great quantity of existing instructional material. In addition, the term *course* does not capture the current variety of possible learning events: for example, structured Internet discussions, workplace learning activities completed over a long period of time, or ambitious systematic training programs for competency development and knowledge management among the members of an organization.

The e-learning system concept I present here aims to address these concerns. It provides for the development of e-learning events such as a course, a module, or an activity, and the development of complex learning event networks such as a curriculum including many courses or a series of integrated training activities within a task support environment. This approach is intended to take into account all types of training in educational, industrial, and commercial environments and does not prejudge or predetermine the types of instructional material (printed, audiovisual, multimedia, courseware, conference calls, automated assistance systems, and so forth) or the technological tools and the organizational infrastructure that may be required to support such a system.

As indicated in Figure 2-1, a learning system is the product of an instructional engineering process. It is the major input to the learning delivery process. A learning system has three main parts:

Figure 2-1. Concept of a Learning System.

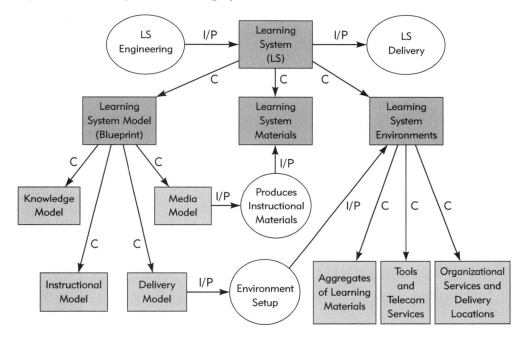

1. The learning system model or blueprint, composed of the knowledge, the instructional, the media, and the delivery models.

2. The learning system materials, or the documents created on the basis of these models, which constitute the "physical" learning system.

3. The environments that support the delivery actors, composed of aggregates of learning materials, tools and means of communication, and organizational services and delivery locations.

The Learning System Model

A learning system model is composed of four specialized models developed during the various design phases. Each describes an important facet of the learning system.

The *knowledge model* describes the learning content and objectives in terms of target competencies. It defines the types of knowledge the learning system makes available and their interrelations and also defines the skills the learners will need to process the knowledge. Both entry and target competencies are defined. The knowledge model may be a graphic model that contains submodels that are then associated with various learning units describing the content and the instruments used in the learning activities.

The *instructional model* describes the learning events network, or to put it another way, the "course" structure composed of events of different granularity. It also defines the learning units, within which instructional scenarios (of any number) describe the learning activities, specify resources available to the learners and assignments learners will use in the activities, and outlines the activities of the trainers and of the other facilitators involved in the delivery.

The *media model* defines the ways tools used in the instructional scenarios are assembled into a variety of media and various types of support: for example, a Web site, optical disks, analog tapes, and printed or 3-D materials. The media model may be represented as a graphic or as a detailed storyboard. It presents the basic media elements (text, picture, sound, animated graphics, and so forth) and their relationships within the media components. (*Media components* are subdivisions such as a module, section, page, or sequence within materials.) The media model also shows the transitional links between media elements, the organizational rules governing them, and the templates or style sheets used to standardize presentations of content.

The *delivery model* defines the actors' roles as both resource providers and users. It describes the main resources that ought to be available in the environment of each actor: the materials, tools, telecom services, and delivery services and locations. The delivery model facilitates the planning of the required technological and organizational infrastructures. It also provides the design for the various delivery processes and the plans to maintain the quality of the learning system.

In distributed learning applications, this model approach is even more necessary than it is in classroom learning, because the absence of a model description will cause the learning system to run inefficiently as soon as many actors—learners, trainers, content experts, managers, technical support personnel—are involved. In addition, as technologies and media continue to evolve, the use of a learning system model means that modifications and component variations can be more easily adopted and there is no need to build everything from scratch every time.

The Learning System Materials

Working mainly from the media model, the development team builds or reuses instructional materials that embody the selected pedagogical approaches. These are the "physical" components of the learning system, those that will be used by the various actors interacting in the system.

The learning system concept allows the use of many types of media and media supports and many different ways to organize instructional material in order to meet the needs of different users. When thinking of the media model, it is helpful to view learning materials as falling into three media categories.

In *monomedia* mode each of the learning materials is delivered in the media in which it was born. The materials are gathered together in a pedagogical package and delivered to the learner, usually by mail. This package might contain printed texts (graphs, manuals, guides, questionnaires); audiovisual material on tapes or CDs; and interactive numeric documents (courseware, simulators, exercise units) on diskettes, CDs, or DVDs.

In *multimedia* mode, regardless of their original media, the various materials (texts, sounds, 2-D, animated pictures, and so forth) are digitized and integrated on a single support, such as a CD or a DVD that is generally shipped by mail or a multimedia server from which they can be published directly on the Internet for viewing and downloading.

In *plurimedia* mode all of the materials are also digitized and stored on media servers, yet they can be published on various supports according

to the material type and the technological infrastructure available
to the users. For example, a text may be printed and shipped by mail,
copied to a CD, or downloaded from Internet files. Audiovisual material or educational software may be delivered on a CD or downloaded
to a learner's workstation from a server. Other techniques, such as
video streaming, allow the delivery of audiovisual material in real
time.

The learning system concept favors the plurimedia approach, yet it also
allows multimedia or monomedia deliveries. Once again, the learning system
approach shows itself to be an adaptable and versatile solution.

Generally speaking, the monomedia delivery mode has the disadvantage
of reducing material reusability, as some materials will not be digitized. It can
be used to deliver bulky materials such as books, complex software programs,
or lengthy TV programs that tend to be difficult to modify. Each of these
materials is in a form suited to its particularities, even though that form renders structural adjustments difficult. Such material can be integrated with
other materials through a printed guide that will have to be revised and
reprinted after each substantial modification of the other material.

In contrast the multimedia delivery breaks the training material into
smaller media components hyperlinked to form a network. Although it is easier in this mode than in the monomedia mode to replace components without jeopardizing the balance of the ensemble, all relevant hyperlinks must still
be processed. In a well-integrated multimedia approach, a media component
may contain links to many dozens of other components. Moreover, the multimedia option can raise some barriers to material reusability as materials generally have to be broken down into smaller units to be integrated into another
format by the selected development tools. They then have to be rebuilt for
the most part to be reused. Finally, content segmented into smaller units also
presents instructional difficulties. Although a flexible and diversified approach
is favored for accessing information, it can prevent more global and con-
structive instructional strategies. The plurimedia delivery is a broader approach that allows the flexible integration of a variety of monomedia and
multimedia components into a coherent collection.

The Actors' Environments

The third and last component of a learning system groups the environments available to the various delivery actors: learners, trainers, managers, content experts, technical advisers, and so on. It includes a series of documents, tools, telecom services, and human services, selected from the delivery model according to the needs of a given actor. These resources are generic in the sense that a given resource, such as an evaluation questionnaire, an e-mail, or a forum, may be integrated into various course environments and made available to various actors.

Most delivery platforms favor a solution in which all the course resources are integrated on a single Web site. I believe, on the contrary, that it is essential to gather them on various sites and then group access to them in a virtual resource center similar to the resource centers found on university campuses or at training institutes. In this approach, library services, telecom services, advising services, and the rules regarding course delivery are not treated as integral components of a course. Instead they are seen as support services that should be constantly available to the individuals engaged in learning activities. (I explain later in this chapter how an actor's environment is viewed as a resource center linked to the actor's roles.)

Also, it is important to emphasize that each e-learning system is not constrained to a single environment. Rather, it contains as many environments as are required by the actors identified in the delivery model. Once this concept is established, it is possible to entrust the construction of the environments to the users themselves. Each user may personalize his or her environment from a bank of simple tools and resources grouped on and available from the Internet.

Actors' Roles and Resources

Let's look more closely at the actors' roles and resources in a virtual learning center.

Actor Types and Generic Roles

As an example, we may consider a generic model that describes a main delivery process in which five types of actors may interact: a learner, a trainer, a manager, a designer, and a content expert. The actor-type concept is useful not only for understanding how the virtual learning center is constructed and functions but also for comprehending a variety of concrete situations. In any given learning center the roles of each type of actor may be carried out by one or many actors, and these actors may be people, media documents, or computerized tools. Also, a given actor may carry out roles belonging to more than one actor type.

Figure 2-2 displays five types of actors (the hexagons), the general processes they govern (the ovals), and the resources they use or produce (the rectangles). Note that the actors who are not learners are identified as "sort of" facilitators (S-link).

Figure 2-2. Interrelations Among Actors in a Virtual Learning Center.

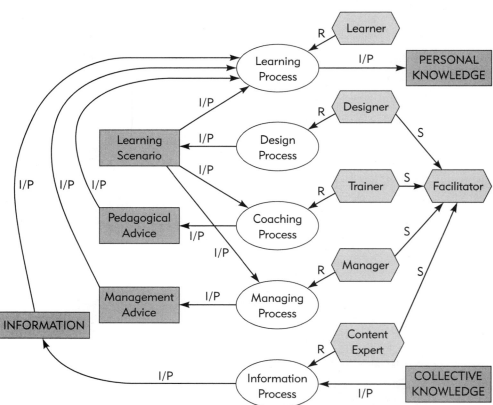

The learning process is governed by an actor type called *learner,* whose task is to transform a set of information into knowledge. By *information,* in this context, I mean any abstract or concrete form of data, perceptible to the senses, and likely to be transformable into knowledge. By *knowledge,* in this context, I mean pieces of information that have been assimilated by learning entities and integrated into their own cognitive systems in relation to a context and a practice. The learner's transformation of information into knowledge suggests an adaptation of preexisting mental schemas or the creation of new schemas. The schemas store knowledge and the context in which it was created. The knowledge is also integrated into some practice, provided it is used in a process that requires the user to perform some actions in his or her environment.

The information is available to the learner because of another actor type, the *content expert.* The content expert may be a person or a group of persons participating directly or via a medium such as a book, a video, software, or any other tool or medium that makes available a section of an individual's or group's knowledge in the form of information that can be used for learning purposes. In this context, *knowledge* means a body of knowledge, socially recognized, structured, and transferable. It may originate from a general domain such as physics or administration or it may be specialized knowledge such as a specific work methodology used by an organization.

These two types of actors are essential to all learning processes. The learners govern a process in which they combine and integrate information obtained from the content experts to build personal knowledge that is internalized in their mental schemas. The content experts govern the information process by which they communicate to learners information related to a section of collective knowledge.

Usually, as Figure 2-2 illustrates, three other types of actors are also present in a learning system. They, like the content experts, are facilitators, bringing information into the knowledge-building process.

The *designer* governs the instructional engineering process and facilitates learning by creating, adapting, and ensuring the correct working order for all the parts in a learning system that integrates various information sources, telecommunications, interaction and communication services used between the actors, and support and assistance mechanisms offered through human trainers, delivery managers, or computerized agents.

The *trainer* overlooks the pedagogical assistance process, facilitating knowledge acquisition and motivating and advising the learner. The trainer's roles are particularly important to the effective enactment and support of the learning scenarios defined by the designer.

The *manager* leads the delivery management process, facilitating learning by managing events and actors and by ensuring a sound delivery process according to the scenarios created by the designing actors.

As the preceding discussion illustrates, each actor type has a specific function (an input and a product). And each of these functions can be divided into subprocesses, or roles. Table 2-1 describes some of these roles. Each one is generic and can be present in the description of more than one actor. For example, *information exploration* certainly falls into the definition of the learner's function, yet it may also apply to other actors as well, even if though for other actors the information may be of a different nature.

Table 2-1. Actor Functions and Roles in a Virtual Learning Center.

Actor's Main Function	*Roles or Corresponding Subprocesses*
Learner: transforms information into knowledge	Navigates a learning scenario
	Explores documentation sources
	Solves problems
	Contracts to complete a project
	Produces tests and essays
	Self-evaluates competencies
	Collaborates with others
	Debates in discussions
	Communicates messages
Trainer: facilitates learning from an instructional perspective	Motivates and guides learners
	Produces diagnostics
	Gives pedagogical advice
	Evaluates learners' productions

Table 2-1. Actor Functions and Roles in a Virtual Learning Center, Cont'd.

Actor's Main Function	Roles or Corresponding Subprocesses
	Assists in the use of learning materials and resources
	Facilitates teams and groups interactions
Designer: builds, adapts, and maintains a learning system	Analyzes training needs
	Builds a knowledge model
	Builds pedagogical scenarios
	Designs and produces learning material
	Plans delivery processes
	Simulates and validates a learning event
Manager: manages actors and events	Supervises trainers
	Manages resources
	Controls delivery processes
	Organizes teams and groups
	Manages the validation process
	Manages the learning assessment process
	Acts as a network manager
Content expert: makes learning information available	Lectures, presents information
	Clarifies knowledge
	Provides mediated knowledge
	Analyzes the content of learning activities
	Analyzes documents and productions

The detailed description of each role allows the identification of the resources that the actors need. For example, for learning self-assessment, a learner will need resources such as a self-evaluation questionnaire or a knowledge acquisition progress report. To participate in a teleconference or a debate, he or she will need asynchronous forum or audio- or videoconferencing tools. To diagnose learners' progress, a trainer will require progress reports and test results. To establish learner teams and groups, a manager will need learners' and trainers' background description documents. To create an e-learning system, a designer will need tools to create knowledge models, to select the media used, and so on. (Chapter Four explains how knowledge modeling is used to create a graphic model of the roles undertaken by the actors during delivery and thus to identify the resources needed in an actor's environment during delivery.)

Of course, the specific names used for the actors are likely to vary from organization to organization as are the ways the main functions and roles are allotted. For example, in a distance education institution, a professor usually takes on most of the designer roles except for the creation and production roles that are performed by Web designers and integration programmers. The professor may also occasionally play facilitator roles during the tutor training sessions or during interactions directly with certain learners. He or she may also take on manager roles when supervising tutors. The tutor is another actor who takes on both trainer and manager roles. On the other hand, on most university campuses the professor's main role is to present the information from a content expert's point of view, although he or she may also take on some secondary roles as a designer, trainer, and manager. This situation is also very common in corporate training. Moreover, participants' roles may evolve during delivery. For example, in a community of practice a learner may take a trainer or manager role regarding a question generated by his or her group, and another learner may take on one of these roles for another question. Such role interchanges are more easily accomplished in adaptable environments.

To summarize, the concept of actor types allows the enumeration of the roles required in a virtual learning center. It also permits the designer to anticipate a corresponding bank of resources to fulfill the actors' needs. However, in each specific learning system each participant takes on a set of roles related to more than one type of actor and uses a series of resources associated with these roles. A participant's environment is thus custom built, according to the roles and resources necessary in a given learning system and in a given organization's context.

Resource Spaces

The resources assigned to an actor can generally be grouped according to the type of interaction shared with other actors. Regardless of the actor type, we can distinguish five virtual interaction spaces, as shown in Figure 2-3. For example, in interactions with the content expert, a learner will need resources for consulting course content information or producing information for his or her own use or for others' use. In the first case, the learner will need documents, a Webography, and search engines. These resources will constitute the learner's *information space.* In the second case, text or graphic editors, database management systems, or courseware will help the learner produce information. These are example of resources that will occupy a second space: the *production space.*

Figure 2-3. Actors and Interaction Spaces.

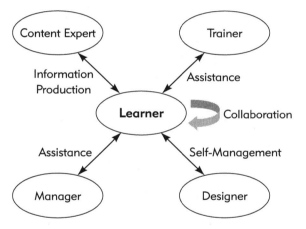

The resources that allow collaboration with other learners for teamwork or group discussions constitute a third space: the *collaboration space.* This space contains synchronous tools and services to support real-time communication, such as chat, audio- or videoconferences, whiteboards, and software sharing. It also contains telecom services that support recorded communication, such as e-mail, video or voice mail, forums, and file transfers.

In the *assistance space,* the learner finds tools and services that will access pedagogical assistance from a trainer or organizational support from a manager. This space may include a directory of relevant personnel and their on-line addresses, various user guides, a list of frequently asked questions (FAQs), or computerized adviser agents that can provide suggestions according to the trace of the learner's processes.

Finally, unlike the classroom setting where events are controlled mainly by the instructor, e-learning requires more autonomy from the learner. The *self-management space* includes resources that allow the learner to get the most advantage out of the learning system and to adapt it to his or her needs, acting either independently or with the help of a trainer. It includes various tools that support learning activity planning, such as a to-do list, a schedule or calendar, and a collaborative agenda. It also includes such information as group and individual progress, lists of consulted documents, tests results, and evaluations from a trainer or from other learners.

Figure 2-4 outlines some of the resources that may be available to a learner, grouped according to the five interaction spaces. Note, in addition, that certain resources may be found in more than one space. This is particularly true of the integrated tools that offer videoconferencing functions or a search engine.

Resources for other types of actors can also be grouped into these five spaces. For example, a trainer also needs information resources related to the course contents. In addition, he or she needs information on the learners' progress. The trainer will have to produce learning diagnostics and interventions that will be supported by resources in his or her production space. He or she may need to collaborate with other trainers using collaboration resources, receive help from the designers or content experts, and self-manage his or her own activities according to the assistance scenario that guides trainer interventions. In the case of the designer or design team the information space is likely to contain a set of documents describing the training framework of the organization or giving access to reusable materials. The production space offers the various tools belonging to the instructional engineering method that supports the production of the knowledge, instructional, media, and delivery models (one such instructional engineering method, MISA, is discussed in Chapter Four). The collaboration space will bring together the communication and group support tools needed by the designer. The assistance space gives the designer access to methodology experts, in the form of either

Figure 2-4. Resources Grouped into Five Spaces.

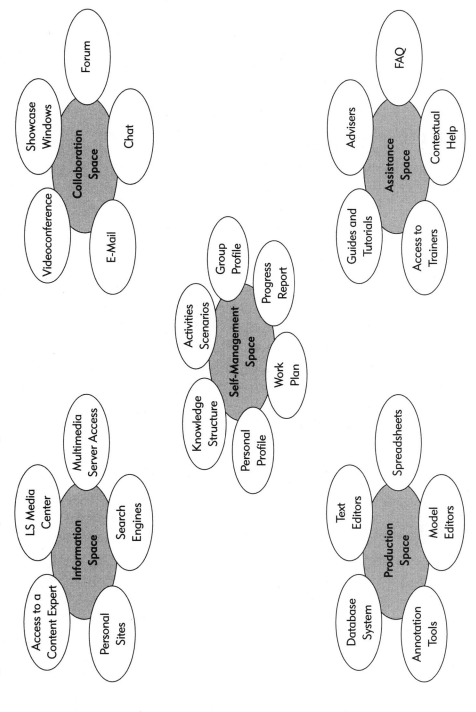

a methodological guide system or an integrated help or adviser system. Finally, the designer self-manages his or her activities through validation of previous design elements, and if the design work is done by a team, through teamwork planning tools.

Explor@: A Web-Based Support System

The model I have been presenting here describes the actors at the moment of delivery of a learning system, the processes they are responsible for, the roles they must take on, and the resources used or produced in what I call a virtual learning center. The virtual learning center is the main component of a virtual campus or a virtual training institution. Other virtual campus functions and services, such as student file management, support personnel management, and resource, course, and network management, are not part of the virtual learning center, which groups and sustains learning system design, material production, resource and environment assembly, and course and learning events delivery and maintenance.

In this section I turn to describing Explor@, which is a system that supports the construction of a virtual learning center that delivers learning events, and ensures that the users share a set of instructional resources (tools, files, documents, telecom services, and so on) maintained by the training institution or the corporation. Explor@ allows the integration of monitoring and advising tools that facilitate both individual and collaborative learning with pedagogical support and training management.

How Explor@ Works

Figure 2-5 shows a view of Explor@ as it first presents itself to users.

This system uses a browser that provides access to the portal of an organization's virtual learning center. When a user chooses to visit the center, a hyperlink takes him or her to the center's welcome page, where he or she obtains a demonstration and information about how the center functions. From here, the user may browse through the technical guide, register for a learning event, and download certain resources.

Figure 2-5. Access Via Explor@ to a Virtual Learning Center.

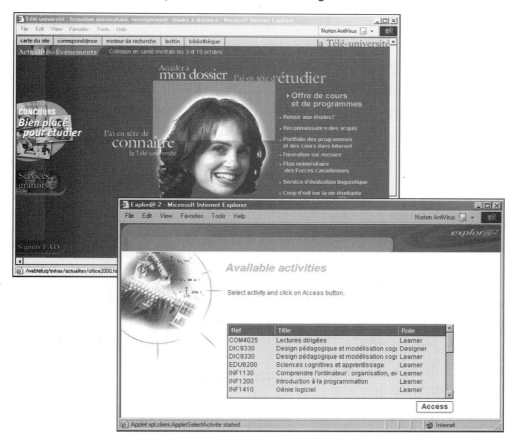

Once this step is completed the user must enter his or her ID and password to begin the activities. The Explor@ system then presents a list of activities available to this user in the virtual center: that is, the list of the programs, courses, or other learning events for which the user is registered as a learner or to which he or she is assigned as a trainer, a content expert, a manager, a designer, or in other roles. There is no limitation on the number and designation of these roles. This gives flexibility to the personnel and the organizations responsible for running and naming the virtual learning center elements.

When the user selects one of the learning events from the list of those for which he or she is registered, two windows are displayed on screen, as shown in Figure 2-6. The first one is the specific course or learning event Web site; the second is the generic virtual learning center navigator.

Figure 2-6. **(1) Course Web Site, (2) Explor@ Browser, (3) Example of a Resource.**

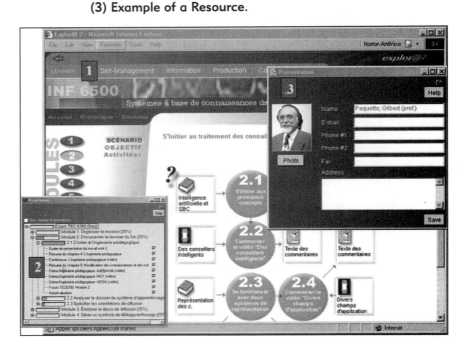

Each learning event has an Explor@ window like the one labeled here with "1," although it will display different content according to the course and type of actor. It offers menus grouping the resources identified as useful for accomplishing this user's roles in the learning event. Selecting a resource opens that resource in a new window.

Again there is no limitation on the number of spaces or on the number of resources of each space. Each user category is offered a group of resources that defines the operational actions available in the learning system. In effect, a user's roles are indirectly and partially defined by the resources presented to that user. These resources have been previously selected by the design team from the central bank of resources it has created. This bank contains resources specific to the Explor@ system and also links to commercial tools (e-mail, forums, and the like) and possibly to proprietary tools specific to an organization.

Example of Resources Assigned to an Actor

Table 2-2 presents an example of a list of resource spaces and resources present in the environment created for a learner who has registered for a course integrated into an Explor@ virtual learning center. This example underlines the versatility and flexibility of Explor@.

Table 2-2. An Explor@ Environment for a Learner.

Space	Resource	Description
Self-management	1. Personal profile	Makes personal information available to other participants
	2. Progress report	Indicates activity progress in the course, modules, and activities; triggers the display of corresponding Web pages
	3. Calendar of events	Allows learner to keep track of activity and assignment dates; indicates corresponding Web pages
	4. Course schedule	Indicates assignment schedule
	5. Evaluation	Presents a questionnaire for course evaluation
Information	6. Texts	Accesses all texts to be consulted or produced in the course
	7. Videos	Accesses all videos used in the course
	8. Webography	Accesses a list of references and Web sites
	9. Search engines	Accesses various Internet search engines

Table 2-2. An Explor@ Environment for a Learner, Cont'd.

Space	Resource	Description
Production	10. Software	Launches software to produce assignment results
	11. Text editor	Accesses actor's preferred text editor
	12. Model editor	Accesses a graphic editor (such as MOT)
	13. Homework	Transfers learner's work to tutor for assessment
Collaboration	14. Group profile	Allows learner to consult other participants' progress to find collaborators
	15. E-mail	Accesses standard e-mail software used by the organization
	16. Forums	Accesses a teleconference system used by the organization
	17. Showcase	Accesses learners' productions and allows a learner to consult other learners' work
Assistance	18. Explor@ guide	Gives detailed information about Explor@ resources
	19. Study guide	Allows learner to read or print a guide that describes course objectives, scenarios, materials, and resources
	20. Technical help	Provides FAQ or other help related to the technological environment
	21. Resource person	Gives e-mail access to various people involved in a course: instructor, tutor, program coordinator, technician, and so on
	22. Adviser	Gives advice based on activity trace or responses to questions

This environment groups twenty-two resources into five spaces, directly accessible and integrated into the Explor@ browser. Most of these resources are generic in the sense that they can be integrated into a great number of actor environments either as is or with little adaptation. The tools specific to the Explor@ system use Java applets linked to a database. Tools such as the progress report, the calendar, and the group profile display the pertinent data from the database for each course. Some of the HTML tools may require some adaptation as they are integrated into different environments, to modify a question on a course evaluation questionnaire, for example, or to revise the list of the available resources. In many cases, tools are integrated into the Explor@ environment rather than into the course Web site. For example, it is more interesting for the user to find a Webography (a list of informative Web sites) in the information space of Explor@ than to search for related Web sites.

Integrating a Learning Event into a Virtual Center

This section describes how a new course or a new learning event is integrated into a virtual learning center. In the most general hardware and software terms, the virtual learning center is a computer system running on an HTML/JAVA server linked to the Internet. It contains management and design tools that facilitate the integration of a new course by adding one or many environments according to the type of user the designer wishes to support. There are two levels of course integration; each is appropriate to a different level of design detail.

Users and Environments

The first level of integration involves the use of Explor@ tools by managers in order to create user accounts that grant users access to virtual center services. Users are identified by name, ID number, password, courses in which they are enrolled, and the roles they are allowed to play in these courses. Once these data are saved in the database, an identification and course selection mechanism is enabled for them.

Other tools allow managers to create groups that contain a certain number of learners and one or many trainers or other facilitators. These data are fed into the tools that enable communication between the members of the group, providing a list of the resource persons, a directory of the members of the group, chat tools, means of exchanging personal profile information, access to a virtual showcase of shared productions, and a means of transferring productions to an evaluator for assessment and feedback.

A third group of tools, integrated into the designer's environment, allows the creation of environments, relevant spaces and resources for each actor, a definition of the course structure and associated resources, and information on course sequencing. With this information in Explor@'s database, other user tools can also be made available.

These first-level operations deal with the functions of the course Web site that are totally independent from the actors' environments. At this level the Explor@ navigator is simply a tool to assemble resources, launch applications, post documents from the user's environment, and facilitate communication among the members of a group.

"Intelligent" Assistance

The Explor@ system also allows the integration of higher-levels tools, those that require coordination between the course Web site and the user's environment. This is the second level of integration into the virtual learning center. It is particularly relevant to the progress report, calendar, group profile, and adviser tools (Resources 2, 3, 14, and 22 in Table 2-2). This more intimate integration requires three operations, which are supported by Explor@ tools that can be integrated in a designer's environment (Figure 2-7).

Description of the Activity and Knowledge Structures. Two hierarchical structures, one derived from the knowledge model and one derived from the course instructional model, are integrated into the Explor@ database. The instructional structure presents a course composed of various modules, units,

Figure 2-7. Some Explor@ Design Tools.

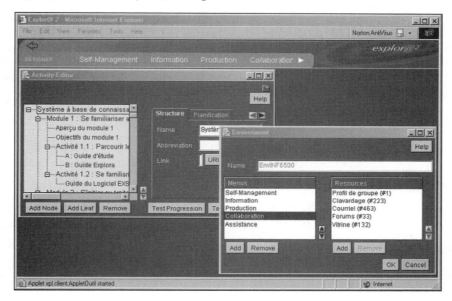

and activities. All these entities are labeled as *instructional units* (IU). The cognitive structure presents the knowledge model covered in the course; its entities are called *cognitive units* (CUs). Web pages are then associated with each IU and each CU.

These two operations activate the tools mentioned earlier. For example, the user has access to a color-coded data system. And he or she can obtain a list of Web pages identified by the activity or the knowledge associated with the page. An option allows the user to open these pages from the list.

Definition of Progress Levels and Transitions Between Levels. For each IU and CU, the designer defines progress levels, using templates. The number of levels defined depends on the complexity of the activity or knowledge. For a simple activity, such as sending a comparative assignment to an evaluator, only two levels are planned: sent and not sent. Other activities require more levels. For example, if a learner had to read two texts, view a video, and pass a test to complete an activity, at least five progress levels would be required: the zero level, meaning that none of the subtasks are completed; and levels 1, 2, 3, and 4, meaning that one, two, three, or all four subtasks are completed. More progress levels will be required when multiple test-score levels need to be tracked.

Once the designer has defined the various levels for each IU and CU to be implemented in Explor@, other user tools become operational and may be integrated in actors' environments, as shown in the progress and group profile tools in Figure 2-8. They present the structure of the course activities to the user in the form of bar graphs indicating a user's progress level. This allows the user to regularly evaluate his or her progress in the course and to take corrective measures. A user may also authorize other group members to view these data for comparison purposes and to identify the other learners they would be interested in working with. It also facilitates the task of trainers and other facilitators who use the group progress viewer and decide on some interaction.

Figure 2-8. Tools Displaying Individual and Group Progress in a Course.

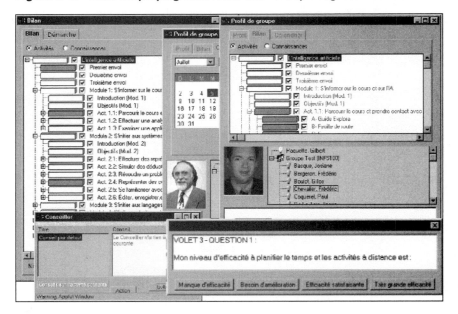

Adviser Definition. The designer can create an even more interactive environment by planning for advisers that take into account the previous actions of a user in his or her environment. This requires defining rules that associate advisory actions with certain progress levels reached by the user in one or more IU or CU. These actions may open short advisory texts on the user's screen. They may launch an external file (a sound or visual message) or initiate a dialogue with the user. The advice may be generated by the user when he or she selects an appropriate option in the Explor@ assistance menu. It may also be generated by the system when certain conditions are met: for example, when the system determines that the learner is completing Activity X without having completed the prerequisite activities or that the learner has received an unsatisfactory evaluation for a certain CU.

Versatile and Flexible Architecture

This chapter suggests a three-level architecture for a virtual learning center. At the first level the designer finds the different instructional material, whether existing or to be built: texts, videos, multimedia, simulations, games, software, and so on. At the second level these materials are integrated into a specific Web site for each learning event. At the third level each Web site is integrated into the virtual learning center, where it is then associated with one or many environments, each grouping information, production, collaboration, assistance, or self-management resources. These resources are selected to match the needs of the course participants according to their roles.

This architecture offers many advantages, both from an instructional and an economic perspective. From the economic perspective the plurimedia approach makes it reasonably simple to reuse existing instructional material. For example, an excellent simulation of a physics process created for a technical training course might be reused in a communication course to give learners the opportunity to analyze this simulation from a media perspective, or it might be used in a pedagogical course so teachers in training could discuss its instructional quality. Thus, instead of investing in onerous new development, a design team has the option of deciding to reuse material that has been successful in the past and to develop only a few new pieces of material for a course.

Instructional quality is related to the information included in the instructional material, but it is even more closely related to the pertinence of the learning activities that are suggested to learners. For example, some wonderful multimedia CDs and Web sites present the masterpieces of various museums. Although this information is interesting, it does not by itself necessarily produce significant learning. It is likely, for example, that a great number of the Internet surfers who have virtually visited many art museums remain incapable of demonstrating any acquired competency on the topic of what they have seen, read, and heard. They would acquire competencies only if their visits required them to engage in learning activities targeting specific competencies, for example, the ability to analyze paintings from various perspectives. The approach proposed in this book requires the course Web sites to provide instructional scenarios that provide access to high-quality materials with which the learner is asked to carry out activities and complete productions in order to construct useful knowledge. Moreover, because material development efforts are reduced as described earlier, more time may be spent designing scenarios and activities that will maximize the potential of a material.

The same concerns generally apply to the resource repositories used to build the environments. Over time these repositories will accumulate new tools, documents, and services that can be reused in other courses. Here again, there is significant instructional and economic value added.

In considering the flexibility and versatility inherent in the relationship between an instructional Web site and its Explor@ environments, we can look at three main categories: the hyperguides, focused on activities; the reference portal, focused on the information; and the resource centers, focused on the resources. When building the Explor@ environments, we must select their resources according to the Web site's general approach, whether it is a hyperguide, a reference portal, or a resource center.

Hyperguides

Hyperguides are Web sites that describe the learning activities rather than the information or the resources to use. This type of interactive site replaces the traditional linear course syllabus and printed study guide. A welcome page presents the course structure and gives the user access to the main course subdivisions, called modules or learning units. Each of these learning units is described in a learning scenario that groups a certain number of activities, the instructional material to be consulted (books, videos, educational software), and the relationships between these scenario components. Each activity is further described by the specific materials to be consulted or used for that activity, and the activity assignments, productions, suggested schedule, and so on, are provided.

At this level the contents of the course are encapsulated in the instructional materials and in the learners' productions. Gradually, each learner's work enriches the content base. His or her productions can be evaluated by peers or a trainer, or both, and then can be reintegrated in the course document database and reused in other activities.

The user's environment is designed to complement the Web site's approach. For example, it avoids integrating a scenario navigator because that would duplicate the Web site pages. However, a knowledge navigator would be welcome to locate activities that deal with specific content. The environment would also avoid duplicating resources available on the Web site, unless they facilitated navigation. For example, the forum would be accessed from the environment rather than the site, unless a particularly significant forum needed to be inserted in a scenario and described locally. Resources shifted to the environment make the Web site lighter, as the number of icons and hyperlinks is decreased, and this facilitates ongoing site revision and adaptation.

Reference Portals

Reference portals are Web sites organized around the structure of the information in a course. The Web pages are structured not according to learning unit concepts, instructional scenarios, or learning activities but according to logical subdivisions in the material, in much the same way a reference manual is structured.

For example, in an art history course, the Web site is likely to be subdivided into periods arranged into schools. For each school, the main artists would be presented, along with their biographies and some photographs of their work or videos demonstrating the techniques they used or invented. Such a site has a certain instructional value, but it does not suggest activities geared toward the acquisition of target competencies. Because the reference portal is similar to a textbook, the designer needs to add a course syllabus in the form of a learning scenario. For example, the analysis of a period using criteria involving color or perspective or the degree of abstract expression in the art of that period could form the basis of a learning scenario.

Explor@ allows a designer to make such additions to a reference portal without modifying it. The designer can integrate an instructional structure navigator that allows site navigation according to the activities to be carried out. Other resources in the environment can also provide synchronous or asynchronous tools that allow reference portal users to hold team discussions or participate in newsgroups.

Resource Centers

Workshops, exhibitions, and laboratories are sites that can take the shape of a *resource center* that favors learning in a particular field of knowledge. The pages of the Web site are then structured for access to resources gathered according to a teaching concept, or metaphor if you will—laboratory, workshop, exhibition, and so forth—rather than organized around learning activities or information structures as in a hyperguide or a reference portal.

For example, a site set up as a virtual exhibition might group pages taking the shape of kiosks that can be visited in an unspecified order. Such a site might address information technologies, investment vehicles, housing, or any other subject amenable to the exhibition format. Among these kiosks the user might find an entry area for registration, spaces for socializing and relaxing (a café forum, for example), interactive demonstrations with simulators or courseware, workshops and discussion groups conducted through forums or videoconferences, multimedia presentations of case studies, and problem-solving clinics using audio- or videoconferencing with a content expert.

Some instructional content, the exhibition topic, is present in each of the kiosks in one way or another, but the site is not structured according to this content. Also, the site lends itself to the use of a variety of learning scenarios.

The participant can view the exhibition in different ways through these different scenarios or by visiting paths on the exhibition site suggested according to user background, user time availability, and content of specific user interest. These scenarios are not in the Web site but are accessed through the Explor@ navigator. A knowledge navigator may also be integrated to help the user select kiosks to visit according to their content. Moreover, duplication of environment resources is avoided as most resources can be integrated into the Web site.

The same concepts apply to a science laboratory or a writing or art workshop. The chemistry laboratory presents various devices and available setups in the pages that represent various lab areas, similar to the exhibition kiosks. In the same way, the writing workshop offers various tools—such as text editors, spell checkers, interactive grammars, and text diagrams of different types—that facilitate the production of various writing projects.

SUMMARY

This chapter examined a distributed learning approach that provides for a diversity of resources, materials, media, and pedagogies and their integration into an Internet Web site structured in different ways depending on course activities, information, and resources. This approach also facilitates the reuse of these items in other courses. This integrated site is completed by one or many environments, each adapted to the role of a type of user called an actor who interacts in the delivery of a learning system.

Such a system constitutes a three-level virtual learning center. The Explor@ implementation of this architecture is currently used to deliver network training in a number of organizations. Each course can be designed according to a different model. The virtual learning center may integrate courses that currently exist on the Web without modifying their format. Or it may facilitate the conversion of traditional courses into Internet training, allowing an organization to gradually transform its training methods.

The central management of resources in environments adapted to the needs of each actor allows the design of course Web sites that compared to more traditional course sites can be created quickly, are lighter in links and icons, and are easier to revise on a regular basis. The load of maintaining the global training environment is also reduced. For example, if a new communication tool becomes available, it is not necessary to update each course. Instead, only a simple substitution is required at the central resource repository. Also, once the first course is carried out, each new course can be summarized in a few Web pages and hyperlinks to existing documents, the majority of the resources being accessible to the users from the Explor@ window.

This chapter reveals a number of basic questions that need to be answered when designing a learning system. Which resources shall we reuse or build? Which delivery model shall we select? Who will the actors be? Which resources will they need? Shall we structure the course according to its activities, its contents, or its resources? These questions and many others like them underline the importance, now greater than ever, for designers to employ a learning system design methodology and supporting tools. These are the topics I discuss in the following chapters.

3

Foundations of Instructional Engineering

WE MUST MAKE a multiplicity of decisions when creating an e-learning system, and the fast evolution of on-line learning is only increasing their numbers. The new and extremely varied pedagogical possibilities available using information and communication technologies constitute the first argument for a methodology adapted to the creation of an e-learning system.

In addition, an on-line learning system is, from a technical perspective, a computer system equipped with software tools, digitized documents, and communication services that are much more diversified than in the past. The development of such systems on the Internet can no longer be considered a handicraft and somehow separated from rigorous methods used in other fields of information science. Software engineering methods are now starting to dominate in Internet applications. They are even more useful when it comes to creating Internet learning systems.

Yet another reason for a systematic approach to learning system creation is the importance of knowledge management in today's organizations. We now recognize knowledge and expertise as the most valuable asset of an individual or an organization. This is the same recognition that contributed to the development of expert systems during the 1970s and 1980s. Since then, techniques and data-processing tools have evolved; knowledge-based systems are integrated into other computer systems. However, the methods of knowledge extraction, formalization, and processing—in other words, knowledge (or cognitive) engineering—remain at the core of knowledge management processes and also, consequently, at the core of learning system design.

In this chapter, I survey the methodological questions that learning system design raises. The results of this examination are then developed in later chapters. which will be developed in other parts of the book. I will present an instructional engineering method, a computerized system of method support, and the use of the method for the creation, the production, and the delivery of learning events in a virtual learning center, such as that presented in the previous chapter.

Instructional engineering may be defined as follows: *A method that supports the analysis, the creation, the production, and the delivery planning of a learning system, integrating the concepts, the processes, and the principles of instructional design, software engineering, and knowledge engineering.*

Systemic Methods

Located at the crossroads of instructional design, software engineering, and knowledge engineering (Figure 3-1), from all of which it inherits its major properties, instructional engineering is a particular systemic method in the field of educational problem solving. Instructional engineering is founded on the science of systems, which defines the concept of a system as a series of units in dynamic interaction, organized in order to achieve specific goals.[1]

The method I am defining here aims to design a series of instructional objects to be built. It includes tasks and operational principles organized to support the creation of a learning system. The latter is a system itself, used by

Figure 3-1. Foundations of Instructional Engineering.

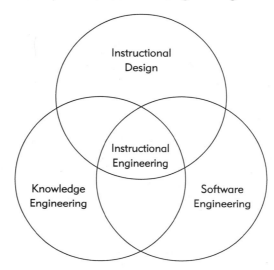

learners and other participants at the moment of delivery. In other words, instructional engineering is a system that aims to develop other systems: learning systems.

Instructional engineering is first and foremost a complex process of problem solving as defined in cognitive science[2] and is sometimes studied as such in educational sciences.[3]

The problems of instructional engineering are first general problems, then design problems (similar to those in architecture or mechanical engineering), then problems of instructional design, and finally, problems of instructional design calling upon the pedagogies of one or many disciplines. The study of each one of these four levels of problems generates a useful framework for the creation of an instructional engineering method.

The general cognitive science model of problem solving leads me to characterize the process of instructional engineering in the following terms:

- Identify a final state: here the learning system to be built, as defined in the previous chapter.

- Identify an initial state: a more or less precise definition of the training problem the learning system must solve.

- Identify operators, or processes: these will allow the transformation of the initial definition of the problem into increasingly precise descriptions until a concrete system is produced.

The systemic approach provides a general methodology to solve complex problems, inspired by the scientific approach and precursory work like Polya's in the field of mathematics didactics.[4] It is applied to various problems in economy, architecture, education, and product design. The systemic approach identifies five main phases or processes through which problem-solving activity evolves, guided by methodological rules. These phases are

- *The definition of the problem,* which means the most precise identification possible of the characteristics and constraints of the solution sought (the final state) and the data or the current situation (the initial state).

- *The analysis of the problem,* which generates possible alternatives for the development of a solution.

- *The development of a solution plan,* which identifies the operations, the stages, the phases, or the means by which the current situation could be transformed in order to reach the final state.

- *The application or the implementation of the solution plan,* which involves assembling the elements of the plan to produce situations that are increasingly close to the final state.

- *The evaluation of the solution and the revision,* which means, on one hand, verifying that the solution obtained corresponds to the solution sought, and on the other hand, examining the solution obtained in order to reuse it to solve other problems.

Polya qualifies this problem-solving process as "heuristic,"[5] which means it is guided by methodological principles that do not guarantee success but that offer "good" leads toward the solution. Such principles can be framed as questions we may ask at each phase. For example, at the problem definition phase we may ask, What is the goal? What are we looking for exactly? Can the unknown be broken down into various units? And which units? What are the available data for the problem? At the analysis phase we may also ask, What conditions or relationships exist between the data and the unknown that would make it possible to pass from one to the other? And at the plan development phase we may ask, Can the problem be broken down into simpler problems? Do we have a solution for an analogous problem? Must the plan process data by successive approximations toward the unknown or, conversely, start from the goal and use regressive reasoning?

This general methodology is useful for instructional engineering because it invites us as designers to deconstruct the training problems, which are seldom simple, into more accessible problems, those for which a solution may be imagined more quickly and then combined with other partial solutions. It also invites us to distinguish between the plan developed (here an instructional model or course syllabus) and its implementation, that is, the production of instructional material, the choice of media supports, and the integration of tools and means of communication. Last of all it invites us to plan an evaluation and revision phase before the implementation of the learning system.

The design problems are similar whether we work in architecture or in physical, software, or instructional engineering. In all cases the solution is the creation of a system that deals with certain constraints that are barely defined at the start and that must be specified in the initial phase and then made more specific throughout the process. After observing engineers working on design problems of various types, Goël and Pirolli identified a certain number of invariable types of strategic knowledge used during the problem-solving process,[6] and their findings relate to the complexity of the instructional design problem.

- The designers engage in intense activity in structuring and restructuring the problem.

- The designers develop several system models, in plans, functional diagrams, and prototypes.

- The fact that there are no "good" or "bad" answers leads to the continual evaluation of the value of a solution or of a component of the solution.

- This evaluation is iterative and carried out by successive approximations.

- The designers tend to gradually specify the contours of the system while trying to preserve a certain latitude.

- The designers deconstruct the problem into permeable modules having intersections and links that are more or less elaborate.

- The designers move from the initial abstract goals toward the final concrete specifications by a series of increasingly precise approximations, until they produce the system that constitutes the solution to the initial problem.

- The designers use symbolic and graphic systems abundantly to describe the intermediate results.

The MISA method presented in Chapter Four was inspired largely by this systemic analysis of design problems. These principles also apply to the three methodologies from which MISA inherits some of its properties: instructional design, software engineering, and knowledge engineering.

Instructional Systems Design

Instruction systems design is also known as *instructional design* (ID), instructional science,[7] and scientific pedagogy.[8] The origin of instructional design goes back to John Dewey, who a century ago sought the development of a "bridging science" between learning theories and educational practices.[9] His demand was heard at the beginning of the 1960s, a date at which we can speak about the beginnings of a new discipline, mainly under the influence of the work of B. F. Skinner, Jerome Bruner, and David Ausubel.[10] Skinner proposed a scientific approach to education by distinguishing it from the study of learning while developing the first instructional intervention model validated on an empirical basis.[11] In contrast to the behaviorist approach adopted by Skinner, Bruner developed an educational instruction theory and intellectual development training courses.[12] At around the same time, Ausubel built an instructional model leading to presentation methods based on cognitive structures.[13]

In the 1970s and 1980s, works aimed at building instructional theories blossomed: we saw the development of a cybernetic approach,[14] the exposure of learning conditions,[15] the identification of instructional strategies based on structuralist learning theories,[16] the development of a cognitive teaching theory through research activities,[17] a theory developed from the analysis of instructional strategy components,[18] and a development theory for task analysis and design.[19]

Because it derives from these various findings, instructional design presents itself today as a collection of theories and models permitting us to understand, improve, and apply instructional methods that favor learning. Compared to the theories developed in educational psychology, instructional design can be seen as a form of engineering aiming to improve educational practices. Its link with educational psychology is analogous to the link between engineering methods and the physical sciences or between the practice of medicine and the life sciences.

The result of the practice of instructional design is a series of plans and models describing the development of learning and teaching activities. These plans and models gather together a series of prescriptions to support learning, rather than descriptions of learning processes. Due to the magnitude of the training problem, the plans and models containing these prescriptions must apply to several levels: for example, the training plan, the training program, the course, the module, and the learning activity.

As a discipline, as a component of educational science, instructional design pursues a goal that requires optimal quality in plans and models. Other fields of educational science are mandated to optimize the development of instructional materials and manage the development projects of a learning system or to implement and manage the training delivery. In this sense the instructional engineering method presented in the next chapter (MISA) falls into the framework of instructional design; it is thus possible for MISA to make use of the knowledge already developed within the models and theories of instructional design, such as those discussed previously. However, according to a growing number of experts in this field, the methods generated by these theories have proved to be, at the very least, incomplete and often inadequate for e-learning. These experts have underlined the fact that it is difficult to find the methods and computerized instructional design support tools that allow designers to efficiently develop programs and courses.[20]

Today it seems necessary to renew instructional design methodology in light of the requirements of the knowledge society and the evolution of learning systems toward e-learning. The existing instructional design models and theories were built on solid foundations and an impressive body of work. The problem lies elsewhere, on the level of the operationalization of the theoretical elements and their integration into a method that is both systemic and cognitivist. In other words, as the main researchers in the field willingly recognize, instructional design methodology has not yet succeeded in filling completely the gap between learning theories and educational practices.

Software Engineering

Software engineering, a branch of information systems engineering, is an interesting field to examine in relation to operationalizing instructional expertise. On one hand, learning systems are information systems that are increasingly computerized and complex; on the other hand, software engineering has been successful at gradually overcoming the artistic tendency in computer programming—that is, the tendency to treat each program as a unique creation of a unique individual—which has proved to be inadequate for building increasingly complex information systems.

The similarity between much existing instructional design and early software engineering can be clearly seen in the following description; just replace the term *programmer* with *designer.*

> The first agents to resist the modern approaches of software engineering are creative and solitary programmers. They can be identified from afar. They seriously delve into their trade, yet they often find it difficult to explain or document their work. They work late at night, with the goal to correct a problem often caused by incomprehensible soft-

ware of low quality, which undergoes frequent repairs. They consider their work a stimulating artistic experience. They have little confidence in the assistance of other programmers, documentation or practices which do not directly relate to their work. The source code they create is unique, elegant and generally incomprehensible to others, which explains why we consider them indispensable [p. 1].[21]

Programming as a personal art is becoming less and less productive because modern information systems require software interoperability and maintenance over long periods of time. More and more, the size, complexity, and vital character of information systems simply exceed the comprehension capacities of a single programmer. The main objective of software engineering has become to provide processes and tools that allow the production of correct, efficient, extensible, flexible, modifiable, portable, reliable, reusable, valid, and comprehensible systems.

An information system, in particular a learning system, is an artificial object (an artifact) built by creating a representation of the activity of a real system, collecting, saving, processing, and making available all or part of this activity in a comprehensible form to an end-user. As one information systems engineer has pointed out: "One of the major difficulties of information systems engineering is that the said systems are more or less immaterial objects. Nobody has ever seen an information system, and this system is visible only from its representations: documentation, models, etc. . . . We must be certain that several parties describing the same object will arrive at the same formal representation, which brings up the fidelity problem of modeling techniques" (p. 27, my translation).[22]

Information systems engineering is a methodology composed of actors, processes, products, and operational principles. It is global, sharing a common language with multiple users and various disciplines. It is dynamic, concerned with the evolution of system components through various processes. It clearly identifies the delivered goods and the products that result from these various processes. It is built on operational principles that consider the characteristics of human design activities, in particular the influential links that are iterative rather than linear and require frequent backtracks, joint acceptance by the *standards breakers* and *system users,* and finally, the diversity of the application modes of these principles, in particular the independence between the method and the computer tools or software engineering support systems.

The methods of information systems engineering suggest a methodological division of a system into modules, phases, or stages that correspond to processes that reflect in-time development without necessarily imposing linear execution. The processes include the following:

Critical observation, statement of the premises, or diagnosis. This process must lead to precise and well-supported recommendations regarding the opportunity to build a system or modify an existing system. The main product is a diagnosis resulting from our reflection on a new system whose equivalent does not exist in the organization or on the reengineering or validation of an existing system to respond to a new problem in the organization.

General orientations, establishment of the operational principles. Starting from a preliminary diagnosis, we study the possible strategies and propose one or many general scenarios for the evolution of a system. This process allows us to define orientation principles describing the selection of the types of resources to be integrated, the activities and the actors to be supported, and the means to place at their disposal.

Preliminary definition. In this process we define, on the basis of our general orientations, one or many operational solutions, considering the products available on the market. Here we will formalize the general orientations, develop an initial model of the target situation, and study and evaluate contrasting setting scenarios, all of which will lead us to recommendations for the design of the system.

Modeling of the system architecture. On the basis of the selected solution, we deal with the problems of composition, organization, computer system structure, choice of resource types, and implementation orientations of the future system. This phase naturally leads to the production of a model or prototype that illustrates, as best as possible, the general operation of the future system. This phase ends as soon as the users and clients, using the prototype, have validated the key technological choices made in the architectural model.

Programming the system. The programming phase consists of transforming the software specifications of the architectural phase into coded components that once assembled become a computer application. In certain cases when an existing system is being reengineered, the use of high-level software engineering tools (or CASE tools) can decrease or even remove much of the use of programming language. In all cases, in a shift from the programming style typical of the early development of the computer sciences, programming becomes a technique rather than an art. It is a milestone, sometimes mandatory, in system development, representing one phase of the many necessary phases of software development.

Simulation and qualification of the system. The simulation design must make it possible to launch the qualification of the system, that is, its validation through tests. The qualification consists of verifying the adequacy of the software to meet the specifications of the architectural plan and the service characteristics expected by the users.

Implementation of the system. The implementation phase prepares for the operation of the computer system in the context of the users. We must not only install the new or revised system but also prepare the structures that will support the software, the materials that will support the information bases, and the management and exploitation procedures that will ensure the quality of the system's operation in the organization.

Exploitation of the system. This process is the final step in information systems engineering, testing in a real setting. It is guided by an evolution plan that generally specifies a system breaking-in period, after which we must expect to revise certain system functions. Thereafter, we continuously observe the system, gather data about system operation in the target environment, analyze and synthesize these observations, and manage the changes that must be made to ensure the maintenance of the system.

In contrast to instructional design, instructional engineering is inspired by the design principles for information systems and adapts them to learning system design. Instructional engineering plans similar processes that are mostly executed in parallel and through successive iterations called *deliveries*. It precisely describes the products of these processes and their contribution to the general model of the learning system. It values developing a sound architecture for the learning system rather than the hasty and artistic development of instructional materials. Finally, it includes careful preparations of the installation and the delivery of the learning system.

Knowledge Engineering

Knowledge engineering was developed in stride with the applications of expert systems and artificial intelligence over the last thirty years. The first systems that qualified as expert tackled complex fields of human expertise in order to create computer systems that rendered this expertise available to a greater number of people than before.

The first expert system, DENDRAL, which was developed in the field of chemistry, used a significant knowledge base focused on analysis of data collected by a mass spectrograph. As this extremely complex knowledge was often poorly understood and applied and never indexed, it was necessary to extract it from human experts and imitate their behavior in the selection and treatment of relevant knowledge. Thereafter other expert systems were developed, in fields such as medical diagnosis (MYCIN), symbolic calculation (MACSYMA), and the relationships between mineral deposits (PROSPECTOR). This knowledge engineering approach was also applied to various types of problems, such as predicting consequences from a description of the situation, planning a series of operations, and monitoring energy power stations to identify failures or to prescribe corrective measures.[23]

Knowledge engineering has also been applied in education to diagnose students' deficiencies and suggest strategies to resolve them. These intelligent tutorial systems[24] are in fact composed of three expert systems: the first employs expert knowledge in solving certain types of problems, the second offers a diagnosis to the student solving a problem of this type, and the third uses tutorial strategies to offer appropriate assistance to the student.

Another application of the expert systems in education directly targets expertise in instructional design.[25] These expert systems have the designer play the role of the student in an intelligent tutorial system. They contain knowledge of instructional design that enables them, for example, to automatically build educational software from the designer's specifications for material content and shape.

During the 1990s, expert systems increasingly took the shape of components integrated into other computer systems, bringing their hosts intelligence by integrating expertise in the form of knowledge base. Thus we speak of knowledge-based systems,[26] advisers, or intelligent agents. As indicated in Table 3-1, the introduction of expert knowledge into computer systems represents a significant evolution at the core of what we now call *knowledge management.*

The terms *data, information,* and *knowledge* label three stages in the evolution of computer systems. At the beginning, the large computerized management systems processed great quantities of numeric and symbolic data. These data were stored in predetermined and fixed formats built by a computer specialist from the information provided by a manager. At the beginning of

Table 3-1. Three Generations of Computer Systems.

Level	Method	Tools	Actors
1	Data management	Central management systems for standard format data	Computer analysts, managers
2	Information management	Relational database systems	Computer architects, content experts
3	Knowledge management	Knowledge-based expert system shells	Knowledge engineers, computer experts, content experts

the 1980s, we became more and more aware of the information contained in the relationships between various data, and we started talking about *information processing.* The relational databases built by computer architects and containing the data provided by a content expert made it possible to dynamically vary the formats of data, relying on links between the tables storing various components of the data. However, the information that resulted remained limited to factual knowledge.

The passage to knowledge processing now makes it possible to manage, in an integrated fashion, not only factual knowledge (data and information) but also more abstract knowledge describing the concepts, procedures, rules, methods, know-how, and models of interest to a group of people or an organization. Knowledge acquisition, modeling, processing, and communication then become essential processes for building an organizational memory, and for developing methods to exploit it and thus render available to the users means of improving their knowledge or making that knowledge available to others.

In this context a new track appears, that of knowledge engineer, and a new discipline, knowledge engineering, which studies the methods and practices for developing knowledge-based systems. The notion of knowledge representation and modeling, which will be covered later on, occupies a significant place in these methods.

Knowledge engineering implies operations like identifying knowledge, explaining it, representing it, and translating it into a symbolic or graphic language in order to facilitate its subsequent use. In a typical situation the knowledge engineer discusses this knowledge with one or many content experts who have the expertise he or she wishes to model. Using systematic interview methods designed for the acquisition of knowledge, the engineer gradually refines a representation of the field, by iterative stages, until he or she captures it in a synthetic form, which will generally be integrated in a computer system.

However, knowledge engineering is also useful independently of this last stage as it facilitates an explicit and structured view of knowledge that can then be communicated directly to users or used as a basis for instructional engineering of a learning system. That is, knowledge engineering can be integrated into an instructional engineering method, as it is in the method discussed in this book. The knowledge engineering processes are adapted and specialized to help designers define the contents, the instructional scenarios, the instructional materials, and the delivery models of the learning system.

On another level, knowledge engineering can also help in defining the instructional engineering method itself. By applying one form or another of knowledge engineering throughout this book, I am identifying the concepts, processes, and principles of instructional engineering. The sources of expertise are the theories and instructional design models of educational sciences and the concepts, processes, and principles of software and knowledge engineering.

A Knowledge Representation System

In instructional engineering the first questions asked are: Which knowledge must be acquired? Which knowledge must be taught? What are the target competencies? The goal of the remainder of this chapter is to delve deeper into knowledge representation and human competencies through an organized system of symbols, to present this system, and describe how important it is for knowledge acquisition and learning system creation.

Graphic Representation of Knowledge

We often hear that a picture is worth a thousand words. That is surely true of sketches, diagrams, and graphics used in various fields of knowledge. With these tools we can strive to generalize and consolidate, using at first the same vocabulary and the various forms of graphic representations that are useful in education: conceptual charts, flowcharts, and decision trees.

Conceptual charts are widely used in education to represent relationships between concepts. By explicitly presenting conceptual network associations, educators aim to facilitate new knowledge assimilation, whether in a context of presentation or explanation by a trainer or in a context of knowledge construction and organization by a learner.

Figure 3-2 displays a conceptual chart, or model, that describes cause-and-effect relationships among various factors that affect climate change. These relationships, or links, reveal a good portion of the knowledge domain and constitute a first synthesis, or a starting point, for building a more thorough analysis using other factors, or links.

Figure 3-2. A Conceptual Chart of Climate Change.

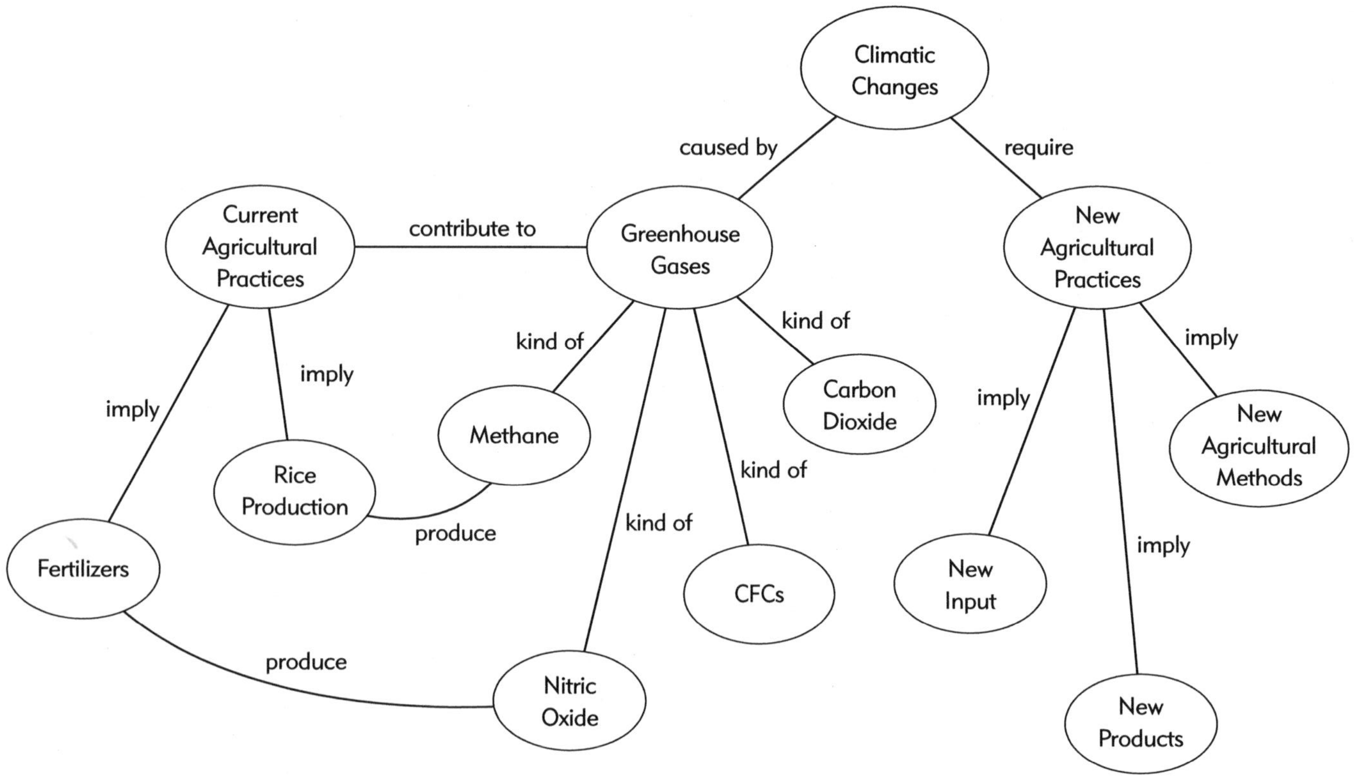

Notice that conceptual charts sometimes use links whose direction of operation is not always clear and that may obscure the interpretation. It is necessary to impose a top-to-bottom and left-to-right reading mode to call on other knowledge contexts that do not appear on the chart, to know that in fact it is the rice production that produces methane and not the opposite. Also, as the vocabulary selection is left to the person who creates the model, inaccuracies can hinder communication and knowledge transfer from one person to another.

Flowcharts, in contrast to conceptual charts, are graphic representations of procedural knowledge, such as algorithms. Flowcharts are used in introductory programming courses and also in other fields of knowledge, such as education. Figure 3-3 presents two simple examples of flowcharts. The first one represents a programming algorithm used to calculate the sum of positive integers, whatever the *N* value provided. The second is a simplified presentation of an instructional engineering method called learner verification and revision (LVR), which validates instructional materials through a number of verification and revision cycles performed by the learners.

Figure 3-3. Two Examples of Flowcharts.

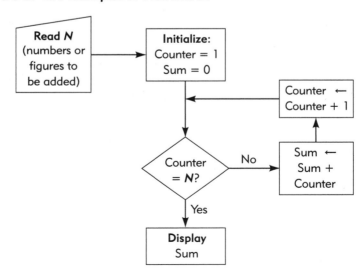

Figure 3-3. Two Examples of Flowcharts, Cont'd.

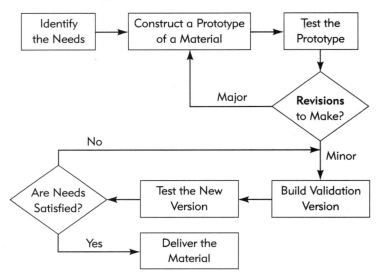

Flowcharts are composed of actions and decisions that lead to a series of actions. They are dynamic rather than static. They unfold in time and contain a number of cycles, or loops, that come to a stop when certain statements are satisfied, for example, that the set of numbers to add is empty, or that the test results indicate the needs are reasonably satisfied.

Decision trees constitute another form of representation used in various fields, particularly in decision-making systems and expert systems, to establish cause-and-effect links between various factors. The decisions are often based on administrative, instructional, or other types of rules. Figure 3-4 presents a section of a decision tree used to detect the causes of automobile breakdowns.

To build such a decision tree, we start with one of the attributes (here, oil level) that influence the attribute we wish to evaluate (here, lubrication problems). We trace an arc for each possible value of the first attribute in relation to a second attribute (here, oil pressure). We repeat this process for this second attribute in relation to a third attribute, and so on. Once all the attributes have been examined, we connect each branch end to the evaluated attribute (here, lubrication), and we determine the value of this attribute in each problem case: normal, temperature, pressure, or oil level.

Figure 3-4. A Decision Tree to Diagnose Automobile Breakdowns.

Source: This example was inspired by Paquette, G., and Roy, L. *Systèmes à base de connaissances*
(*Knowledge-Based Systems*). Montreal: Télé-université and Beauchemin, 1990.

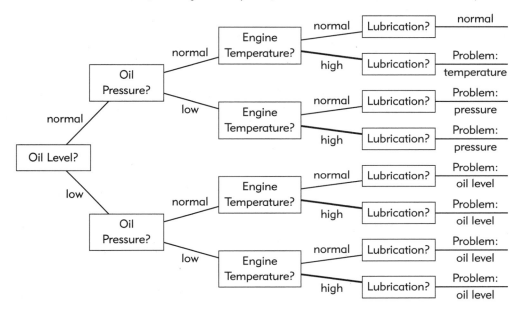

In fact a decision tree allows the user to build a series of rules (knowledge in the form of principles) that will constitute the knowledge base of an expert system. We can obtain the following rules that summarize the decision tree in Figure 3-4:

If oil level = normal and oil pressure = normal and engine temperature = normal

Then lubrication = normal

If oil level = normal and oil pressure = normal and engine temperature = high

Then lubrication = temperature problem

If oil level = normal and oil pressure = low

Then lubrication = oil pressure problem

If oil level = low

Then lubrication = oil level problem

MOT: A Language Representation Tool

The Modeling with Object Types (MOT) knowledge representation technique that I have developed, and its corresponding MOT editor, provide a way to build graphic models showing knowledge types and the relationships between them. It has become a useful aid for instructional design both for academia and the workplace.

MOT models are composed of up to six types of knowledge and seven types of relationships. They deal with knowledge broadly defined: not only factual and abstract knowledge, concepts, procedures, and principles but also the cognitive skills that are considered meta-knowledge. Indeed, anything that can be learned by humans, including cognitive, motor, or socioaffective skills, may be called knowledge.

In MOT diagrams, each knowledge type is represented by a different geometrical figure. Abstract knowledge is an object class that organizes facts into more or less complex coherent sets. MOT distinguishes three types of abstract knowledge: concepts, procedures, and principles (see Table 3-2).

Table 3-2. Definitions and Symbols for Abstract Knowledge Types.

Abstract Knowledge	Symbol
Concepts, or conceptual knowledge, describe the nature of the objects of a field (the "what"); they represent an object class through their common properties, each object of the class distinguishing itself from others through the values these properties take.	Concept
Procedures, or procedural knowledge, describe the series of operations used to act on objects (the "how"); they are concerned with the action combinations that can be applied to several cases, each case distinguishing itself from the others through the objects to which the actions can apply and the transformations they undergo.	Procedure

Table 3-2. Definitions and Symbols for Abstract Knowledge Types, Cont'd.

Abstract Knowledge	Symbol
Principles, or strategic knowledge, are statements that describe the properties of objects, to establish cause-and-effect links between objects (the "why") or to determine which conditions apply to a procedure (the "when"); principles generally take the form: "if condition X, then condition Y or action Y."	Principle

Facts are data, observations, examples, prototypes, production processes, or statements that enable us to describe specific objects. We can distinguish three types of facts: examples, traces, and statements (see Table 3-3).

Table 3-3. Definitions and Symbols for Facts.

Facts	Symbol
Examples are obtained by specifying the values of each attribute of a concept, obtaining a series of facts describing a very precise, concrete object.	Example
Traces are obtained by specifying the variables of each action in a procedure, obtaining a very precise series of particular actions called an execution trace.	Trace
Statements are obtained by specifying the variables of a principle, thus obtaining cause-and-effect links among the particular properties of an object or among the properties of a particular object and a specific action to carry out.	Statement

Table 3-4 presents examples of the ways the graphic symbols just defined can be interpreted and thus what they can be used to represent. The general utility of a representation system depends on the flexibility with which we can interpret the symbols when they are used in various contexts. The MOT knowledge representation system can be used to present various categories of objects from the real world, as displayed in Table 3-4.

Table 3-4. Interpretation Examples for Three Types of Knowledge.

Type	Interpretations and Examples
Concept	Object classes: countries, clothing, vehicles . . . Types of documents: forms, booklets, images . . . Tool categories: text editors, televisions . . . Groups of people: doctors, Europeans . . . Event classes: floods, conferences . . .
Procedure	Generic operations: add up numbers, assemble an engine . . . General tasks: complete a report, supervise production . . . General activities: take an exam, teach a course . . . Instructions: follow a recipe, assemble a device . . . Scenarios: the unfolding of a film, of a meeting . . .
Principle	Properties: the taxpayer has children, cars have four wheels . . . Constraints: the task must be completed within twenty days . . . Cause-and-effect relationships: if it rains more than five days, the harvest will be destroyed . . . Laws: any metal sufficiently heated will stretch out . . . Theories: all the laws of the market economy . . . Rules of decision: rules to select an investment, . . . Prescriptions: principles of instructional design, . . . Regulating agent or actor: the writer who composes a text, . . .

It should be noted that abstract knowledge is always interpreted by classes of objects, actions, or statements. Concepts, procedures, and principles must consider the variability of objects, actions, and statements. If only one occurrence is possible, if there is no variability, we are dealing with fact or a series of facts: example, trace, or statement.

The knowledge relationships in MOT diagrams are represented by arrows bearing a letter that specifies the type of relationship. There are seven basic types of knowledge relationships, or links. The first link, the instantiation, connects abstract knowledge and facts. Five other links connect the various types of abstract knowledge. A seventh link connects knowledge to skills and is presented toward the end of this chapter.

> *The instantiation link (I)* connects abstract knowledge to a fact obtained by giving values to all of the attributes (variables) of the abstract knowledge. Each concept, procedure, or principle instantiates in a series of facts (examples, traces, or statements).
>
> *Example:* "Renault cars" has as an instance "John's car."

> *The composition link (C; "is composed of")* connects knowledge to one of its components or one of its constituent parts. We can then specify the attributes of an object as components of some specific knowledge by connecting the object to each of its attributes with a composition link. (In other representation systems, the C-link has the meaning "is a component of." It has a broader sense here.)
>
> *Examples:* The "automobile" is composed of a "body," a "price," a "color."

> *The specialization link (S; "a sort of")* connects two items of abstract knowledge of the same type where one is a particular case to the other one. In other words, the second one is more generic or more abstract than the first one.
>
> *Example:* A "convertible" is a kind of "automobile."

> *The precedence link (P)* connects two procedures or principles of which the first one must be completed or evaluated before the second starts or is applied.
>
> *Example:* "Drafting a plan" precedes "writing the text."

The input-product link (I/P) connects a concept and a procedure. Considering the relationship from the concept toward the procedure, the concept is an input to the procedure. Considering the relationship from the procedure toward the concept, the procedure produces the concept, which generally represents the class of object resulting from the procedure.

Examples: "The plan" is input of "writing the text"; "writing the text" has "the text" as a product.

The regulation link (R; "rules" or "governs") is used from a principle toward another item of abstract knowledge, which may be a concept, a procedure, or another principle. In the first case the principle defines the concept by constraints to be satisfied (sometimes called *integrity constraints*), or it establishes a law or a relationship between two or several concepts. In the second and third cases, the regulation link means that the principle controls, from the exterior, the execution of a procedure or the selection of one or more principles.

Examples: "The layout principles on the page" govern "the plan"; "traffic control laws" govern "get a plane off the ground"; "the project management principles" govern "the design principles to apply."

Types of Models and Examples

Object-oriented representation systems allow the modeling of a variety of knowledge systems. The types of abstract knowledge—concepts, procedures, and principles—and the three types of facts can be combined into increasingly complex systems of structured knowledge. Figure 3-5 presents five classes of knowledge models that can be divided further into sixteen types of models.

Table 3-5 presents definitions of the five first-level types.

Figure 3-5. Taxonomy of Knowledge Models.

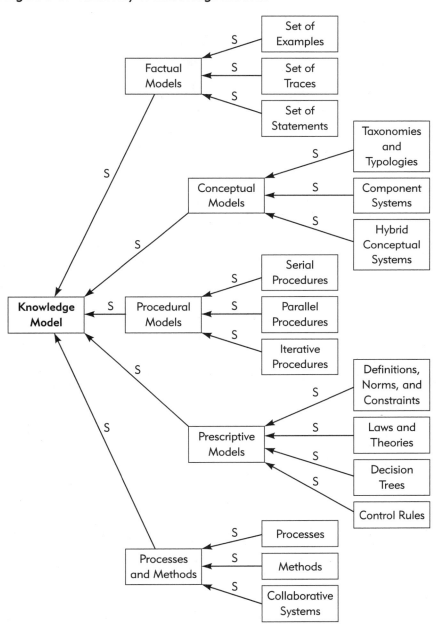

Table 3-5. Main Model Categories.

Class	Definition	Examples
Factual models	Most of the knowledge is facts.	A multiplication table; the execution traces generated by processing a form; a network of relationships among people.
Conceptual models	Most of the knowledge is concepts.	A car, its subsystems, and their components; the animal kingdom taxonomy.
Procedural models	Most of the knowledge is procedures.	An income tax calculation procedure; the procedure used to solve an equation with two unknowns.
Prescriptive models	Most of the knowledge is principles.	A feature checklist used by prospective home buyers to select a house; the laws of gravity; the theory of natural selection.
Processes and methods	No knowledge type is prevalent.	A project management process or method; the experimental method; the MISA method presented in Chapter Four.

Figure 3-6 presents a MOT model of the same knowledge that is displayed by the conceptual chart presented in Figure 3-2. This example clarifies the distinction between knowledge types in MOT. Here, the current and new agricultural practices are presented as procedures, because the author of the model considers them to be a set of human activities. Certain subcategories (S-link), such as the use of fertilizers and the production of rice, produce (I/P-links) an increase of gases such as methane or nitric oxide that

Figure 3-6. MOT Model of a Conceptual Chart.

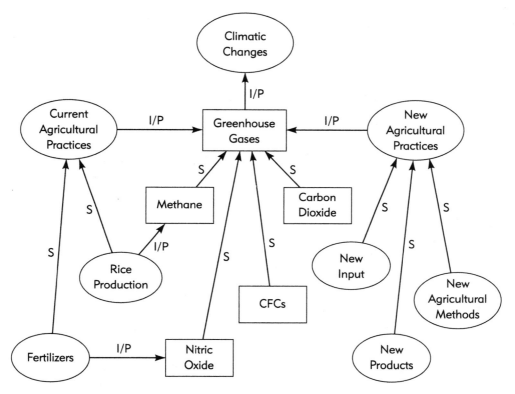

contribute to the greenhouse effect. The same sort of reasoning applies for the new agricultural practices, which can produce a reduction in greenhouse effect gases. The model also emphasizes the categories of greenhouse gases and the fact that they are inputs of climate change.

Figure 3-7 presents the MOT model of a development procedure for instructional material, which has as much expressive force as the flowchart presented in Figure 3-3.

Figure 3-7. MOT Model of an Algorithm.

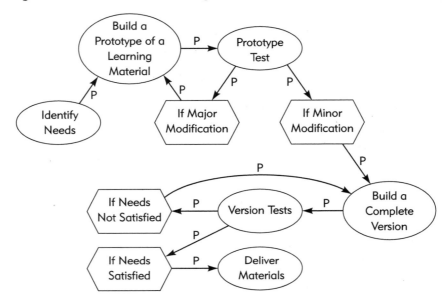

Figure 3-8 presents in MOT language the decision tree displayed in Figure 3-4. It explicitly reveals the principles that govern each procedure in order to identify the specific cause of a car breakdown in the case of a lubrication problem. Here, the model author has chosen to state the rules in the form of four relational principles, each one being a component of the "Lubrication Rules." Each of these principles has two components: a condition, which states certain properties of the attributes influencing the result (here, oil level, oil pressure, and engine temperature), and a conclusion stating a property of the target attribute (here, lubrication).

A set of rules that permitted the user to discover other possible reasons for a car breakdown, such as those related to the engine, the fuel injection system, or the electrical system, could be stated in the same way. Compared to Figure 3-4, the model displayed in Figure 3-8 clearly highlights the level of decision of each group of rules. It allows the user to interpret the rules directly rather than indirectly.

Processes relate to the dynamics of a system such as the operations of a factory or the tasks leading to the diagnosis of a medical or mechanical prob-

Figure 3-8. MOT Model of a Decision Tree.

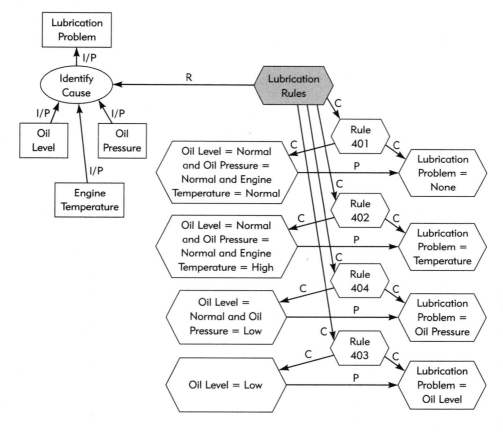

lem, the cash flow forecast of a company, or the performance evaluation process of a department. Here, the input-product link is essential between concepts, which represent the objects or products to be treated, and the procedures that transform them. Decision principles control the passage from one procedure to another in the process. They are precise principles with a descriptive character, which is necessary for understanding the process. Figure 3-9 presents a MOT model to diagnose a defective sound system. The action of repairing a defective stereo is composed of five procedures, numbered one through five on the figure. The basic development of the process is indicated by the chain of I/P links, indicating the procedures' input and products, and by the P-links between principles and procedures.

Figure 3-9. MOT Model of a Diagnostic Process.

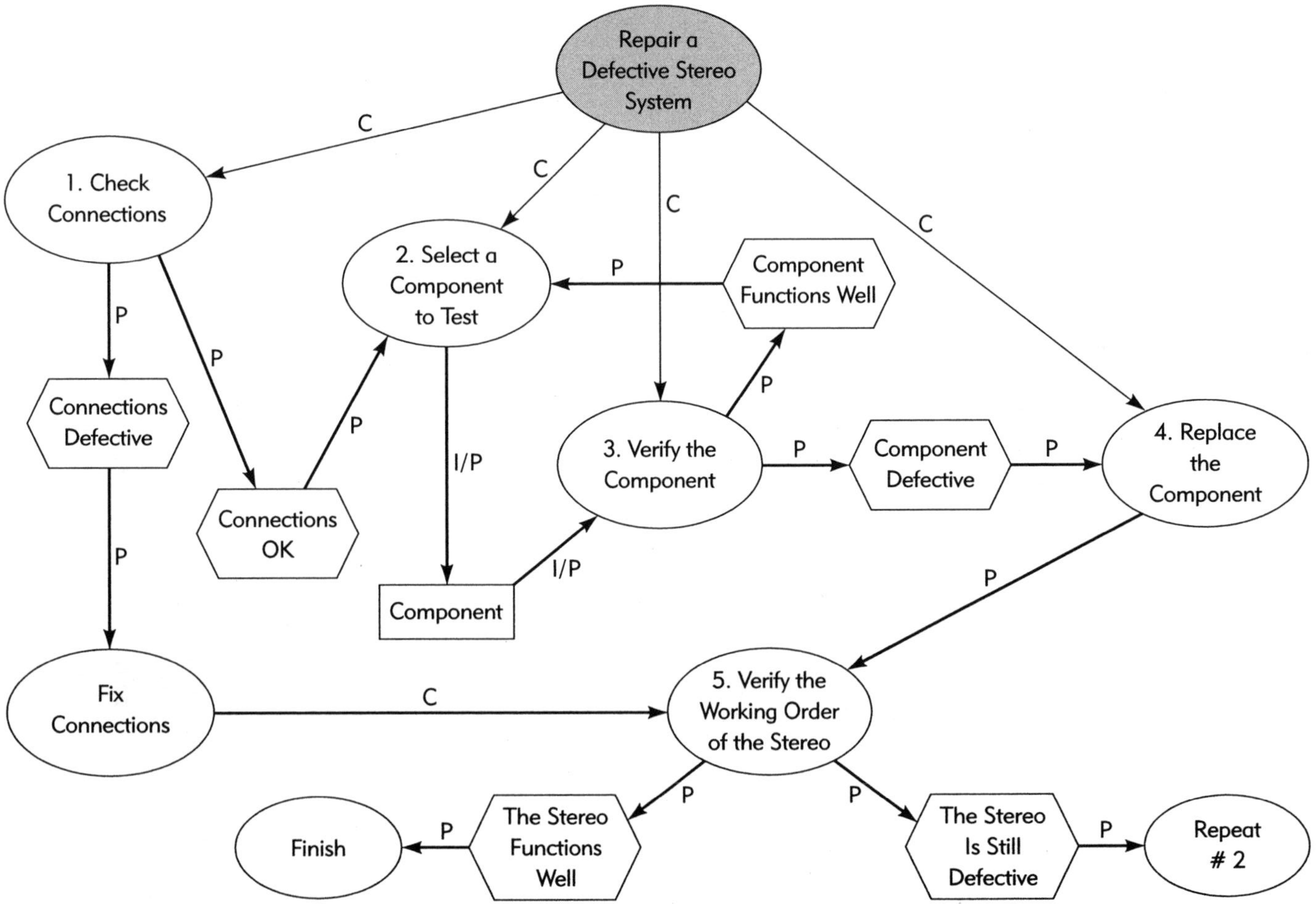

Most processes and methods require the cooperation or collaboration of several people or agents. Figure 3-10 presents a MOT model of a collaborative writing process to produce a document for a customer. The various tasks are represented as procedures. The information sources and the productions are represented as concepts. The agents are represented as principles: the group leader overlooks the plan and revision of the text; the customer validates the final text; each writer composes one section of the text (cooperation); the writing team, composed of the group leader and the writers, establishes the work plan and integrates the text.

The agents are represented as principles in order to highlight their roles in the control of the process. They could also be represented as concepts, enumerating the attributes that describe them such as their names, professions,

Figure 3-10. MOT Model of a Collaborative Process for Writing a Text.

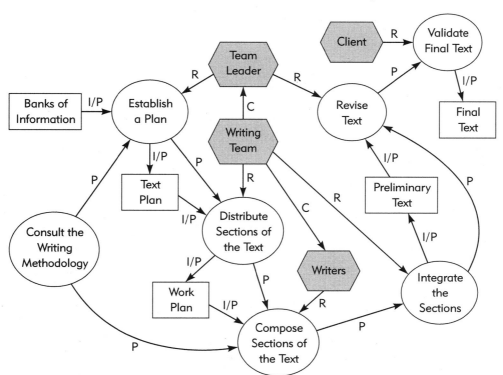

competencies, and so on. Nevertheless, the role of the agent is described mainly by the principles he or she uses to intervene in the tasks that concern him or her. It is therefore this dimension of the agent that is considered important here.

Skills and Competencies

Knowledge, skills, and ultimately, competencies are the desired results of learning. In instructional engineering each of these results has a distinct definition. At the same time, knowledge, skill, and competency must be defined in respect to each other. I define a competency as a statement of principle establishing a relationship between a target audience, or actor, a skill that actor is able to execute and the knowledge to which this skill is applied. In the following sections, I define a skills taxonomy, then represent these skills with graphic models, and finally, represent the concept of a competency.

A Skills Taxonomy

A skill can be defined from three different perspectives: as a generic problem-solving process, as active meta-knowledge, or as an information processing objective. However, the resulting classifications of skills converge, providing the basis for my skills taxonomy. I propose defining the various skill types by integrating these three perspectives as a generic problem-solving processes. This taxonomy treats skills as a kind of generic knowledge that we can describe, analyze, and evaluate as such or in relation to specialized knowledge of various fields. Hence, skills must be part of our knowledge models if we wish to designate them as learning activity targets, just like the knowledge of a specific domain.

Figure 3-11 presents an overview of the skills taxonomy I propose (note that some skills mentioned in this chapter do not appear on this figure). Three layers are shown here, reading from left to right, from the generic to the specific. (The second and third layers are numbered in this overview to facilitate references to the taxonomy in the remainder of the chapter.) The most general skills (in the first layer out from the root of the tree) correspond to phases of

Figure 3-11. A Skills Taxonomy.

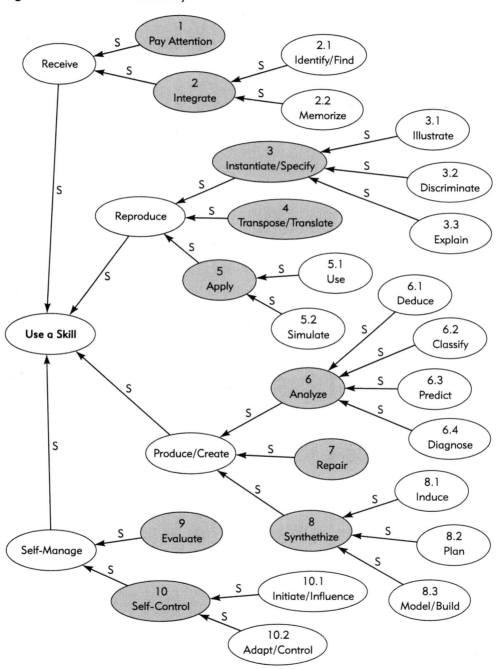

the information-processing cycle. Although terminology varies across writer on this subject, there is a rather broad consensus on the set of skills that characterizes human learning and action.[27]

The first step is an *input,* or *reception,* phase, where perception is mobilized following external stimuli: we pay attention, or notice, objects, and we access relevant information in our memory to find a referent for each stimulus, and we memorize some of this information.

The reception phase is generally followed by a *reproduction* phase, where memory is managed to select relevant knowledge to prepare a possible reaction, through explicit, transferable, and applicable processes, or skills.

Then the superior intellectual processes of creation and production, of analysis, repair, and synthesis, may be mobilized to create or produce the plan of the possible reaction and to develop a response or a solution.

Expressing this response in the environment leads to self-managing one's mental, corporal, emotional, and social actions through the expressive means of speech, movements, expressions, and so on. This process starts with an evaluation of the situation, which leads to initiation or orientation, influencing others, controlling a situation, and adapting to events. This is what I call the *self-management* phase.

Representation of a Skill

A skill description limited to the description of the inputs and the products is far too rudimentary to adequately define an instructional strategy. Because skills are generic processes, however, we may represent them through MOT models. Here are some examples.

A Generic Simulation Process. Simulating a process (Skill 5.2) amounts to using a process model to produce an execution trace for one or many particular cases. Figure 3-12 presents a model of the skill "to simulate."

From the description of the process we aim to simulate (upper left-hand corner of the figure), we first produce examples of all the inputs to this process. This is an application of the illustration skill (3.1). Then we find, through discrimination (3.2), a relevant subprocedure of the process that is applicable, in other words, for which all the inputs are available. We perform this

Figure 3-12. Model of the Skill "to Simulate."

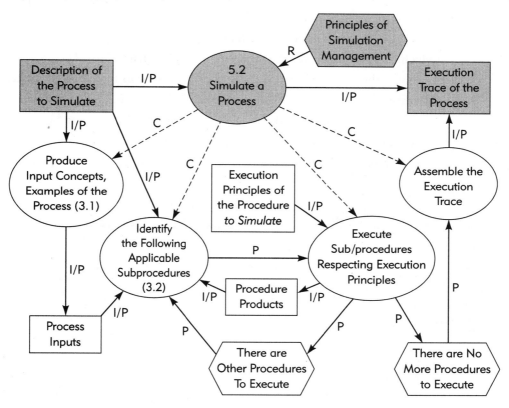

procedure by considering the principles that govern the process "to simulate." We thus obtain a product that can now be used as input for other subprocedures. If any subprocedure remains to be carried out in the process we are simulating, the cycle starts over again. If a final subprocedure is reached, and all of the final subprocedures are carried out, we assemble the trace and produce the result of the simulation.

A Generic Deduction Process. The skill of deducing a solution (6.1) consists of applying a certain number of procedures (operators) to concept instances (*data*) in order to produce another concept instance (*goal*). For example, we apply algebraic operators to an equation with two unknown factors in order to find a solution; we apply permitted actions to a Rubik's Cube in its initial state to obtain the final state that satisfies the game conditions; we create an academic schedule by reusing last year's schedule and applying substitutions that satisfy new constraints.

Figure 3-13 displays the model for a generic deduction process (6.1), which is a specific case of the more general skill "to analyze" (6). The first procedure of the generic process is to examine the operators relevant to the data. We therefore call upon the application skill (5). Then, we choose one of these operators and apply it to the data. If the product of this procedure is an instance of concept occurrence-goal, we obtain a one-step solution. If we do not, we repeat the steps by seeking another operator to apply to the product,

Figure 3-13. Model of a Deduction Skill.

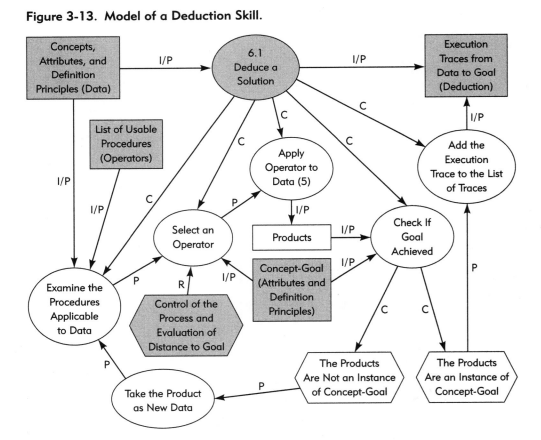

and so on, until we obtain a solution, an execution trace of a sequence of procedures that transform the initial data into a goal.

A Generic Evaluation Process. Evaluating (Skill 9) knowledge of a field of application consists of allotting values. The concepts of validity, priority, interest, and degree of acquisition are examples of these values, or knowledge properties. These values are meta-concepts, in the sense that they are external to the field of application and can be used to qualify knowledge regardless of the field. They represent knowledge about knowledge, which Pitrat qualifies as "knowledge properties."[28] Figure 3-14 presents a simplified model of a generic evaluation process of knowledge acquisition. It is a model that generalizes the concept of "model by overlay" used in several intelligent tutorial systems.[29]

Figure 3-14. Model of the Skill *Evaluation of Knowledge Acquisition*.

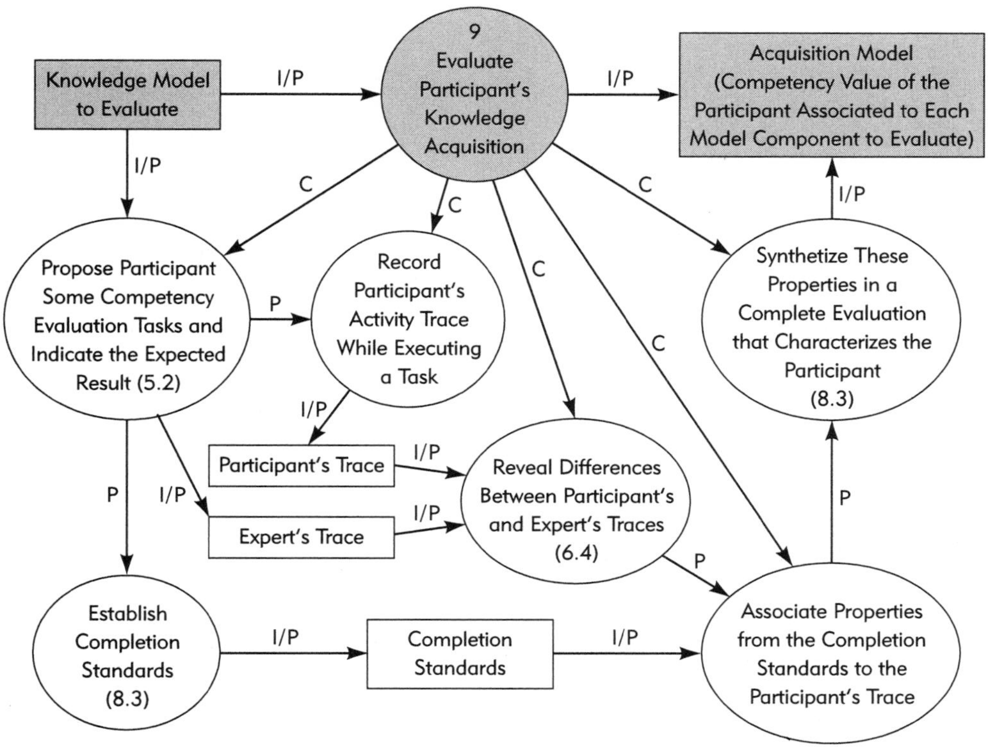

We start with a knowledge model that the learner is to have acquired and that we are now to evaluate, for example, a taxonomy, a component system, or a process. From this model, we simulate (5.2) the tasks that will evaluate the competencies of a participant in relation to the knowledge, and we specify the result by asking an expert to perform these same tasks, thus giving us a representation of excellent performance. Then we collect the trace produced by the activity of the participant and compare it with the expert's activity trace. The differences between the two traces are diagnosed (6.4) in order to evaluate the extent and nature of these differences.

In addition, we build (8.3) a set of success criteria that can be used to allot knowledge competency values in areas where we have identified a difference between the participant and the expert trace. These competency values can be based, for example, on the capacity to execute certain skills in regard to specific knowledge. By combining a certain number of these partial values, we can synthesize a participant model (8.3) that coherently gathers the specific evaluations obtained in the previous step.

The Concept of a Competency

When we define the competencies a learner should possess, we state the objectives to be reached regarding the knowledge to process. Competencies also state the general skills learners are to build and the learning they are to acquire through similar problem-solving processes. Figure 3-15 presents, in a MOT model, the generic concept of competency that is used in the rest of this book. Specifically, a competency is a statement of principle governing the relationships among a target audience, or actor, a skill, and a field of knowledge. Thus a competency emerges out of the convergence of three fields.

The field of knowledge is described using a model composed of concepts, procedures, principles, and specific facts, with which we describe the practice of a role or task. A professional competency profile for a field of knowledge such as nursing, for example, would relate to knowledge from the health sector or about actual practice of the profession. In a multimedia production competency profile, it would relate to knowledge specific to the techniques, inputs, and products involved in multimedia software creation.

Figure 3-15. The Concept of a Competency.

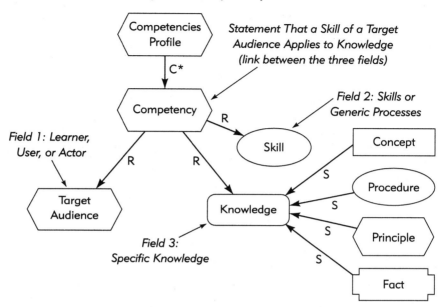

The field of skills describes the processes that can be applied to a field of knowledge to perceive, memorize, assimilate, analyze, synthesize, evaluate, and so forth. They are meta-processes, which means they have a generic character. They are independent from the field in which they are being applied at any given moment and relevant to many different fields. A skill is generally described by an action verb, which may be accompanied by other parts of speech such a direct object, adjective, or adverb, describing an application context or a specific use. For example, in the medical field a skill could be stated as "to establish a diagnosis," "to establish an exhaustive diagnosis," or "to establish a diagnosis in an urgent situation." In each case the skill can be applied to various medical knowledge such as "a skull fracture" or "the birth of a child."

The field of the target audience contains a description of the actors and their properties, functions, tasks, and especially, competencies. We can associate with each target audience the basic competencies required to perform a role or task and a profile of current or target competencies. This definition implies a number of underlying hypotheses that allow the concept of competency as it used here to be situated within the framework of action theories.[30]

- The people to be described through competencies are not simple operators or factors to be evaluated; they are defined actors, individuals equipped with intentions and placed in a cognitive and social context.

- Competencies describe activities specified by a function, a role or a specific task qualified by the level of excellence of the observed performance and validated through social sanctions.

- At the core of a competency is the association between skills, seen as generic cognitive processes, and a model for representing knowledge; this association avoids a dissociation between knowledge and know-how and the atomization of competencies.

- Skills can then be interpreted as generic knowledge that allows a person to act in various ways. The cognitive and meta-cognitive aspects necessary for well-thought-out human actions can then be integrated.

- Competencies can be used to evaluate individuals, but the criteria are no longer reduced to graduated scales of juxtaposed immediate behaviors. Competencies are functionally structured and can be used as objectives for individual development rather than only as means to control behaviors.

Interpreting a Competency Profile

Now that we have defined knowledge, skill, and competency, we can analyze a series of competency statements (that is a *competency profile*), or build them in a standard fashion, by determining the relevant actor, skill, and the knowledge pertaining to that skill. In order to illustrate this process, I will use a competency profile for a multimedia producer as an example.[31] At this first stage it is important to define the actor through a number of properties, particularly those related to the task description, such as the one presented in Table 3-6.

Table 3-6. Example of a Task Description.

Tasks of a Multimedia Producer

Take responsibility for managing the interactivity components of the creation process

Participate in defining the client's specifications and requirements

Prepare detailed documentation describing the finished product

Participate in the technological choices

Develop the production method

Ensure product coherence

Ensure the content remains well adapted to the established objectives and target groups

Document the project evolution in writing

Maintain team communication

Lead the project team

Ensure coordination between the client and the project team

Participate in the selection of external suppliers

Ensure quality control for products delivered by external suppliers

Ensure quality control for deliveries to the client

Ensure adherence to the budget and deadlines

Ensure technology watch and competitive intelligence

These tasks are not statements of competency but descriptions defining necessary knowledge of the field. For example, "Take responsibility for managing the interactivity components of the creation process" contains no skill whatsoever. This statement describes a role, a process in which the actor will be implicated. The same applies to all the other statements in this task description. Using mainly a task description of this type, we can model an actor's required knowledge. Within the framework of MOT knowledge representation, tasks are also knowledge (of a procedural type), and we must also distinguish the other types of knowledge present in the definition of an actor's task. These will provide a foundation on which to graft the required skills.

Figure 3-16 presents a knowledge model corresponding to the task definitions in Table 3-6. This model is mostly procedural, but it could be supplemented by adding concepts and principles required to perform the tasks. By adding certain procedures (the shaded ovals) and grouping tasks, it sets forth three main functions, or processes, that must be governed by the media producer: the development of the production method, the management of the creation and production process, and the control of product quality.

We can now identify various skills that will be associated with the tasks in this knowledge model:

The development of the production method requires mainly knowledge creation skills—analysis, synthesis, conceptualization, and creativity—applied to multimedia knowledge resulting from the technology watch and competitive intelligence.

The management of the creation and production process requires cognitive self-management skills—the ability to be methodical, to manage emotions, to resist stress, and to be flexible—and especially social skills—the abilities to lead, to work in teams, to manage interpersonal relationships, to persuade, and to be open-minded to criticism.

The quality control of the finished product requires mostly cognitive skills—critical capacities and the ability to be methodical.

We still have to specify these general skills and their context of use in order to generate more precise competency statements. To do so, we simply further develop the knowledge model shown in Figure 3-16 to bring out the various concepts, procedures, and principles with which skills may be associated. Figure 3-17 takes this step for a section of Figure 3-16 for the task "Develop a production method," the first of the three main tasks. We can associate an appropriate skill with each area of knowledge related to the central task of the model. For example, for the production method, an appropriate skill is "to build," for the project definition, "to plan," for the approaches and the uses, "to transpose" (to a present situation), and so forth.

Figure 3-16. Model of the Tasks of a Multimedia Producer.

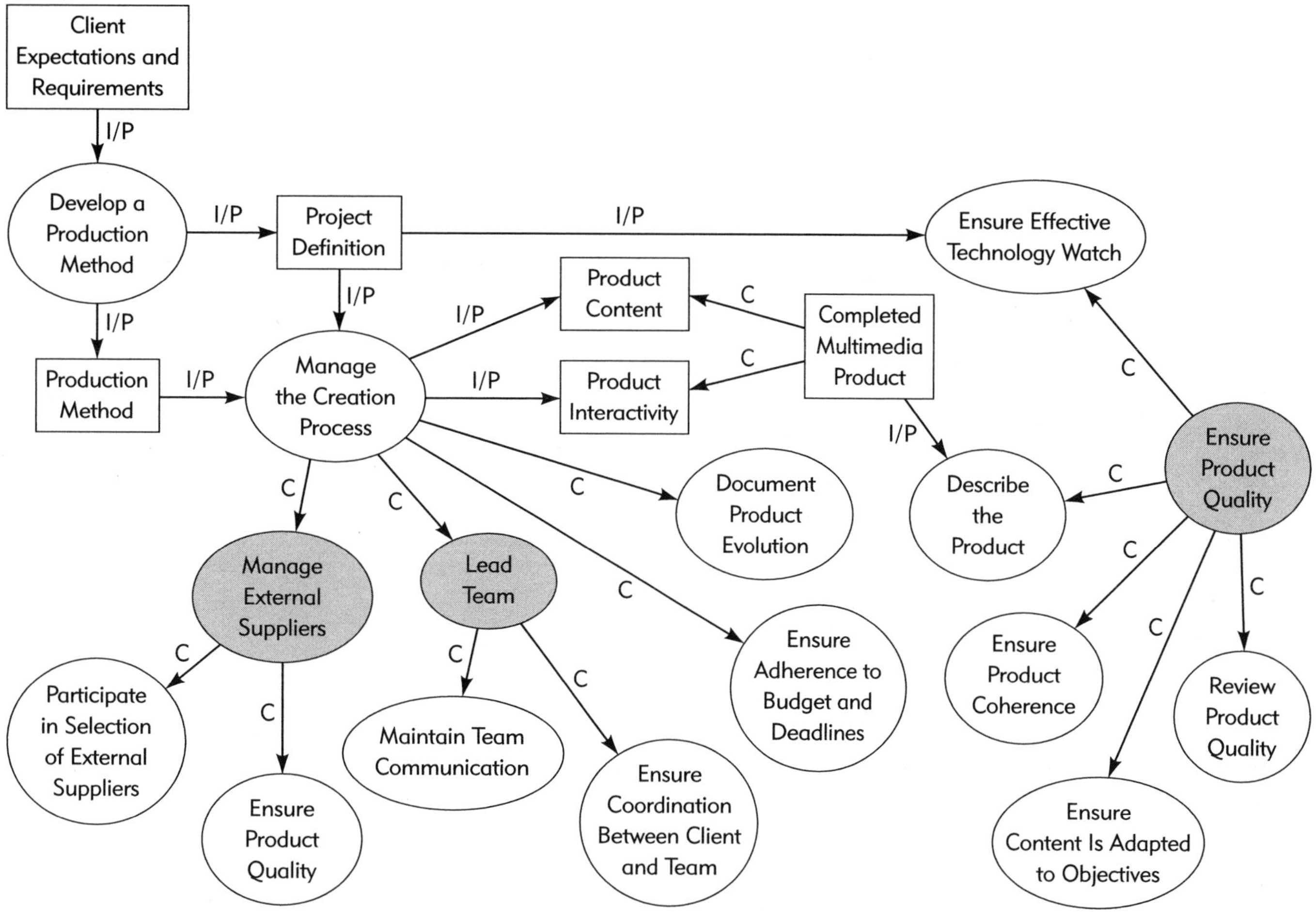

Figure 3-17. Subknowledge Model and Associated Skills.

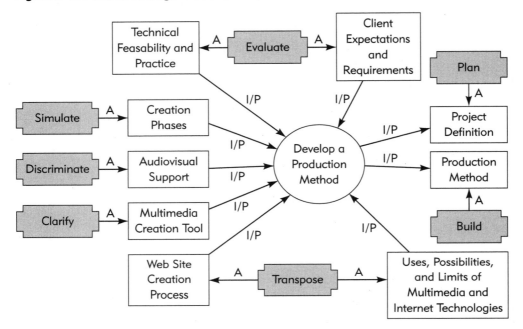

This work enables us to formulate the competency statements more precisely by giving them a standard interpretation, as illustrated in Table 3-7. Notice that the initial statements (before our analyses) began with words such as *capacity* and *knowledge,* which indicates that many of these statements mentioned knowledge without specifying the skill to perform. Moreover, some important knowledge, in particular the expected products of the central task "Develop a production method," is not related to any statement. Note that in Table 3-7, Type "C" means "cognitive." Competencies can be cognitive, affective, social, or psychomotor. In this example, all competencies are cognitive.

The last three competencies in the first column of the table are stated as they were in the original multimedia producer's profile. They begin with words such as "capacity" and "knowledge," which are vague and underline the fact that elements are missing in the definition. Many statements only mention knowledge without specifying the skill to perform on that knowledge. These

Table 3-7. Interpretation of Statements of Competency for a Multimedia Producer.

| Competency Statement | | Interpretation | | | | |
Initial	Reformulated	Actor	Skill	Type	Related Skill	Knowledge
(Nonexistent)	Build a production method	MM producer	Build	C	Synthesize (8)	Production method
(Nonexistent)	Plan the project definition	MM producer	Plan	C	Synthesize (8)	Project definition
Capacity to evaluate technical and graphical feasibility	Evaluate technical and graphical feasibility of a project	MM producer	Evaluate	C	Evaluate (9)	Technical and graphical feasibility of a project
Knowledge of each production step	Broadly simulate each production step	MM producer	Simulate broadly	C	Apply (5)	Production steps
Knowledge of audiovisual support	Discriminate between properties of the various audiovisual supports	MM producer	Discriminate properties	C	Instantiate/specify (3)	Audiovisual supports

three competencies are reformulated in the second column on the basis of our knowledge modeling effort. Furthermore, the model presented in Figures 3-16 and 3-17 has helped us identify important competencies that were missing in the original competency profile, in particular "Build production method" and "Plan the project definition."

SUMMARY

Knowledge models and also competency statements that associate skills with knowledge to acquire are essential components of instructional engineering. To say that a person must "know" something or that a person must "acquire" such or such knowledge is not sufficient. We have to ask ourselves, Up to what level? In what way? In which context? And for which use?

Knowledge modeling is a critical component of instructional engineering. It is at the core of the definition of the content to be learned, the instructional scenarios, the learning and teaching materials, and the delivery resources and processes that make up a learning system. The method that allows designers to determine these objects relies mostly on graphic representations of knowledge. This graphic language is generic, is applicable to various fields of knowledge, and facilitates the representation of various types of models: taxonomies; component systems; procedures in series; in parallel, or performed iteratively; definitions, laws, theories and decision trees; processes, methods, and collaborative multiagent systems.

The association of skill and knowledge within a competency statement makes it possible to specify which of the cognitive, emotional, social, and psychomotor processes must be mobilized to process knowledge. The competency statement thus provides not only learning objectives but also the means to put them in place to acquire knowledge and skills.

The systematic interpretation of competencies using a skills taxonomy builds a bridge between competency profiles and instructional engineering. For each main area of knowledge to be acquired, the gap between the learner's actual competency and target competency guide the construction of knowledge models. The target competencies and the associated generic processes provide a foundation to define the learning scenarios. They also make it possible to build scenarios for the other actors in an e-learning system, and also to design multiactor scenarios to improve coordination between actors and offer them resources adapted to their roles in these scenarios.

4

MISA: An Instructional Engineering Method

BY THIS TIME, I hope to have convinced the reader that there is a large set of interrelated decisions to make when we build e-learning systems. Among these decisions are the following: What kind of e-learning delivery model shall we use, or what mixture of these models? What kind of learning scenarios do we need for this course? Should they be predefined, offer multiple learning paths, or be learner constructed? Which actors will interact at delivery time, what are their roles, and what resources do they need? What kinds of interactivity or collaboration should be included? Will we use multimedia or plurimedia materials? What materials can be reused, and which ones must be built from scratch? How will we manage distributed resources on the networks? What standards will be used? How can we support interoperability and scalability of the e-learning system? How do we take into account the different levels of technical ability among groups of users in the target audience? How can we promote the reusability, sustainability, and affordability of our Web-based learning system?

To help us make these decisions thoughtfully and effectively, an instructional design methodology based on graphic modeling is needed now more than ever. This chapter presents an example of such assistance, a new instructional engineering method called MISA (*méthode d'ingénierie de systèmes d'apprentissage,* or method for engineering learning systems). This method is the result of both research in the field of instructional engineering and practical experience acquired through the development of many e-learning courses.

This effort started in 1992, and a first version of MISA was produced in 1994, embedded in a computerized support system for designers called AGD.[1] The method was thereafter validated by instructional designers and content experts in nine organizations and was rebuilt according to the results and observations gathered during these validations. In a parallel process we extracted and rebuilt MOT (the tool for knowledge modeling discussed in Chapter Three) to support a central aspect of the method. After another round of validation, we turned our attention to learning object typologies, defining seventeen of them: knowledge models, a skills taxonomy, learning scenario types, learning material categories, delivery models, and so on. This effort led in 1998 to MISA 3.0. In MISA 3.0 these typologies gave learning system designers many alternatives to choose from. Finally, the method was restructured in terms of six phases and four axes, under which the main design tasks were distributed. MISA 4.0 has been built in coordination with ADISA, a new Web-based support workbench for instructional engineering that is presented briefly in the next chapter.

Overview of the MISA Method

MISA 4.0 supports 35 main tasks and some 150 secondary tasks. Its main objectives are the following:

- To take fully into account the requirements of distance training, and to integrate knowledge modeling into its processes, its products, and its operational principles.

- To make the instructional engineering process visible, and to structure it so that it allows both process and product quality control.

- To facilitate communication and obtain consensus among the various actors who participate in the development, through the integration of operational principles inspired by those of software engineering.

- To discipline the engineering process without restricting the creativity essential to the design of effective instructional and media strategies.

- To facilitate the production of learning systems that offer learning paths that can be adapted by the learners, the trainers, and the training managers.

- To facilitate the production of a learning system that is comprehensible, complete, and user validated.

- To support the reusability of learning system models and model components in subsequent projects.

- To maintain the coherence of the learning system, in its contents (knowledge and competencies) and other dimensions and in the various models they share.

Because the method was entirely modeled using MOT, it guarantees coherence and renders visible the various processes while offering hyperlinked access to the tasks to be carried out. A precise definition of the products as documentation elements, thanks to the integration of the seventeen pedagogical object typologies, guides the efforts and reduces design time.

MISA 4.0 is structured with six phases and four axes (see the MOT model in Figure 4-1). The axes are the knowledge model; instructional model; media or learning material model; and delivery model..

The *knowledge model* distinguishes various types of links and knowledge, including the competencies to be developed. Moreover, in this model the concept of *competence* is reconciled with concepts of knowledge, skills, and learning needs; a skills typology allows the integration of the cognitive, emotional, social, and psychomotor domains.

The *instructional model* guides the creation of learning units. Moreover, the concepts of resource and educational instrument and the identification of a set of instructional strategies describing the learning activities offer a precise and broad definition of the central concept of the instructional scenario.

The *media model* makes it possible to carry out the macro-design of the instructional materials without prejudging the decisions that will be taken later by specialists as the various media are built (micro-design). Thus reinvesting these materials models in various development tools or other projects becomes possible.

The *delivery model* covers the delivery infrastructures and the training management tasks and processes necessary to access the learning system. MISA can then provide data to a computerized training management system, such as Explor@ (presented in Chapter Two).

The MISA method embodies the following types of knowledge:

Conceptual knowledge (concepts, represented as rectangles in the MOT model in Figure 4-1) allows the description of the objects the designer must use or produce, what I call the documentation elements, which make up the blueprint and specifications for a learning system.

Procedural knowledge (procedures, represented by ovals) aims to define the actions to be performed on these objects, or how the designer achieves each task necessary to the production of the training system: for example, an analysis of the training needs for a target audience, the definition of a learning activity, the macro-design of an instructional material, and so forth.

Strategic knowledge (principles, represented by hexagons) consists of statements to help the designer decide when or why to make a particular choice during the application of a certain procedure: for example, principles to assign knowledge to learning units, principles of coherence between training needs and target competencies, and principles leading to the choice of an instructional strategy or certain media, and so forth.

Figure 4-1. MISA: High-Level Representation.

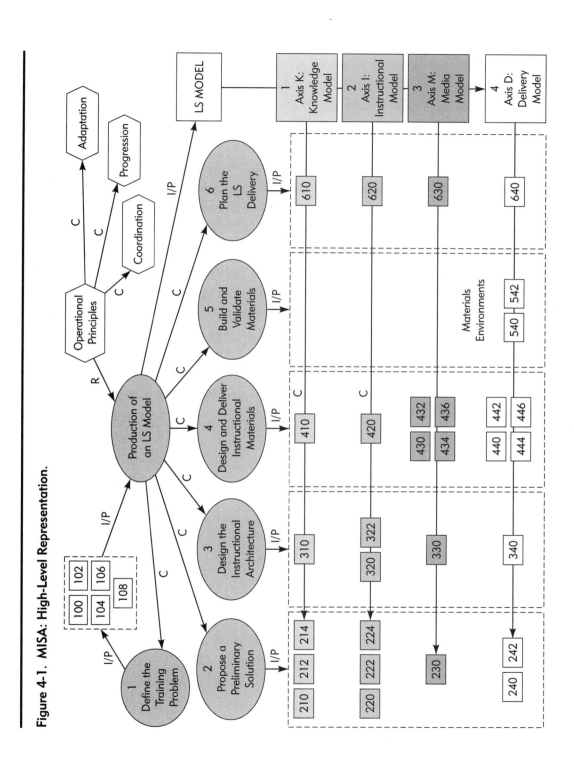

Figure 4-1, then, presents a synthesis of the main elements of the method. Three types of MOT links are used here: the C-link ("is composed of") connects two objects where the second is a component of the first; the R-link ("rules" or "governs") connects two objects of which the first is a principle that governs (controls) the second; and the I/P-link (input-product) connects an input concept to a procedure or a procedure to a concept that is a product resulting from the execution of the procedure.

The main task "To produce a model of a learning system" results in a blueprint for the learning system, grouping all its specifications. It is governed by operational principles and broken into smaller units in two complementary ways, according to whether we examine the six progress phases or whether we consider the models of the four axes.

> *Progressing through the phases* allows designers to construct a learning system through six main processes, or phases: define the training problem, propose a preliminary solution, design the instructional architecture, design the instructional materials, build and validate the materials, and plan the delivery of the learning system.

> *Developing the LS model by axes* provides a mode of progression, orthogonal to the first, according to four dimensions: the creation of the knowledge model, the instructional model, the media model, and the delivery model.

In both approaches, these main tasks are broken down into smaller tasks. MISA 4.0 comprises thirty-five basic tasks, each producing one *element of documentation,* and numbered from 100 to 642. These components of the learning system model are distributed according to the six phases and four axes, with the first digit in a number indicating the phase and the second digit the axis (Task 210, for example, is keyed to Phase 2 and Axis I). The small number of elements of documentation planned in Phase 5 indicates clearly that MISA is centered on the macro-design of the learning system model rather than on the micro-design of the system's instructional material. Other methods must be used to produce these materials, each depending on the material type (printed, audiovisual, courseware, multimedia, and so forth). Also, as indicated in Figure 4-1, the elements of documentation are fairly equally distributed between the axes.

Three groups of operational principles govern the processes, providing instructions on how to use the method:

The *adaptation principles* allow the selection of a set of tasks according to the training problem and the considered solutions.

The *progression principles* govern the transfer of control from one phase to another.

The *coordination principles* define the interactions between the four main components of a learning system model: the knowledge model, the instructional model, the media model, and the delivery model.

Conceptual Levels of a Learning System

The learning system conceptual model consists of thirty-five elements of documentation. They are selected according to the training problem and the characteristics of the target learning system. The learning system model can be structured in folders, gathering the elements of documentation by phase, by axis, or according to other criteria such as the intended user (project manager, media designer, content author, delivery manager, and so on).

The elements of documentation (EDs), a concept inspired by software engineering methods, constitute the core products of the MISA method. Certain EDs are graphic models resulting from knowledge engineering relating to one of the axes of the method; others are forms with accompanying annotations describing the components of the learning system to be built and their properties. Each form is further deconstructed into a number of attributes and their values, for a designer to select.

Figure 4-2 displays a model of an ED 222 (a learning event network) for a course. In other words, this is a description of the instructional structure of the future learning system. The course is broken up into seven interconnected *learning units* (LUs), or modules, linked by the three assignments requiring the user to send work in for evaluation. Figure 4-2 also shows form ED 224, describing the properties of a learning unit (LU-3) created in ED 222. Among the attributes, or properties, of any learning unit are its name, its suggested duration, the percentage of the course evaluation it accounts for, the importance of collaborative activities in the unit, the type of learning scenario it

Figure 4-2. Two Examples of Documentation Elements.

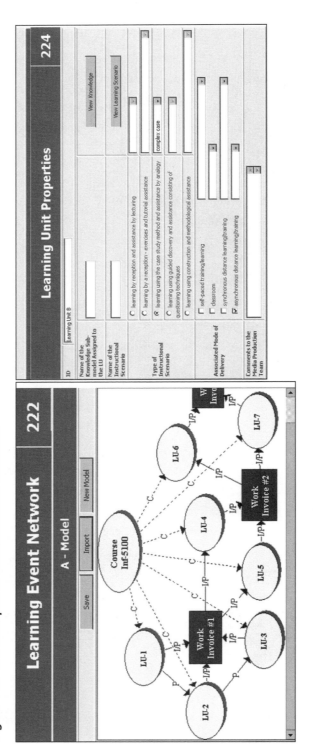

uses, the associated knowledge submodel describing its contents, its delivery mode, and the media designers who will produce its materials.

Table 4-1 lists (by phase) the thirty-five documentation elements shown by their reference number in Figure 4-1. Each one of these EDs is composed of attributes—a title, a number, a text, a list of objects, a graph—that can take different types of values. Each attribute and its value(s) describe a property of the learning system. The learning system model thus contains the following conceptual levels:

Learning system model
> Folder grouping elements of documentation
>> Element of documentation
>>> Attribute of the element of documentation
>>>> Value(s) of the attribute.

Table 4-1. Documentation Elements of MISA 4.0 (by Phase).

Phase 1
100 Training framework of the organization
102 Objectives of the project
104 Target audiences
106 Current context
108 Documented resources

Phase 2
210 Knowledge orientation principles
212 Knowledge model
214 Target competencies
220 Instructional orientation principles
222 Learning event network
224 Learning unit properties
230 Material orientation principles
240 Delivery orientation principles
242 Cost-benefit analysis

Phase 3
310 Learning unit content
320 Instructional scenarios
322 Properties of learning activities
330 Development infrastructure
340 Delivery planning

Phase 4
410 Content of learning instruments
420 Properties of learning instruments and guides
430 List of learning materials
432 Learning material models
434 Media elements
436 Source documents
440 Delivery models
442 Actors and material packages
444 Tools and means of communication
446 Delivery services and location

Phase 5
540 Assessment planning for the learning system
542 Revision log

Phase 6
610 Knowledge and competencies management
620 Actors and groups management
630 Learning system and resources management
640 Maintenance and quality management

Table 4-2 presents another view of the elements of documentation, this time sorted by axis. The elements of documentation that contain graphic models are shaded. Each axis is built around a model whose objects will be described subsequently in other elements of documentation (forms). The task

Table 4-2. Documentation Elements of MISA 4.0 (by Axis).

Knowledge Modeling	Instructional Modeling
210 Knowledge orientation principles	220 Instructional orientation principles
212 Knowledge model	222 Learning event network
214 Target competencies	224 Learning unit properties
310 Learning unit content	320 Instructional scenarios
410 Content of learning instruments	322 Properties of learning activities
610 Knowledge and competencies management	420 Properties of learning instruments and guides
	620 Actors and group management
Material Modeling	**Delivery Modeling**
230 Material orientation principles	240 Delivery orientation principles
330 Development infrastructure	242 Cost-benefit analysis
430 List of learning materials	340 Delivery planning
432 Learning material models	440 Delivery model
434 Media elements	442 Actors and materials packages
436 Source documents	444 Tools and means of communication
630 Learning system and resources management	446 Delivery services and locations
	540 Assessment planning for the learning system
	542 Revision log
	640 Maintenance and quality management

of building each model is preceded by a statement of the orientation principles that will guide model development.

Processes and Tasks

Each element of documentation produced by MISA is at the crossroads of a phase and an axis. It is produced by a task, or subprocess, that is a process component of both a phase and an axis. For example, ED 222 and ED 224 are components of both "Propose a preliminary solution" and "Design the instructional model."

Each task is defined by its context, that is to say, the EDs that influence its execution, the ED that results as a product, and the other tasks influenced by this product. As an example, consider the task context of "Define the learning unit properties" (shown in Table 4-3), which produces ED 224. The elements of documentation 102, 104, 220, and 222 influence the definition of the learning unit properties (ED 224), with the definitions of the target audience (ED 104) and the learning event network (ED 222) having a significant influence. Each learning unit is indeed created in the learning event network (ED 222) for one or more of the target audiences defined in ED 104. Furthermore, once content has been associated with a learning unit (ED 310) and an instructional scenario (ED 320), the definition will be completed in Phase 3 (ED 224–3). In

Table 4-3. Task Context "Define the Learning Units."

Source		Destination
102 Training objectives		310 Learning unit content
104 Target audiences		320 Instructional scenarios
220 Instructional orientation principles	224	322 Properties of learning activities
222 Learning event network		340 Delivery planning
310 Learning unit content	224-3	410 Content of learning instruments
320 Instructional scenarios		420 Properties of instruments and guides

addition, once ED 224–3 is completed, the learning unit properties thus defined will influence tasks that define ED 410 and 420.

Each of the thirty-five basic tasks of the method can be broken into activities corresponding to one of the attributes of the corresponding ED. For example, the task "Define the learning unit properties" can be separated into these activities:

- Choose an identifier for each learning unit.

- Identify the target audience for whom the learning unit is designed.

- Evaluate the duration for each target audience.

- Establish, for each target audience, the percentage of the course evaluation allotted to the learning unit.

- Estimate the time devoted to the collaborative activities for each target audience.

- Select the type of instructional scenario.

- Select the delivery mode of the learning unit.

- Write a comment message for the material designers.

From a procedural perspective, we carry out the engineering of a learning system (method) as follows:

Progress through the phases (process)
Create the products of a phase (for each of the six phases)
   Produce one of the elements of documentation (for each of the thirty-five tasks)
      Define a property of one of the elements of documentation (until all activities for each of the EDs are defined)
Progress through the axes (process)
   Create the products of an axis (for each of the four axes)
      Produce one of the elements of documentation (for each of the thirty-five tasks)
         Define a property of one of the elements of documentation (until all activities for each of the EDs are defined)

Operational Principles

This process, task, and activity outline highlights two processes: one by phase, the other by axis. We may also work directly at the level of the elements of documentation. Hence a great number of operational principles are needed to guide the processes.

Adaptation of the Method

The adaptability of the MISA method allows designers to construct different projects that are highly diverse. For each project, they construct a preliminary configuration of the elements of documentation at the onset of the project or after the first phase. This allows them to select the necessary elements of documentation and the level of detail desirable for each ED by choosing some or all of the attributes. Thus they can create an activity path adapted to the nature of each project. Here are some examples.

> The main goal of the method is to provide an operational base for the cognitivist and constructivist theories of learning. Therefore, if the designer uses the rather traditional pedagogical approach of information presented in a classroom, he or she can concentrate on modeling the knowledge and can avoid most of the work related to the other three axes.

> The choice of delivery mode is also critical. A classroom delivery mode, even if constructivist, will exempt the designer from defining the majority of specifications concerning the media, tools, or telecom services. Conversely, a distance education or a self-training program using computerized tools will require special attention to these specifications.

> The choice of an individual training program rather than a collaborative one will considerably reduce the definition work required on the telecom services and on certain aspects of the learning scenarios—for example, the learning activity instructions.

> The scope or the complexity of the instructional engineering project also affects design requirements. Thus developing a curriculum comprising several courses will require constructing a vast model of

knowledge. The design project can be limited mostly to the analysis and architectural phases. Once the curriculum is designed, then the first five phases will have to be covered for each course. In contrast, when developing a learning unit of a few hours, the designer can proceed quickly through the analysis and architectural phases to concentrate on the main aspects of Phases 4, 5, and 6.

Progression Through the Phases

Once the process path for a given project has been determined, it has to be managed according to the project characteristics. Although the engineering process presented here is structured in phases, axes, tasks, and activities, the activities are not completed in a linear sequence. The design problem-solving process is more akin to a spiral than a straight line and benefits from successive iterations.

The instructional engineering process works from abstract to concrete specifications. We start with an abstract definition of the requirements of the future learning system, which were established at the training definition stage, in Phase 1. Then in Phase 2 this definition is clarified through orientation principles and general models. In Phases 3 and 4 the system takes shape through definition of the central elements of the model. Phase 5 consists of actual production of the materials and environments according to the model.

This project approach, borrowed from software engineering, allows gradual rather than block construction of a learning system's specifications. Once the architectural design is completed in Phase 3, we can group certain components of this design into folders, to constitute one or many Phase 4 deliveries (recall that deliveries are made to various participants during the design process as well as to learners in Phase 6). The development process can then be broken up according to the scope of the project. For example, a first delivery might aim to create a prototype that defines the first learning unit, a second delivery might produce an initial grouping of three of the five learning units of the course, and a third delivery might group the entire series of learning units. Deliveries may also relate to various types of materials: a first delivery might be all of the printed and video material; a second delivery, the course Web site; a third delivery, the integration of the materials into the Web site; a fourth delivery, the integrated Web site and a resource environment that groups the other course resources.

Thinking in terms of multiple deliveries during the design process encourages the application of iterative development principles and the synchronization of teamwork. Thus, on the basis of the delivery plan (ED 340), Phases 4 and 5 will be iterated as often as the number of deliveries. This provides for the design, creation, and validation of the material delivery by delivery, item by item.

The definition of the orientation of each of the four models that make up the learning system blueprint—knowledge (210), instructional (220), media (230), and delivery (240)—ensures the coherence of the learning system. (As outlined in Chapter Three, orientation principles describe the selection of the types of resources to be integrated, the activities and the actors to be supported, and the means to place at their disposal.) Orientation principles are particularly useful when the development spans several deliveries and requires the participation of several types of multidisciplinary specialists and teams. Generally, an understanding of shared orientation principles reduces the time it takes to transfer information from one team to another. Moreover, it facilitates communications between the teams.

The decision to pass from one phase to another is governed by the level at which the objectives have been met in each phase. We pass from Phase 1 to Phase 2 once clear recommendations have been stated regarding the opportunity (106) to produce the learning system. We move from Phase 2 to Phase 3 once the cost-benefit analysis (242) allows us to select one of the Phase 2 preliminary solutions as the basis of the architecture. We go from Phase 3 to Phases 4 and 5 once the architecture is sufficiently advanced to undertake the design of the materials in one or more deliveries (340). We move from Phase 4 to Phase 5 once all the learning system materials are defined (430) and the delivery models are built (440). We move from Phase 5 to Phase 6 once the resources and material have been tried, tested, validated, and revised for all the deliveries. Phase 6 is completed once the various components of the development and installation plans allow the first global delivery of the system.

Coordination Between the Axes

The processes corresponding to the axes of the method lead to a definition of the four basic models of the learning system. Although they are independent, these processes are of course interrelated.

The knowledge model defines the target knowledge and competencies, thus determining the contents of the learning system—that is to say, the facts, the concepts, the procedures, the principles, and the skills to be learned. It is important in this axis to avoid pedagogical considerations, media choices, or delivery orientations that would hinder this model's independence.

On the basis of the content defined in the knowledge model, the instructional model defines the instructional tasks, a process that in turn leads to the description of the learning events, the ways they interact, and the paths by which the learner will acquire the targeted knowledge and competencies. This instructional model is constructed independently of choices of media and infrastructures that will assist the learners in their learning. For example, a learning scenario might include an activity asking the learners to simulate a certain phenomenon. This is sufficient description for the instructional model. Later on, in the media model, we will determine whether this simulation will be carried out in a laboratory, through role playing, or through a computer simulation.

Defining the media model requires describing the various materials in terms of their properties and internal structure and the contents they make accessible. This model of the learning materials must take into account the results of the knowledge and instructional models, which provide the contents to be included in the media formats and the context of their acquisition through learning activities. This is where the learning system ultimately takes its concrete form, through the selection, adaptation, and construction of a variety of media.

Finally, tasks centered on the delivery processes consist of deciding how the materials and the other resources (tools, documents, telecommunication methods) will be made available to the various actors at delivery time. Again a certain independence from the other models is necessary. For example, depending on the quality of the technological devices available to the users, digitized instructional material could be delivered by mail on a CD-ROM or DVD, downloaded from a media server, or consulted directly on the Internet.

Although they are independent in key ways and play different roles in a learning system, knowledge, instructional, media, and delivery specifications must be well coordinated in order to create a learning system that fulfills its goals. The knowledge model plays a significant unifying role in this respect. A knowledge submodel is associated with each learning unit (310), thus defining the content on which instructional scenarios will rely. Each of these learning unit content models is then distributed (410) between the instructional instruments present in the instructional scenarios of that learning event.

The instructional model is also coordinated with the media model through the learning scenarios, where the learning instruments to be formatted as media are associated with the learning activities. The instructional model provides the media model with a definition of each instrument and its relevant material context.

It is highly important that designers synchronize the development of the four models. Synchronization can be ensured by the progressive development of each phase. Phase 2 is especially devoted to the development of the knowledge model and the definition of an initial learning events network. The orientations of the media and delivery models must take into account the content of these two models. Phase 3 focuses mostly on the instructional model, yet designers also progress on the other three models during this phase, particularly through the revision of the orientation principles. Phase 4 concentrates mainly on the media and delivery models, but it also leaves room for designers to review the other two models.

Context and Frontier

The MISA method does not cover all of the tasks necessary to the production of a learning system. The instructional engineering process supported by MISA must be coordinated with three other important processes: project management, production (micro-design) of the instructional materials, and delivery management. These processes have their own tools and methods, and the study of these tools and methods goes beyond the realms of this book. However, the following sections sum up MISA's interaction with these processes. As indicated in Figure 4-3, although specifically destined to be used by content experts and instructional designers, MISA produces plans and models that feed the relevant actors involved in the other three processes. In return, MISA receives data that are produced by actors in these three processes and that feed MISA processes.

Figure 4-3. Contextual Model of the MISA Method.

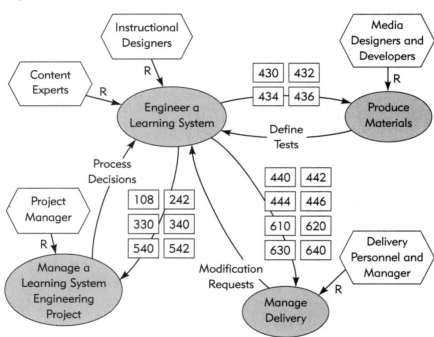

Material Production

MISA 4.0 does not produce the actual learning system materials, but it provides model creators, graphic designers, and programmers with material models and specifications to be produced or adapted (430, 432, 434, 436). Once the materials are produced, MISA defines testing and, if applicable, revision support (540 and 542) of the materials produced by developers.

Instructional Engineering Project Management

MISA 4.0 is not a project management method, yet it provides the instructional engineering project manager with some of the data necessary to manage his or her team. EDs 108, 242, 330, 340, 540, and 542 constitute inputs that are essential to the project management process. In return, the project manager, working either alone or with the engineering team, proposes adaptation and orientation principles for the instructional engineering activities and, later on, for the production of the learning system materials.

Delivery Management

MISA 4.0 is not directly employed when the first delivery of the learning system starts. However, one of its most significant tasks consists of planning that delivery. The main content of the delivery model is a description of the delivery model (classroom, distance education, self-training, and so forth) and their main elements: roles of the actors, materials packaging, technological and organizational tools and infrastructures, and the other services and environments that will support the work of these actors (440, 442, 444, and 446). Indeed, the last phase of MISA 4.0 is entirely devoted to the immediate preparation of the delivery of the learning system. MISA provides suggestions from the design team to facilitate knowledge and competency management, actor and group management, the management of the learning system and its components, and finally, the maintenance and quality management of the learning system (610, 620, 630, and 640). In return, the delivery manager and other personnel may provide modification requests to the instructional designers and content experts. These modification requests are integrated as changes to the problem definition in Phase 1, thus triggering the beginning of a new instructional engineering cycle in which the MISA method will be used.

SUMMARY

This chapter, the midpoint of this book, completes the methodology loop. Starting with the social and economic context of e-learning in the knowledge society and the technological and e-learning models that can be used, I have defined a general and open e-learning model, a virtual learning center, and a system (Explor@) that assists in the creation of such centers. I hope Chapters Three and Four have convinced the reader of the importance of an instructional engineering method that allows the designer or a designing team to define, with flexibility and coherence, a series of models and plans that favor the creation of quality e-learning systems.

The MISA 4.0 instructional engineering method presented in this chapter is founded on a number of the basic principles discussed in the previous chapters:

> Learning necessarily implies the construction of the learner's knowledge through information processing; however, cognitivist and constructivist principles can be implemented through a variety of instructional approaches and strategies.

> Knowledge modeling is essential to elaborate the plans and specifications for a learning system, particularly if it involves problem-solving activities. Otherwise designers and content experts end up being guided by a simple list of subjects whose relationships are inefficiently defined and interrelated, making it difficult to structure training adequately.

> A distributed learning system such as an e-learning system can integrate various live or remote activities, with significant or limited use of information technologies, in an individualized or collaborative mode. Only objective analysis of the training itself, the characteristics of the target audience, and the context in which the training will be offered make it possible to make enlightened choices for this system. A learning system may also offer various options so that different segments of the target audience can at certain points choose among different approaches.

> Learning materials are best grouped in a plurimedia mode and offered on various media supports, integrated as interactive multimedia on a compact disc, on a Web site, or in a hybrid format (CD and Web). Instructional engineering makes it possible to define delivery principles to ensure the most appropriate materials are supplied for each given situation.

A learning system built with MISA can be integrated into an information-processing task support system at home, in a workplace, or in a public school, college, or university, using various material design systems and delivery management systems. It is critical to analyze these systems as part of establishing a coherent learning system model.

The components of a learning system can be reused in other learning systems when modular and nonlinear principles are applied to system design. Without such principles the maintenance of courses and programs may be so challenging that designers and content experts may prefer to start over with each new course or program, an expensive proposition, or may continue to use teaching materials long after they have became obsolete.

The next chapter discusses the use of Web-based tools that support the principles and tasks of instructional engineering.

5

Instructional Engineering on the Web

THE RAPID EVOLUTION of e-learning models has increased the number of decisions that have to be made when developing Web-based learning systems. As a consequence, designing these systems is more and more the affair of teams instead of single designers. This chapter examines how a design team distributed on the Internet, with members working from different workstations, can use the MISA method to build e-learning environments. Owing to the need to support this kind of collaborative work, my colleagues and I have built ADISA, the learning systems engineering distributed workbench (Atelier Distribué d'Ingénierie de Systèmes d'Apprentissage). ADISA is a series of design tools, grouped into an instructional engineering workbench and accessible through a Web browser.

I present the main components of the ADISA system first, to establish the workings of an instrumentation approach, and then I examine how the workbench tools can be used to define and build the components of an e-learning environment for learners, trainers, content experts, and managers.

ADISA is a Web-based system for a project team designing an e-learning system while team members work together through the Web. It is based on MISA 4.0 (described in Chapter Four) and provides tools for carrying out MISA's thirty-five main tasks, through which the user will produce the design specifications of a learning system, describing knowledge, skills and competencies, learning scenarios, activities and resources, learning materials, and finally, delivery processes. ADISA supports knowledge modeling through an integrated MOT knowledge editor (described in Chapter Three). It offers a set of Web-based forms for producing the MISA documentation elements (EDs) and also offers data propagation between the design components, embedding software engineering principles to support a design project team.

General ADISA Features

This instructional engineering workbench is a design support system created for the users of MISA 4.0. It gathers interrelated series of tools to channel and support the instructional engineering tasks. Its goal is to enhance coherence among the products of the method and to provide quality control over the various components of a learning system. Like MISA, ADISA is independent specific from delivery platforms, instructional strategies, media, and knowledge. Its main role is to assist content experts and designers to choose, adapt, and integrate these various components and approaches.

ADISA is the first instructional engineering support system that integrates knowledge modeling to fulfill the requirements of e-learning engineering. Other instructional engineering support systems exist, such as Designer's Edge, but they are based on more traditional methods that do not use knowledge modeling and that cover many fewer aspects of e-learning system design. AGD, the ancestor of ADISA, integrated knowledge modeling, but it supported only the tasks used in the initial version of the method, MISA 1.0. Moreover, AGD was a local system that did not provide distributed support to a design team.

As illustrated by Figure 5-1, ADISA is accessible to design team members via a Web browser. The left part of the screen is used to access the workbench functions. Four menus and a chart allow users to select one of the thirty-five MISA tasks that lead to elements of documentation. The right-hand section displays a tool that assists the user to create a selected ED—here, the learning event network (ED 222). In this case the corresponding editing tool opens up the MOT model editor so the user can construct a model representing the structure of a course composed of several modules, or learning units.

Figure 5-1. ADISA: An Instructional Engineering Workbench.

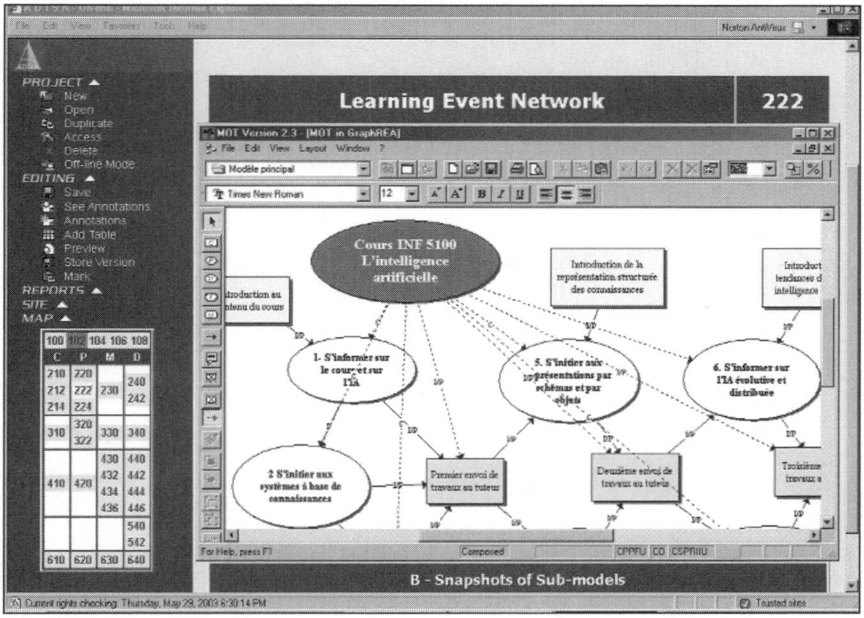

Other elements of documentation appear as forms, such as the one (ED 224) displayed in Figure 5-2. The four menus on the left of the screen access software functions.

Figure 5-2. Example of an ED Form (224).

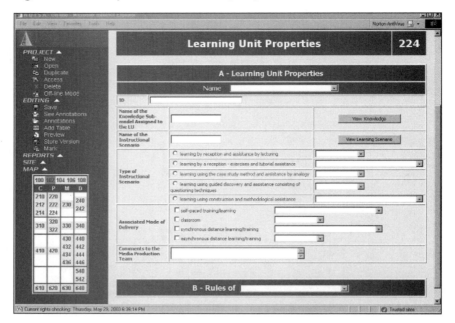

The *Project* menu is used to create, open, copy, or delete a learning system project. This menu also manages access rights, so team members can work on various elements of documentation prior to their integration. Because ADISA is entirely accessible through the Internet, users can work on-line, storing models on a server, or they can download ADISA and work off-line, using local storage space. The two copies that result may be synchronized using another option of the Project menu.

The *Edit* menu offers various options for building a documentation element selected from the chart. The ED can be saved and annotated, and users may also add a table of additional properties. They can indicate document completion or validation, and also view and archive documents, saving several copies representing various stages for the production of reports.

The *Reports* menu allows the grouping of document versions to create reports by phase, by axis, by author, by intended receiver, by element of documentation, or any other grouping criterion chosen by the user.

The *Site* menu allows users to search ED forms and models. It also offers a help option and on-line assistance. Through this menu ADISA may be downloaded from a server to a customer's computer for off-line work. Finally, this menu grants access to a browsing function accessible with any Web browser. This allows people performing a validation function to view an element of documentation under construction without modifying its contents and to annotate it with suggestions to the designers.

On a technical level the workbench uses the basic functions of Windows 95, Windows 98, and Windows NT, and DHTML and file data storage in XML. The DHTML format allows designers to create dynamic forms, modifiable according to the user's previous decisions. Once completed, the DHTML forms, just like the MOT models, are stored in XML files. This method facilitates the propagation of data between elements of documentation, the integrated ability to search for keywords in the models or the forms, and communication with various database formats and other systems used for the production of the instructional material or training management.

The high-quality graphics of the workbench provide a global and a structured view of the instructional objects, which facilitates the design. The fact that all the tools are integrated in the same workbench and can share data avoids a separate process of data transfer from one tool to another, saving time and eliminating transcription errors and inconsistencies from this source.

ADISA is based on a large quantity of instructional knowledge from the MISA 4.0 method, especially the seventeen instructional object typologies, each thoroughly researched. These typologies are integrated in the properties forms as options, reminding designers of the various possibilities from which they can choose. As for the models, a standard model library can be made available to start the modeling process.

The data entered by the user in the forms or the MOT editor can be transferred to another element of documentation in various ways. Figure 5-2 illustrates this fact. The DHTML form describes the properties of each learning unit defined in the LEN network (see Figure 5-1). The first attribute is the name of the learning unit. It is selected from a list read from the LEN network (ED 222) and transmitted to ED 224. The data are propagated automatically between the two elements of documentation.

The next two lines of the form in Figure 5-2 describe duration, evaluation weight, and amount of collaboration in a learning unit proposed to two target audiences, here labeled as IAO and ITIE. They illustrate another automated data propagation feature, this time from ED 104, where these target audiences are first defined. The names IAO and ITIE (students registered in two programs) are transmitted automatically to the ED 224 form.

Other data on the first three lines are entered directly on the form by the user. Lines 4 and 5 of the form in Figure 5-2 illustrate another form of propagation, this time nonautomated. Once the knowledge model (line 4) or the learning scenario (line 5) has been created, the name appears on the form and it can be displayed on screen to help the designer identify the type of scenario. In the next section of the form, the designer chooses a tutor-type scenario with ramified course (offering choices) and a free pace of learning activities (decided by the learner). The designer can verify whether the model of the scenario corresponds to this description.

ADISA seeks to create a balance between automated data propagation and user propagation. On the one hand automated propagation is convenient as it avoids replication of data already created in another ED. Without automatic propagation, using MISA and ADISA would often become tedious. On the other hand automatic propagation complicates teamwork, as conflicts may occur between two designers when one is modifying data used by the other who is involved in building another ED. Unfortunately, this situation would force the designers to work sequentially rather than in parallel. Moreover, automatic propagation is not the best solution when the user is the best actor to make certain delicate choices.

For example, a significant task of the designer (ED 430) consists in grouping all the instruments appearing in the instructional scenarios within a certain number of instructional materials. These instruments can be grouped in different ways, using different media, according to a training program need: a reference handbook, videos, multimedia, or Web sites. To assist the designer in this task, ADISA provides a table, such as the one illustrated in Figure 5-3. Here, the system groups the instruments appearing in the models of the learning

Figure 5-3. A Tool to Sort Instructional Materials.

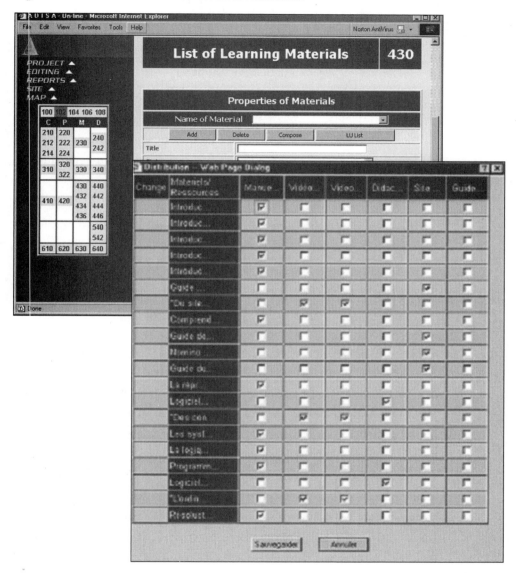

scenarios (320) and presents them on each line of the table. The columns represent the materials to be built, as defined by the user in ED 430. This interface enables the designer to choose the instruments that he or she will group in one or more materials, just by clicking the appropriate boxes. For example, a designer could choose to group all reference information related to the contents of the course both on a Web site and in a printed guide.

In sum, ADISA offers users three ways to propagate data from one element of documentation to another.

Automated propagation happens without any user interventions. The data from a source element are transferred directly into one or more fields on the form of the target ED.

Source-type propagation consists of transmitting data from one or more source elements for a user to decide which data will be integrated into the target ED.

Information-type propagation consists of displaying on the screen a model or a form that is particularly useful in the construction of the target ED. The user is free to take it into account or to ignore it.

Designing the Main Components of a Virtual Learning Center

This section discusses the use of MISA and ADISA specifications to build learning events in a virtual learning center (as defined in Chapter Three). Figure 5-4 illustrates the interactions between the MISA specifications and the possible components of a concrete learning system in a virtual learning center, built with Explor@. (Using another learning content management system [LCMS] would involve similar operations.)

The integration of a learning event in an Explor@ Virtual Center requires a more or less elaborated Web site giving access to the learning activities and corresponding resources, together with one or more environments linked to the Web site, each grouping the necessary resources needed by an actor at delivery time. Some of these resources are grouped according to two main tree structures: the knowledge, or cognitive, structure and the instructional structure (see Chapter Two). These structures are used to model and assess learners' progress, to provide them with activity reports and advice, and to give them access to the information, production, and collaboration tools actors need to interact with other actors.

Figure 5-4. Transfer from MISA and ADISA to a Virtual Learning Center.

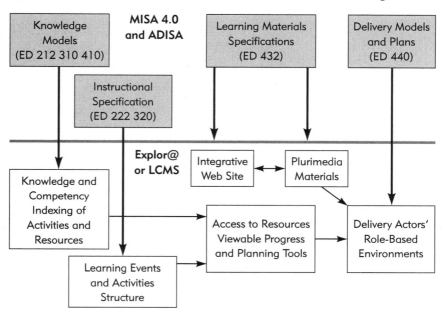

Media Model and On-Line Materials

In MISA, ED 432 constructs a graphic representation of each material used in a learning event (program, course, module, activity), including the model of the integrated Web site as defined in Explor@. Figure 5-5 shows a model of an integrated Web site. The rectangles represent the components (Web pages or sections of pages) and the media elements—such as video clips, graphs, texts, or hypertexts—that provide access to the contents of source documents (boxes with cut corners) built by an author. (Some of these source documents may be described with a similar model.) The circles represent the hyperlinks, for example, from a course scenario to the pages of the modules, which will then be similarly described, by submodels. The hexagons represent layout principles or style sheets defining (ruling) the format of the media elements.

Once this media model is completed by the instructional designer, it is transmitted to the production team who will produce the Web site. This

Figure 5-5. Model of Web Site Material in MISA and ADISA.

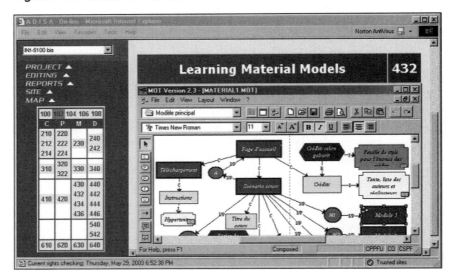

model and the complementary EDs, such as a table of media elements grouping them by media type or a table of source documents, can be distributed to the computer analysts, graphic designers, and content authors to give them a precise and structured view of the intentions of the designers, a step often lacking in many projects. This model and its documentation is used as a tool for communication between the instructional designers and the production team. The fact that the model is conceptual, that is to say stripped from its precise context, allows both the graphic designer and the programmer to use their creativity. In a media model the instructional designer indicates the hyperlinks he or she would like to see between the various components. However, the designer does not specify how to present these hyperlinks in the user interfaces. This decision is left to the production team, who may decide that the hyperlink will be most effective when presented as a button, in a menu, in a text, or in an animated graphic.

Time has shown that the best materials result from respecting the capacities of the project team members, so it is important to ensure that the design team decides on the structure of a material in light of the relevant knowledge and the instructional approach selected. Also, the production team is responsible for establishing the media standards and the look-and-feel of the user's interface. The team can then validate this interface with tests (MISA Phase 5) that will result in appropriate modifications to the media model of the Web site or modifications to the interface or other site functions.

Delivery Models and Actor Environments

In MISA the delivery models (ED 440) provide the elements required to create one or many Explor@ environments, thus supplementing, or even completely replacing, the Web site created from the media, or learning material, model. At this point, the design team can identify the main actors in a general delivery model: one or many types of learners and one or many types of facilitators, such as trainers, content experts, managers, technical advisers, and so forth. The team can then build a specific delivery model for each actor for whom it wishes to build an environment. Figure 5-6 displays such a model, intended for an actor identified as "trainer-tutor."

Figure 5-6. Delivery Model for a Trainer.

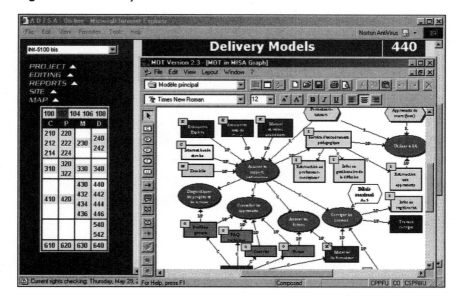

In a delivery model the actors are represented by hexagonal figures and their roles or operations at delivery time by oval shapes. The resources they need or produce in each role or operation appear in rectangles. The actor is linked to each one of his or her roles by an R-link ("rules" or "governs"). An I/P link connects input resources to an operation to be used by the actor responsible for the role or connects a role or an operation to a resource to be produced by that actor. In the example presented in Figure 5-6, the trainer-tutor actor must produce an evaluation of the learners. He or she must also provide several types of feedback: to a learner about that learner's progress, to the registrar in order to transmit the grades obtained by the learner, and finally, to the designer and to the training manager about the quality of the course, together with general feedback at the end of each session.

This trainer-tutor delivery model indicates the resources needed to complete this actor's productions and fulfill his or her roles. These resources could be integrated in an Explor@ environment accessible by the participants personifying this actor. In addition to the Web site and materials identical to those available to the learners, the trainer-tutor will also need a group profile tool as an aid in viewing the learners' progress and diagnosing their deficiencies. To give advice to the learners, he or she will also need a tool to maintain a frequently asked questions file, and some e-mail, forum, and audio- or videoconferencing tools. With the help of a forum tool, this trainer-tutor can act as a group facilitator. Finally, for all of the role's tasks, this actor can access an Internet connection from home.

Knowledge and Instructional Models for Course Management

The media and delivery models provide the production team directly with the essential specifications of the physical learning system, comprising Web sites, other plurimedia materials, and Explor@ environments. The two other models produced by MISA, the knowledge and instructional models, are also very useful during the delivery.

The knowledge model, describing the knowledge, the skills, and the competencies to acquire, is clearly essential for evaluating the success of the instruction. The instructional model describing the learning events structure, the courses, the instructional units, the activities, and the resources to be used or produced is also necessary to evaluate the learners' progress and provide them with feedback according to the work they have accomplished. In MISA, the instructional model starts with the learning event network (LEN) (222). It is thereafter supplemented by the instructional scenarios (320) associated with each learning unit of the LEN, such as the instructional scenario, presented in Figure 5-7.

Figure 5-7. Example of an Instructional Scenario in a Learning Unit.

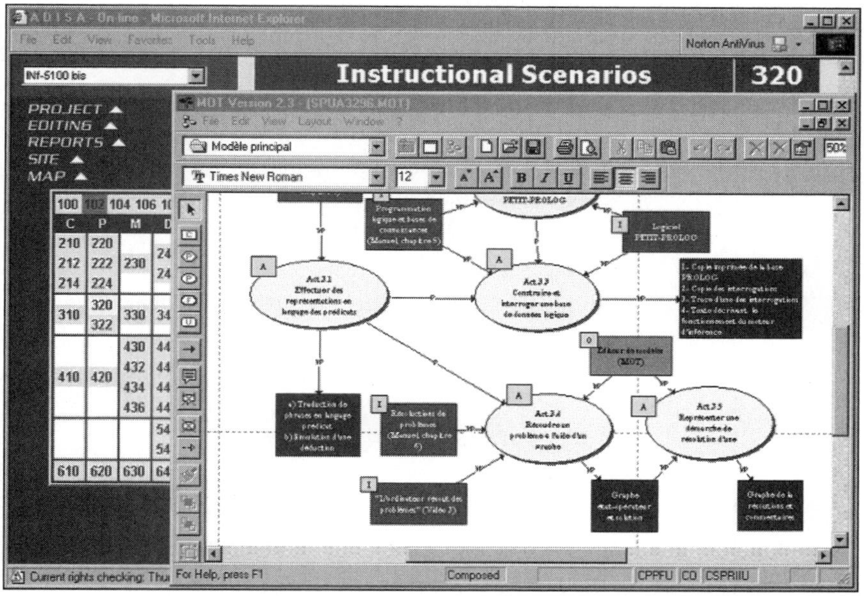

By grouping the LEN and the instructional scenarios, we can build the *instructional,* or *pedagogical, structure* used in Explor@. To do so, we use the LEN structure. We follow the C-links until we reach the learning units, and then we continue to develop the tree structure using the instructional scenario to integrate the activities and the surrounding resources. A sample of a section of this work is presented in the following box. The first part of the tree structure is based on the LEN in Figure 5-1, and the development of the LU-2 subtree is based on the instructional scenario in Figure 5-7. The development of the tree structure for the other learning activities is constructed in the same way, from their respective instructional scenarios.

PEDAGOGICAL STRUCTURE (PS) FOR THE COURSE "ARTIFICIAL INTELLIGENCE"

LU-1: Getting Acquainted with the Course and AI

LU-2: Introduction to Knowledge-Based System

    Activity 2.1: Knowledge Representation

        Knowledge representation (Chapter 2)

        Representation exercises

    Activity 2.2: Deduction

        Knowledge representation (Chapter 2)

        Deduction exercises and comments

    Activity 2.3: Problem Solving

        Knowledge representation (Chapter 2)

        Problem-solving exercises

    Activity 2.4: Rule-Based Knowledge Representation

        Expert systems (Chapter 3)

        Electronic advisers (Video 2)

        Rule-based representation exercises

    Activity 2.5: Getting Acquainted with the RULES Software

        RULES software

    Activity 2.6: Editing, Saving, and Testing a Knowledge-Based System

        RULES software

        Rule representation on paper

        Copy of the RULES base and deduction steps

LU-3: Introduction to Logical Databases

LU-4: Introduction to Natural Language Processing

LU-5: Introduction to Schema and Object Representations

LU-6: Introduction to Distributed and Evolutionary AI

LU-7: Evaluation of the Impacts of AI

This structure reveals how the learner progresses through each instructional unit and what needs to be associated with each level. With the information in this user progression model, Explor@ can provide learning activity assessments to the learner and trainer. The trainer can use this kind of assessment when interacting with the learner. Explor@ can also provide advice to assist learners as they work through the training events.

Some information is lost when we transform the instructional model built in MISA into an instructional tree structure. We lose the P-links shown in the LEN, for example, and the activity prerequisites that the instructional scenarios revealed. However, these elements can be taken into account as we formulate the conditions that define the levels of progress.

Knowledge Models and Cognitive Structure

Although instructional models permit the evaluation of a learner's progress, they do not indicate whether the learner has acquired the target knowledge and skills. To learn this, we need to use the knowledge model.

In MISA, the knowledge model for a learning event (a program, course, or activity) is built gradually. In ED 212, the designer first builds a preliminary general model of the contents of the instructional event, then in ED 310, the designer develops this model by producing a submodel for the content of each learning unit, and finally, in ED 410, he or she further refines the general model by producing a knowledge submodel for each instrument in the learning scenarios of the learning units. Figure 5-8 shows the knowledge submodel for a learning unit.

Figure 5-8. Learning Unit Submodel in a Course Knowledge Model.

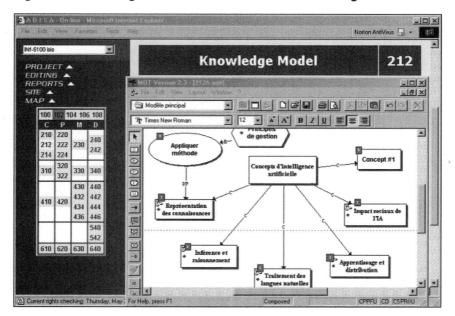

The cognitive structure that follows is the knowledge model for the pedagogical structure shown in the previous box. It demonstrates that the knowledge model for an instructional structure is not necessarily unique to that structure nor is it necessarily an architectural match for that structure. For example, a subject like "structured representation" may occur in more than one learning unit, especially in spiral models of instruction or in project-based learning. Or a course may be subdivided into three instructional units—a presentation, a project, and a group discussion—each one covering the entire content of the knowledge model.

COGNITIVE STRUCTURE (CS) FOR THE COURSE "ARTIFICIAL INTELLIGENCE"

Inferences and Reasoning Processes*
State-operators models*
Knowledge processing*
Multiagent systems*

Knowledge Representation
Expert systems
Propositional logic
Predicate logic
Structured representation
Object representation
Programming paradigms

Natural Language Processing
Sentence analysis
Generative grammar
Semantics

Learning and Distribution
Machine learning
Neuron networks
Multiagent systems*

Social Impact of AI
AI and education
AI, work, and economy
AI, culture, and society

The passage from the main knowledge model and its submodels in MISA to the cognitive structure that the designer has created earlier in Explor@ is not as direct as in building an instructional structure. In the former case, the designer examines only the *principal* knowledge, that for which target competencies will be defined and for which learning evaluations will be carried out. The asterisks (*) in the cognitive structure displayed here indicate the principal knowledge units, those labeled "P" on the knowledge submodel shown in Figure 5-8. (This submodel of course displays only part of the complete cognitive structure.)

In addition, along with the instructional structure, the cognitive structure assists in defining progress levels in the acquisition of knowledge and criteria for assessing the learning level achieved at a given time. As discussed in Chapter Two, we can define a user model as composed of progress levels for the activities achieved according to the instructional model and the knowledge and competencies acquired according to the knowledge model and the cognitive structure. This user model allows Explor@ to launch various "intelligent" tools, such as knowledge and competencies assessments or group profiles for the trainer. These tools can then be integrated in the Explor@ environments according to the roles played by each actor.

SUMMARY

In contrast to most proprietary systems, which are limited to the production of courseware on the Web, MISA and its support system, ADISA, allow the construction of large-scale learning systems that integrate several courses, each one composed of several activities, documents, or resources, using a variety of media formats.

After this brief overview of instructional engineering, readers may feel that the topic is highly complex. It is true that instructional engineering overall is not an easy task; however, it can be simplified though the use of integrated tools such as ADISA and the application of well-chosen instructional engineering operations and principles. Moreover, this impression of complexity comes mainly from the fact that the method discussed here is general. It was designed so it could be applied to multiple and extremely diverse situations. My experience has been that each single project carried out with MISA and ADISA has used only a fraction of the functions available. In other words, individual projects are highly unlikely to have this level of complexity. This is demonstrated through the case studies presented in Chapters Six, Seven, and Eight.

6

Reengineering a University Course for the Web

THIS CHAPTER PRESENTS the first of three case studies.[1] It
describes how the instructional engineering method MISA 4.0 was
applied to transform a university course so that it could be delivered through
a Web site in a virtual learning center. The course Inf-5100, Introduction to
Artificial Intelligence, is taught in three Télé-université programs. It was
offered for the first time in 1990, and has achieved a certain success because
over two thousand students have registered in the following years. From 1990
to 1999, the course underwent two minor revisions. At the beginning of
1999, it was reengineered to update the contents, to integrate new collaborative activities, and to provide Internet delivery of materials and on-line
tutoring. The design of the new version of the course began in April 1999
and was completed by November 1999. The course has been offered in this
Web version since these modifications took place.

Definition of the Project

Table 6-1 presents the tasks that were planned in the first phase of MISA 4.0 and the tasks that were actually carried out. The decisions taken in this effort were guided by three main factors. First, my colleagues and I wished to respond to the dissatisfaction of many students with obsolete course content. Second, the Télé-université wanted to offer greater course accessibility, better tutor guidance, and more student interactions, in order to increase students' persistence. Finally, decisions were affected by time and resource limitations: the planned improvements were carried out, the less essential modifications (video updates, delivery model documentation) had to be postponed.

Table 6-1. Tasks Accomplished in Phase 1 of the Project "Introduction to Artificial Intelligence."

Phase 1	Task Planned	Results
Elaborate the profile of the organization (ED 100)	Identify the current situation and the expectations of the organization regarding the content, the pedagogy, the technological tools, the training management, and so on.	We decided to update the contents, to introduce a more collaborative pedagogy, and to deliver the entire course on the Internet.
Identify the resource documents (ED 108)	Sort all documents that could be used in the engineering of the learning system (LS) and all materials that could be used or recycled in the new LS: training plans, programs, courses, and activities already available; task descriptions and analyses; instructional materials; technical guides; promotional materials; and so forth.	The existing activity guide (to be replaced by a Web site), the manual (to be reused), certain chapters to be replaced by PDF documents; the video and the courseware were delivered in digitalized form.

Table 6-1. Tasks Accomplished in Phase 1 of the Project "Introduction to Artificial Intelligence," Cont'd.

Phase 1	Task Planned	Results
Describe the desired situation (ED 102)	Identify the general training objectives and priorities, type of training, scope of the LS, its life span, its delivery date, and so forth.	Not carried out; desired situation is similar to that of the source course. Life span: revision in 3 years. Delivery date: beginning 2000.
Describe the target audience (ED 104)	Build learners' profiles: languages, availability, mean education level, learning styles, main gaps to be filled, and so forth.	Not carried out; target audience similar to that for the source course.
Describe the current context (ED 106)	Identify the frontiers of the future LS; the human, material, financial, and organizational resources available; and the constraints that may have an impact on LS development.	The human resources are limited: a part-time designer, a small budget for updating the courseware, a small production team whose members must create three other courses.
Adapt MISA	List the retained EDs and their priority attributes.	Available knowledge in the manual; main focus on the instructional model and the media model.

Preliminary Analysis

The main orientation principles of the solution were established in the second phase, as shown in Table 6-2. As we were reengineering this solution, most of the instructional materials were left intact, allowing a rapid progression to the architectural phase. Our main preoccupations for Phase 2 were related to the instructional orientations and to the reorganization of the course into seven learning units, as shown in Figure 6-1.

Table 6-2. Tasks Accomplished in Phase 2 of the Project "Introduction to Artificial Intelligence."

Phase 2	Task Planned	Results
Define the knowledge model orientation principles (ED 210)	State the knowledge model orientations (type of knowledge and principles) to develop a structured knowledge and competencies model of the learning system (LS).	Knowledge mainly conceptual; procedures found in the practice exercises.
Build the knowledge model (ED 212)	Build a graphic and structured representation of the LS in conjunction with the evaluation of the users' current and target competencies (ED 214).	Postponed to Phase 3; to be done at the same time as the definition of the instructional scenarios (ED 320).
Identify discrepancies between target and current competencies (ED 214)	For the main knowledge of the knowledge model, determine the discrepancies between the current and target competencies.	Not completed because course objectives were mainly satisfactory.
Define the instructional model orientation principles (ED 220)	State the instructional orientations that will allow the development of a structured learning event network (LEN). Also, state the principles for the instructional processes, the evaluation approach, the learners' level of collaboration, and the adaptability of the instructional scenario.	LEN: 2 levels; the course is split up into LUs called "modules." Instructional strategy: concept presentation (texts and videos), paper or exercises with course software; continued collaboration between the learners, even more pronounced in LU-7. Evaluation according to learner productions submitted to a tutor.

Table 6-2. Tasks Accomplished in Phase 2 of the Project "Introduction to Artificial Intelligence," Cont'd.

Phase 2	Task Planned	Results
Build the LEN (ED 222)	Structure a series of learning events (LEs) and the rules that govern the progress between them.	LEN split up into 7 LUs, progress into 3 phases where learners submit their productions (see Figure 6.1).
Define the learning unit properties (ED 224)	Describe the proprieties of each learning unit (LU) for the target audiences, the length, the weight of the evaluations, the collabo-rative activities, the learning scenario type, and the delivery mode.	Postponed to Phase 3, to be done in conjunction with defining the properties of the learning activities (ED 322).
Define the media development ori-entation principles (ED 230)	State the principles that will guide the media selection: media type, material interaction, media support. These elements will be useful for the cost-benefit analysis (ED 242).	Postponed to Phase 3 (many orientations already stated in Phase 1).
Define the delivery orientation principles (ED 240)	State the principles that will guide the delivery decisions.	Postponed to Phase 3 (many orientations already stated in Phase 1).
Analyze the cost, benefits, and im-pacts (ED 242)	Provide project management with the basic elements to evaluate project feasibility in relation to associated costs, benefits, and impacts.	Task not completed, as these data were known from the start.

Figure 6-1. Result of Task ED 222: A Network of Seven Learning Events.

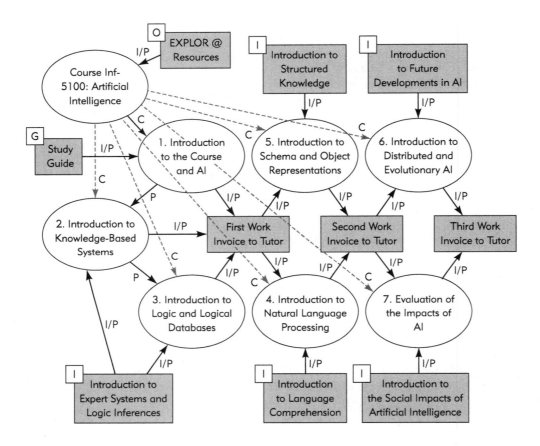

Figure 6-1 shows the series of resources we designed (labeled I) and then integrated into an Explor@ environment, to support a series of course activities. They are subdivided into seven modules, or learning units, each one described by an introductory document. The module titles display themes that confirm the conceptual orientation of this introductory course. The first three modules are ordered sequentially; the work produced by the students in these modules will be bundled and sent to the tutor for a first evaluation early in the course. Modules 4 and 5 can be completed in parallel; here learners will generate documents that will be grouped for a second evaluation. Modules 6 and 7 can also be studied in parallel and learners will produce results that will be used for a third and last evaluation.

Architecture

Several important decisions were delayed to the architectural phase (Phase 3). A main knowledge model was built through retro-engineering, mainly from the contents of the chapters of the handbook that were reused and also from new documents created to replace the obsolete chapters.

Figure 6-2 presents the knowledge submodel associated with LU-2, on the subject of knowledge representation. It displays the main topics as concepts and also displays two procedures to be applied using the course exercise software. Figure 6-3 presents the submodel associated with LU-6, which highlights three main knowledge units (labeled "P"), which are to be presented in new documents available from the course Web site.

Figure 6-2. Knowledge Model for LU-2.

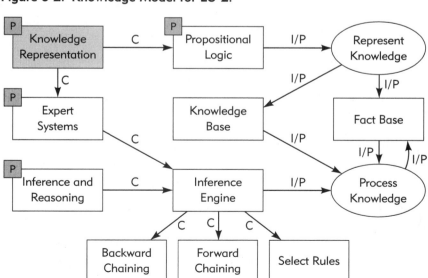

Figure 6-3. Knowledge Model for LU-6.

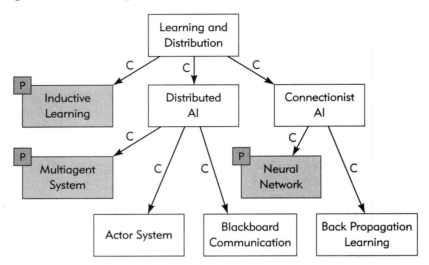

Table 6-3 presents the task results from Phase 3, in which the architecture of the learning system is designed.

Table 6-3. Tasks Accomplished in Phase 3 of the Project "Introduction to Artificial Intelligence."

Phase 3	Task Planned	Results
Identify the learning unit content (ED 310)	Build a submodel of the knowledge associated with each learning unit.	Produced through retro-engineering of the contents of the textbook and new texts (see Figures 6.2 and 6.3).
Define the instructional scenarios (ED 320)	For each learning unit (LU), build a structured model of the activities, the resources, and the instructions given to the learners and the facilitators.	Learning scenarios were built for all 7 learning units (see, for example, Figures 6.4 and 6.5).

Table 6-3. Tasks Accomplished in Phase 3 of the Project "Introduction to Artificial Intelligence," Cont'd.

Phase 3	Task Planned	Results
Define the learning units and learning activities properties (ED 322, ED 224)	Describe the properties of each instructional activity of the learning units.	Property description forms were produced for all 7 modules and 36 activities (Figure 6.6).
Revise the media and delivery orientations (ED 230–3, ED 240–3)	Revise, if necessary, the media and delivery orientations to take into account the instructional scenario instruments (ED 320).	The main media and delivery orientations were produced.
Develop the infrastructure (ED 330)	Provide the project manager with information to guide the selection of the human and material resources required to create and produce the LS.	Not completed, as the usual methods and tools are used, as well as MISA, MOT, and Explor@.
Plan the learning system (LS) delivery (ED 340)	Coordinate the creation, the production, the tests, and revision schedules to determine the various delivery dates of the LS components (including, if applicable, one or more prototypes) for the target organization.	Delivery 1: a prototype limited to LU-2. Delivery 2: the Web site and the materials. Delivery 3: the whole course integrated into the Explor@ environment.

Figure 6-4 displays one of the seven learning scenarios. It concerns predicate logic representations and contains five activities; the first three have two input instruments (labeled "I"): chapters of the handbook and the pedagogical software (PETIT-PROLOG) used to produce small logic programs. The inputs for the last two activities are a video and another chapter of the book. A tool, the MOT model editor, is used to build a knowledge model to solve logic problems. This scenario confirms the choice of a strategy based on information consultation followed by practical work. The scenario for LU-7, illustrated in Figure 6-5, makes use of asynchronous teleconferencing. Each student selects two of four topics (7.1 or 7.2, and 7.3 or 7.4). Then he or she consults the information provided in some of the six texts and the two videos; a list of Web sites is also provided in Explor@. The student then produces an analysis, a comment, or an opinion that he or she integrates into a discussion forum (Activity 7.5). Finally, the student uses the information from that forum to write a synthesis (Activity 7.6) of the impacts of artificial intelligence. This text will be evaluated by the tutor in the third submission of work for evaluation.

Figure 6-4. Learning Scenarios for LU-3.

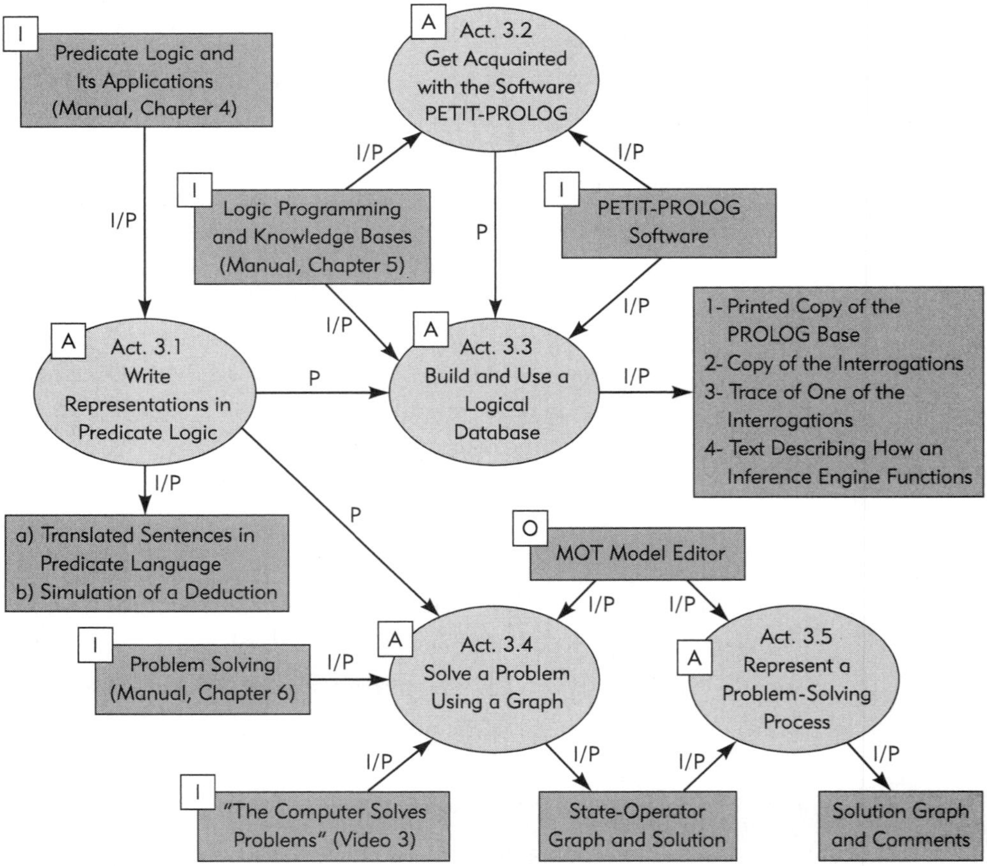

Figure 6-5. Learning Scenario for LU-7.

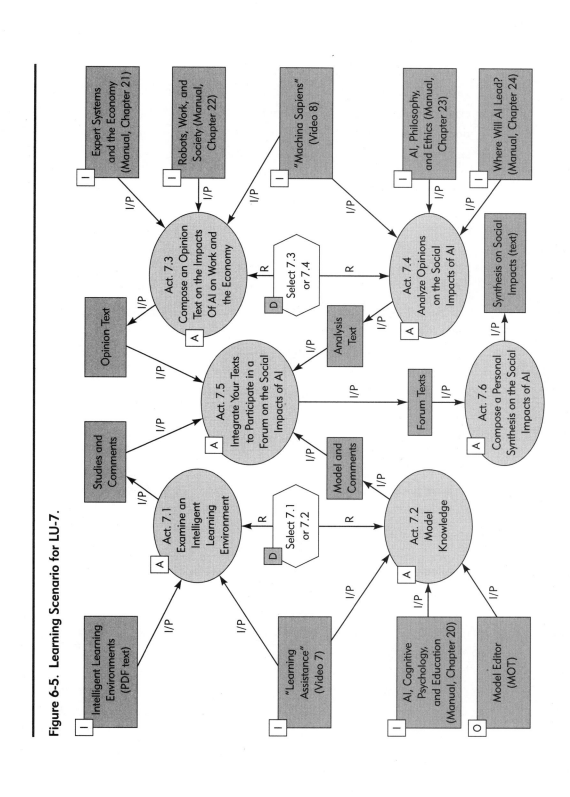

Note that both scenarios contain only learning activities (labeled "A"). Usually an instructional scenario will also contain the trainers' activities. However, in this case these activities could be deduced from the property description forms we built (ED 322) for each of the learning activities. Figure 6-6 is an example of such a form for Activity 7.6.

Figure 6-6. One of the Thirty-Five Activity Property Description Forms.

Learning Activity Property Form	
Identifier **Act. 7.6**	Title **Produce a personal synthesis on the impacts of artificial intelligence.**
Description	Synthesis exercise on the impacts of AI
Input materials	Your opinions produced in activities 7.1 or 7.2 and 7.3 or 7.4. The information obtained from the discussion forum for activity 7.5.
Production	Synthesis of the social impacts
Time: 1 hour	**Evaluation:** 20 % **Activity Type:** Production (written)
Instructions	Compose a synthesis of no more than five pages about your thoughts on the impacts of artificial intelligence structure in your text in three sections, corresponding to the topics covered in this module.
Collaboration	This assignment must be produced individually.
Evaluation	This is a graded activity; to be included in your third and final evaluation. Use the template available on the Web site to send your text to your tutor.

The following lists state the orientation principles of the media and delivery models. The media principles provide the selected material types, their media supports, and their general interactivity characteristics. They show that the materials are texts, a Web site (network hypermedia), videos, and on-line text or graphic courseware. The Web site is supported by a server; the videos are broadcast on-line and also sent on videocassettes to accommodate learners who do not have access to a broadband connection; most of the texts remain in their original printed format, due to the quantity, although new texts are available on-line as PDF files. Note that the principles suggest the use of a function (in Explor@) that provides personalized ("intelligent") assistance.

ORIENTATION PRINCIPLES
FOR THE MEDIA MODEL

- Some of the materials are network hypermedia, text/graphic course-ware, videos, or static texts/graphics.

- Some of the digitized materials are available on a Web server. Some of the materials use analog support of the videocassette type; others are in a printed reference manual.

- Some of the materials are dynamic, allowing the user to navigate on a network of hyperlinks; others offer keyword search functions. Some of the materials offer personalized ("intelligent") assistance, and others enable remote user interactions.

The delivery orientation principles identify the selected delivery model first: that is to say, asynchronous training with remote communication, a network means of communication (generally broadband), and mail (for printed materials and cassettes). The last seven principles indicate the selected delivery moments and locations, the start-up groups and their composition, the instructional personnel, the administrative and technical support required, and the objectives, means, and agents for evaluating the course and assessing learners' work. It was also decided to split the evaluations into two groups. A learner's self-assessed activities (formative exercises) were transmitted via an Explor@ tool and did not count toward the student's final mark. A learner's evaluated activity (graded work) was not available to other students and was sent only to the tutor, because it did count toward the final mark.

> ### ORIENTATION PRINCIPLES FOR THE DELIVERY MODEL
>
> - All of the learning events use an asynchronous distance education delivery model with remote communication.
>
> - Certain telecom tools are broadband connection and narrowband modem access. Other communication tools are the phone and public mail.
>
> - All of the learning activities are delivered at the moment chosen by the learner.
>
> - All of the learning activities are delivered at the location selected by the learner.
>
> - All of the learning units can accommodate groups that start up any time the minimum number of learners is reached (minimum 5, maximum 15).
>
> - All learning units require the intervention of instructional trainers who provide assistance to many groups of learners, and require remote contributions from the administrative and technical support personnel.
>
> - All of the LUs will be evaluated by a remote tutor for purposes of issuing training credit.
>
> - Some of the training activities are evaluated only by the tutor; others are self-assessed by the learner himself or herself.
>
> - All of the learning events are reevaluated at least once a year and they are revised at least every two years. They are evaluated by the learners and trainers, through forums and questionnaires integrated into the material.

Design of Learning Materials

Our design of the new instructional materials and the other components of the delivery environment (Phase 4) was based on the decisions taken in the architecture phase. Our plans and results are presented in Table 6-4.

Table 6-4. Tasks Accomplished in Phase 4 of the Project "Introduction to Artificial Intelligence."

Phase 4	Task Planned	Results
Define the content of the learning instruments (ED 410)	Associate a knowledge submodel (which describes the content) with each instrument resource that appears in the LEN (ED 222) and in the LU scenarios (ED 320).	A draft plan based on a knowledge submodel was completed for the three new texts.
Define the properties of the learning instruments and guides (ED 420)	Describe the properties of each instrument and each guide for the LEN (ED 222) and the LU scenarios.	A text to insert on the course Web site was produced for each instrument.
List the learning materials (ED 430)	List and group the learning system (LS) materials and describe their main properties.	The instruments were grouped in a series of materials according to their media.
Build the learning material, or media, models (ED 432)	For each instructional material that has to be adapted or produced (ED 430), build a graphic representation of its structure and contents for the authors and media team.	Not completed. The Web site and the new texts were built directly from the scenario model of each LU.
Describe the media elements (ED 434)	Describe the properties of the various media elements that appear in each material model (ED 432) of the learning system.	Not completed (except for the models representing each LU and the model captions).
Describe the source documents (ED 436)	Describe, for all the LS materials, the properties of the source documents that appear in the material models (ED 432).	Not completed, except for the new texts, as all of the Web site content was defined by the instructional model.

Table 6-4. Tasks Accomplished in Phase 4 of the Project "Introduction to Artificial Intelligence," Cont'd.

Phase 4	Task Planned	Results
Build the delivery models (ED 440)	Build graphic models that feature the relationships between the actors and the resources upon the LS delivery.	Not completed, although the delivery orientations (ED 240) have been applied.
Define the actors and material packages (ED 442)	Describe the properties of the various delivery actors in the LS (especially the learner groups and the main resource providers) and the series of materials used to access the LS knowledge and activities.	Two series of materials were defined: one by mailing CDs or tapes with the manual, the other entirely on the Web (except for the manual), with material downloads and video streaming delivery.
Define the telecom services and tools (ED 444)	Describe the properties of the telecom services and tools of the delivery model (ED 440).	This is where the resources to be integrated into the Explor@ environment were selected.
Define the delivery services and locations (ED 446)	Describe the properties of the services and locations of delivery model use (ED 440).	Not completed, because the delivery orientation principles were sufficiently clear.

This phase, which aims to prepare for the media production, focused on the resources of the Explor@ environment and the Web site, which replaced the original printed guides. This Web site, a hypermedia guide, was structured from the instructional model: after the welcome page, the user obtained a page similar to the LEN model (Figure 6-1), providing access to any of the modules (LUs) and to their scenarios (Figures 6-4 and 6-5). Then, from these scenarios, users were granted direct access to the description of the activities, the input instruments (texts, videos, courseware, tools), and production templates for students' work (formative exercises or graded assignments).

In addition, resources were listed and integrated in the five spaces of the learner's Explor@ environment, as follows:

Self-management: personal profile, calendar, progression, course syllabus, course evaluation

Information: Webography, text summaries and three PDFs and videos

Production: tool to send graded work, text editor, MOT, six courseware (RULES, PETIT-PROLOG, Syntax, Semantics, Animals and Blocks)

Collaboration: showcase window, e-mail, forum, group profile

Assistance: directory, technical capsules, study guide, Explor@ guide

Development and Validation

During Phase 5, MISA does not cover the details of learning material production. The production process is determined by the earlier choice of development tools and the delivery plans established in Phase 3. In this case the Web site components were integrated directly, using HTML programming, and the graphic elements were produced with tools such as Photoshop. The designer and the linguist, using a Web editor, carried out the revisions. Table 6-5 presents the plans and results for this phase.

Table 6-5. Tasks Accomplished in Phase 5 of the Project "Introduction to Artificial Intelligence."

Phase 5	Task Planned	Results
Use various production tools	Micro-design and produce materials.	HTML programming, graphic tools, Dreamweaver-2 editor, Explor@ design tools.

Table 6-5. Tasks Accomplished in Phase 5 of the Project "Introduction to Artificial Intelligence," Cont'd.

Phase 5	Task Planned	Results
Plan the trials and tests (ED 540)	Describe the trials and test for each delivery (ED 540), plan the tests, and identify the resources necessary to analyze the learning system (LS).	Not completed; the tests were limited to linguistic and content revision by the designer-author.
Tests and Revision Log (ED 542)	Provide the project manager with data related to the modifications of one of the LS deliveries. Facilitate the evaluation and follow-up of the modification requests.	Not completed, but a follow-up table of the various components of the site and the Explor@ resources was built and regularly updated.
Revise the LS materials	Working from the Revision Decision Log (ED 542), modify the instructional materials and the other resources of the LS.	Not completed, although many elements were modified.

Figure 6-7 displays two of the pages produced for the Web site. The first corresponds to the model for the learning scenario of LU-3 and the second presents the description of Activity 3.2 in this module. The activity inputs and products are identified by icons corresponding to the type of learning material. In addition, the activity page corresponds to the form built in ED 322.

The production of the Explor@ environment required us to configure some of the Explor@ Java tools. It was decided to integrate visualization tools for the learner and the trainer-tutor environments, such as a calendar, a progression report, and a group profile, and to offer personalized help functions. Here are the main steps in this process:

Figure 6-7. Two Pages from the Course Web Site.

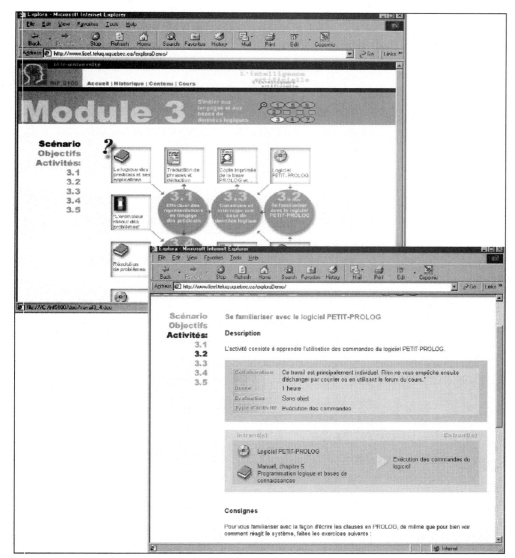

- Construction of two tree structures: the instructional structure, built from the learning event network and the instructional scenarios, and the cognitive structure, built from the knowledge model, as explained in Chapter Five.

- Attribution of a number of progression levels for each instructional unit and each cognitive unit of the two tree structures, according to the number of task components or activities associated with each unit in the course Web site.

- Design of the transition conditions for moving from one learning unit to another, for moving from one level of progression to another, and the design of help capsules displayed at certain progression levels.

These design activities configure generic Explor@ tools, according to the characteristics of the project under development, as complements to the Web site content.

Delivery Planning

Phase 6 tasks were carried out in an informal fashion: some testing was conducted with learners through short documents or e-mails, a learner evaluation guide was produced by one of the tutors and shared with the others. We mainly relied on the regular operation of the delivery services at Télé-université. Table 6-6 contains our plans and results for this phase.

Table 6-6. Tasks Accomplished in Phase 6 of the Project "Introduction to Artificial Intelligence."

Phase 6	Task Planned	Results
Prepare the knowledge and competency management (ED 610)	Provide information to the target organization to facilitate research, updates, and reuse of the knowledge and competencies.	Not carried out, as the course had mainly the same contents as previously.
Prepare the actor and group management (ED 620)	Provide instructional information to the target organization for the registration and training of students, actor and group management, and learning assessment.	Informally produced, in collaboration with the coordinator of the tutor.

Table 6-6. Tasks Accomplished in Phase 6 of the Project "Introduction to Artificial Intelligence," Cont'd.

Phase 6	Task Planned	Results
Prepare the LS and resource management (ED 630)	Provide information to the target organization to facilitate archival storing and updates of the learning system (LS) and its components. Recommend ways to provide the learners and assistants with a series of materials and other resources available to promote and maximize the use of the LS.	Informally carried out through communication with Télé-université's services.
Prepare the maintenance and quality management (ED 640)	Provide information to the organization to initiate the first delivery, to continue to evaluate the quality of the LS and its resources, and to prepare periodic revisions of the LS models, materials, and environment.	Informally carried out through communication with Télé-université's services.

Discussion

Our use of the MISA method in this project resulted in carrying out eighteen of the thirty-five tasks of the method. Some of these eighteen tasks, especially those relating to the knowledge and media models, were carried out partially. The delivery model was also partially carried out, with an accent on the delivery orientation principles and the selection or creation of learner-centered Explor@ resources. This process turned out to be efficient, as it allowed part-time resources (totaling approximately four person-months) to complete the reengineering project in eight months, including the production of new materials (texts and revised courseware) and the Web-based learning environment.

With the advantage of hindsight, I can comment on three significant gaps in this project. First, our direct transition from the instructional model to the production phase, skipping the design of the media model of the Web site, caused much misunderstanding and duplicated work for the designer and the production team. Undoubtedly, frequent revisions during development could have been avoided if the instructional specifications had been translated into media terminology for the production team.

Second, the absence of structured scenarios for the tutors and also of a specific Explor@ tutor environment caused several problems. For example, in the learner's environment, an Explor@ tool was used to send graded work to the tutor. However, the tutor did not have access to an equivalent tool to provide feedback. As a result, certain tutors asked the students to bypass the transfer tool and to use e-mail instead. This of course does the job, but because there is then no central registry of the work sent, it is not a secure and easy way to exchange documents on which the evaluation of students depends.

Third, the informal processing of Phase 6 might have been justified for the first delivery of the course, but the absence of a structured delivery plan has the potential to cause problems with the quality of service to the students, especially if there is staff turnover between deliveries. If this course had been supported by a less experienced distance learning institution, such a gap might have been catastrophic.

7

Engineering a Vocational E-Learning Environment

THE SECOND CASE I examine is a project in which my colleagues and I designed, produced, and implemented a pilot course, titled "Improve Your Efficiency with New Information and Communication Technologies," for three professional corporations in Quebec. The professionals were accountants, notaries, and certified administrators. This project, started in February 1999, was completed in March 2000. Unlike the reengineering project discussed in Chapter Six, this project required the complete engineering of a professional training program in a new technological environment, a *virtual continuous learning center.* This learning center is an environment built with Explor@, accessible to the professionals from their offices via the Internet. It contains the resources users require to carry out the activities for this course and, eventually, other vocational continuing education courses as well.

We decided to produce, if possible, all of the MISA engineering deliverables. (In the case discussed in Chapter Six, where we were reengineering, we produced selected deliverables.) Using MISA 3.0, because ADISA and MISA 4.0 were not yet developed when this project started, we organized the method to produce thirty elements of documentation (EDs) distributed within the six phases of the project. Modeling, the process at the heart of the method, was carried out with the MOT software.

The discussion of this project is also organized differently from the discussion in Chapter Six. Rather than presenting comparative tables of the planned and completed tasks, I use a more discursive approach, reflecting the descriptions of the elements of documentation for each phase contained in the final project report.[1]

Definition of the Project

The definition phase of this training project consisted of gathering the information that would guide our decisions about learning content, instructional scenarios, and media and delivery dimensions. A team of seven people was formed, with designers from the LICEF Research Center of Télé-université and representatives from the professional corporations. The team completed the EDs related to the steps of the first phase at an initial meeting on February 23, 1999. The report on the results of Phase 1 was presented on April 3, 1999.

The general objectives of the project were both individual and organizational. At the individual level, it aimed to lead the members of the three professional organizations to acquire new competencies related to working in the emerging knowledge economy. It also aimed to get these learners to adopt the new information technologies in their work as a result of using them in the framework of their continuing education activities. These new capabilities were expected to generate new thoughts and actions in the workplace, particularly among professionals concerned with their career development and their ability to understand and use information technologies in a professional environment.

At the organizational level these project objectives were related to changes sought by the professional corporations themselves as they reexamined their trainers' roles and the manner in which they supported their members. Thus the project also aimed to help the corporations to adopt new training technologies. Finally, the project was to carefully evaluate results in order to transfer the acquired knowledge to other training activities and other professional corporations.

Therefore, from the operational perspective, we decided right at the first phase that the course would be created with the following terminal objectives in mind:

- Facilitate the use of information technologies by the three kinds of professionals.

- Integrate content directly related to the professional contexts and tasks of the corporations.

- Propose training activities adaptable to the learner's level of competence (beginner or intermediate).

- Digitize and deliver training completely at a distance, on the Web.

- Use a modular approach to allow the learner to progress according to his or her entry level.

- Guide and support the learner's progression by a combined use of system tools and trainer support.

- Build new competencies progressively, to lead the participant toward autonomous use of the technologies.

Preliminary Analysis

Phase 2 consisted of defining a preliminary solution to the training problems identified in Phase 1. Here, we established the guidelines of the training project (the course), according to the four axes of the MISA method. An initial knowledge model and instructional model of the course were completed using MOT software. The media and delivery orientations were stated. Although Phase 2 ordinarily includes an initial costs-and-benefits analysis, it was agreed with the representatives of the three professional corporations to postpone this evaluation until the end of Phase 3. A Phase 2 report was presented on May 10, 1999.

In each corporation, the design team held discussions that helped to guide the elicitation of the content and the specific tasks where the use of information technologies would be beneficial. Then the team analyzed specific tasks common to three types of professionals. Next the first knowledge model and course instructional structure were completed, validated by the content experts of each corporation, and documented by the project team.

The knowledge model focused on the training objectives identified in the previous phase. We decided to build a generic knowledge model, that is, one common to the three types of professionals, though we would also design training activities that could be adapted to each of the three work contexts. In this respect the selections made by the content experts were of the utmost importance as they provided contexts, professional tasks, and appropriate examples. The knowledge model also had to consider the fifteen-hour duration limit set on the course.

The skills and competencies to be developed by the three target audiences were to be ones they would apply in the framework of their professional practice. That is, they would learn applications of generic information technology functions like organizing useful information, communication with clients, or preparing documents. The skills to be developed were to be targeted on the information and communication technology (ICT) processes beyond particular techniques or tools in order to promote the autonomy of the learners.

The knowledge model presented in Figure 7.1 illustrates these orientations. The main model (top of the figure) underlines the basic procedural orientation. It also suggests examining some conceptual knowledge (the definition and types of ICT), although the primary course objective is to increase the procedural competencies or, more precisely, "to optimize the use of technological tools within the framework of the professional practice." This model, the main training target, contains two subprocesses, the first of which is modeled at the bottom part of Figure 7-1.

The instructional model, presented in Figure 7-2, features learning activities selected according to the participants' needs and interests. This learning

Figure 7-1. Initial Knowledge Model and One Submodel for the Project "Improve Your Efficiency with ICT."

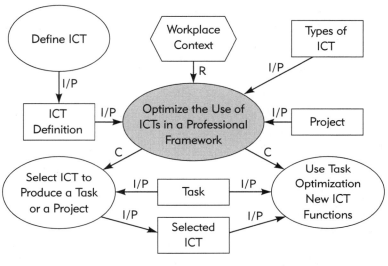

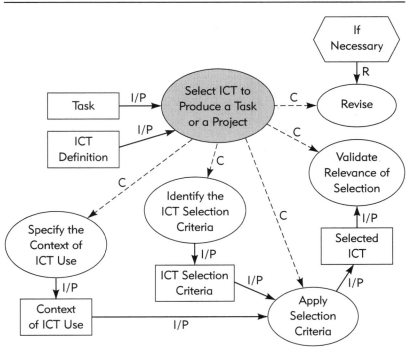

event network (LEN) allows learners to progress through modules centered on professional tasks. The design team used a metaphor, the ICT Exhibition Show, as an integration concept when identifying the orientation principles of the instructional model and establishing an initial LEN. This LEN includes seven learning units. Units LU-0, LU-1, LU-2, and LU-3 are brief introductions to the course contents, activities, and materials. A self-diagnosis allows the learner to plan the following learning activities. Unit LU-4 explores the technological tools, and continues in parallel with the last three learning units, which group the main activities of the course: establish a communication network, conduct a search on the Internet, and produce presentation documents.

Figure 7-2. Initial Instructional Model for the Project "Improve Your Efficiency with ICT."

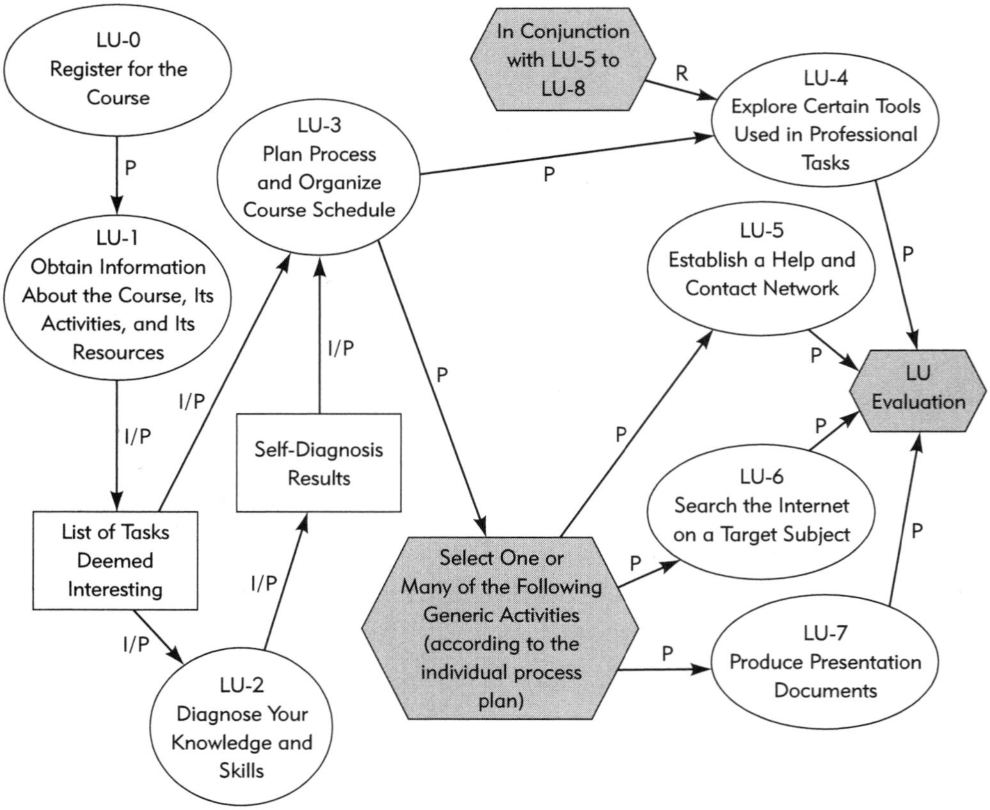

In preparing the media model, it was determined that some of the materials were common to the three groups, such as the course Web site, which presented the material to the learner as the ICT Exhibition Show. Other materials were specific to each group of professionals, in particular the documentation used as input to the generic assignments, which had to be related to the occupational practice of each corporation. An interactive model of the exhibition that had been introduced to the representatives of the professional corporations was discussed and validated during this phase, directing future media work.

We determined that various delivery models would have to be considered to ensure flexibility and accommodate the variety of technological equipment used by the organizations. The delivery type for each learning event remained to be defined in Phase 3. We suggested using a single platform to minimize development costs. As for the tools selection, we sought to privilege the most widely used software to avoid premature obsolescence. We planned to offer a training session to the managers and trainers to prepare them for the changes the implantation of the course would generate in their work habits.

Architecture

In the third phase the design team consolidated the work of the previous phases through reexamining the knowledge model, the instructional model (in the form of a LEN), and the media and delivery orientations. This was followed by the creation of the instructional scenarios and the revision of the course structure. A Phase 3 report was presented to the project management committee on May 31, 1999. As a result of this work, the general knowledge model was further elaborated, guided by an estimation of the competency gaps to be fulfilled. The new model was then distributed into the course's learning units, thus defining their content. Figure 7-3 presents, as a hierarchical structure, the knowledge model and its distribution into four course modules (LUs). The learning event network produced in the previous phases was also revised. The first four LUs shown in Figure 7-2 were grouped into Module 1 (the introduction) and LU-5 was removed so the course would comply with the fifteen-hour constraint imposed at the onset of the project. Hence, from this point on, the course structure contained only four modules.

Figure 7-3. Knowledge Assigned to LU Modules.

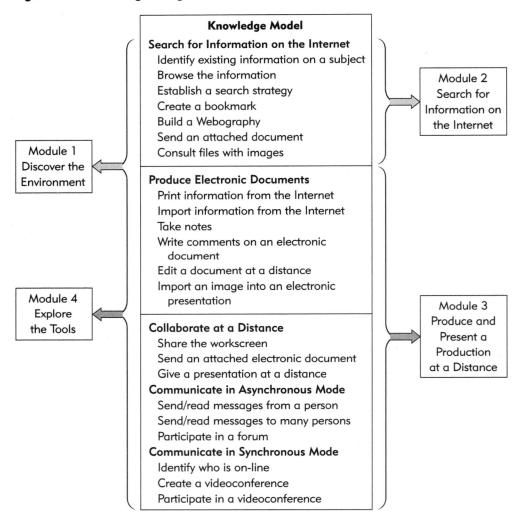

Knowledge Model

Search for Information on the Internet
Identify existing information on a subject
Browse the information
Establish a search strategy
Create a bookmark
Build a Webography
Send an attached document
Consult files with images

Produce Electronic Documents
Print information from the Internet
Import information from the Internet
Take notes
Write comments on an electronic
    document
Edit a document at a distance
Import an image into an electronic
    presentation

Collaborate at a Distance
Share the workscreen
Send an attached electronic document
Give a presentation at a distance
Communicate in Asynchronous Mode
Send/read messages from a person
Send/read messages to many persons
Participate in a forum
Communicate in Synchronous Mode
Identify who is on-line
Create a videoconference
Participate in a videoconference

Module 1
Discover the
Environment

Module 4
Explore
the Tools

Module 2
Search for
Information on
the Internet

Module 3
Produce and
Present a
Production
at a Distance

As indicated in Figure 7-3, Modules 1 and 4 cover almost the entire knowledge model yet from different perspectives: Module 1 by a self-diagnosis of one's competencies in all areas; Module 4 by search, examination, and evaluation activities with the technological tools. Module 2, in contrast, is centered on the submodel "Search for information on the Internet," and Module 3 is centered on the competencies needed to produce and present electronic documents and to make collaborative use of synchronous and asynchronous means of communication as part of that process.

Once the knowledge model had been restructured, instructional scenarios were built for each of the four learning units, in order to define instructional activities that would help learners acquire the content described in each corresponding part of the knowledge model and the target competencies. The model for each learning scenario groups the activities and identifies the learners' productions as well as the instruments necessary for their production. Figure 7-4 presents the scenario for Module 2. This scenario was composed of three activities represented as procedures (ovals). The instruments to be built by the engineering team, represented as input concepts (rectangles), were to be integrated into the Web site or the Explor@ environment. Notice that the initial Work File must be produced in three different instances, one for each professional group. The output concepts (rectangles) correspond to learner productions. The learner's task consists of creating a Webography of interesting sites, corresponding to the initial instructions. Because this task will be different for each of the three groups of corporate participants, the design team had to produce three different series of documents as materials for some of the instruments.

In this phase the media orientations established during the previous phase, more specifically the tools selected to produce the appropriate activities, were revised. We noticed that certain tools were more useful or accessible to professionals who had some previous computer knowledge. We also produced a more realistic estimate of the scope of the instructional material in regard to the available content and the media resources. A user-friendly interface that allows all users to navigate quickly and accurately has a positive impact on the success of an open learning system, such as the one defined here.

Figure 7-4. Instructional Scenario for LU-2.

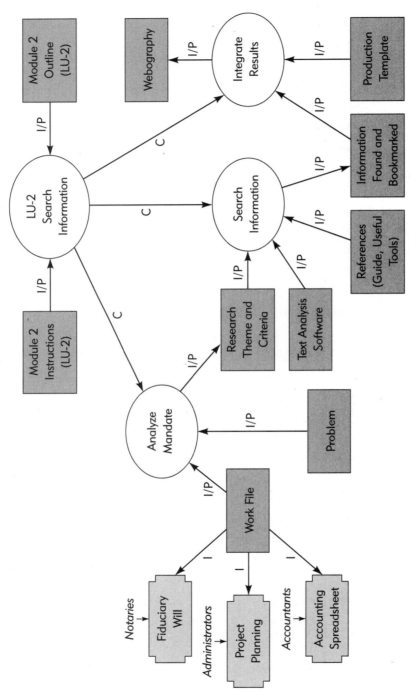

The delivery orientations established during the previous phase were specified in ways that underlined the importance of the paradigm shift needed from the training managers of the three professional corporations and that stressed the need to ensure training for the trainers. We also underlined the need to ensure regular updates of the learning system and to promote the course effectively. Finally, we did opt for a high-level technological platform to avoid premature obsolescence, and negotiations were undertaken with telecom suppliers to obtain reduced prices for the duration of the pilot project.

The cost-benefit analysis, postponed from Phase 2, generated an estimate for the full development costs and a break-even point. The anticipated benefits involve increased access to training, freed from space and time constraints; application of just-enough and just-in-time training principles; development of new skills and professional effectiveness through the use of ICT; emergence of communities of practice among the professionals, and greater efficiency in achieving a main mandate of the three professional associations: to undertake continuing education that improves the professionals' services to the public.

Design of Learning Materials

The fourth phase consisted of linking the knowledge model to the instructional scenario materials in order to elaborate the media and delivery models and complete all the plans for the physical production of the learning system.

The Knowledge Model

The challenge in the task of modeling the knowledge contents of this course was to create a single generic model adaptable to each corporation. Although the instruments supporting the common instructional activities are all of the same type, some have to be produced in three versions. The instruments' knowledge model thus takes different colors, suitable for the professional practice of each corporation. For example, for an activity with communication tools in the module "The effective communicator" (shown on the media model for the Web site, in Figure 7-5), the accountants would collect client data to create a balance sheet, the administrators would use client data to produce a human resource analysis, and the notaries would carry out a similar activity to finalize a deed drawn up by a solicitor.

The Instructional Model

The instructional activities likely to help learners acquire the competencies in the knowledge model were described in Phase 3, when the instructional scenarios were defined. On that basis, we established the properties of the instruments and guides appearing in the instructional scenarios. These will be grouped to build the instructional materials in the subsequent phase.

The Media Model

Using the media orientation principles proposed in Phase 2 and revised in Phase 3, we specified the types and shapes of the course materials and the approximate number of each required at delivery time. For the most important material, we built a media model presenting the media components and elements, transition links, and organizational rules and templates. Our media model for the course Web site is presented in Figure 7-5. From the Explor@ system, the student accesses the Web site's welcome page (the transition link numbered "2" on the figure) and simultaneously enters a learner or trainer environment, depending on his or her role in the course. The site welcome page gives users access to an introductory video clip (which is different for each professional corporation) and to the Web site map, which mimics an ICT exhibition show.

The site contains seven transition links (labeled "a" through "g") for accessing the welcome pages of the four course modules—now named Introduction, The Fruitful Prospector, The Effective Communicator, and The Informed Explorer—and three virtual communication environments (the Idearium, the Auditorium, and the Coffee Shop), each of which plays a precise role in each of the modules. These seven welcome pages are media components that will eventually be developed to access specific activities within the modules or the virtual communication tools and services. In Figure 7-5,

Figure 7-5. Media Model for the Project "Improve Your Efficiency with ICT."

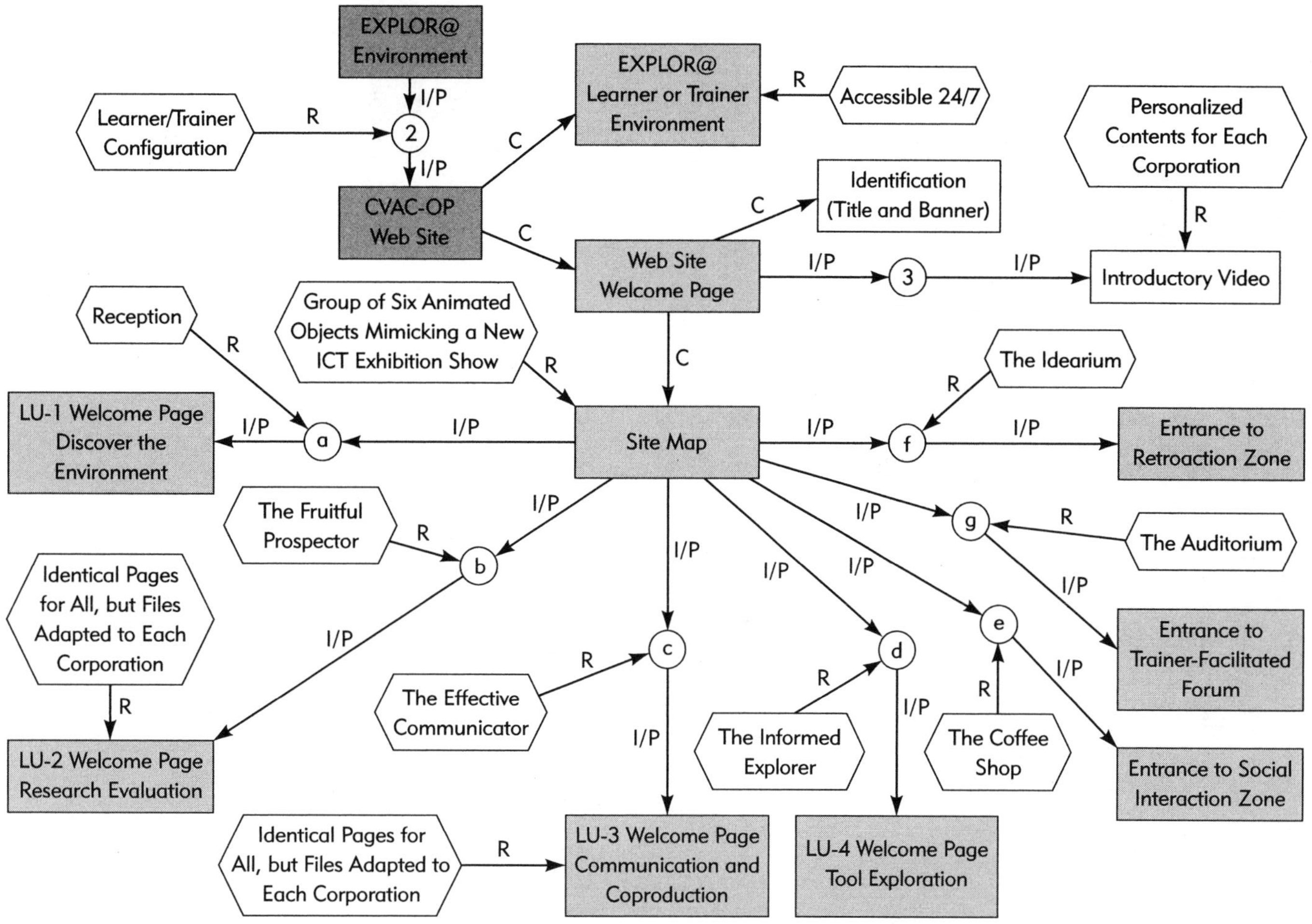

note the principles (hexagons) that govern the pages, the site components. Some give a name to the transitional links; other indicate contents adapted to the target audiences.

Two significant constraints influenced the production of the media model. Thus for the Web site we opted for a single interface common to the three professional corporations to minimize development costs. However, we wanted each corporation to have access to its own specific tools and materials. The challenge, then, was to organize the materials so that the main model presented only the generic materials common to all and the submodels presented all the specific materials.

This media model is generic in more than one respect. It makes the instructional scenarios concrete while retaining their generic definitions. In fact, the same media model was used by our team to create two different versions of the Web site, sharing the same structure but having different media instantiations. The model could also be reused with very different content simply by replacing the instruments or replacing documents or tools.

The Delivery Model

The delivery model was produced in conjunction with the media model. The delivery orientation principles stated in Phase 2 and revised in Phase 3 allowed us to identify the infrastructure and the related services necessary for course implementation. The model identifies the groups of users and the series of materials they use. Part of the content of the delivery model is shown in Table 7-1, where a list of resources (learning objects) are grouped in five categories or Explor@ spaces. These resources will be inserted in an Explor@ environment comprising a set of five corresponding menus giving access to the learning objects in each category. To take into account the three target audiences (accountants, notaries, administrators), some of the learning objects will be different in each environment, but most of them will be common to all three.

Table 7-1. Explor@ Resources for the Project "Improve Your Efficiency with ICT."

Explor@ Spaces	Resources	Description
Self-Management To self-manage the course activities	Self-diagnostic	Evaluate your information technologies user profile.
	Assessment	Display progress in the course activities.
	Schedule	Find the activity dates.
	Road map	Indicate the distribution of the activities in time.
	Idearium	Transfer comments and course evaluations to the coordinators.
	Agenda	Access Outlook software and its management tools.
	Personal profile	Introduce yourself to the other participants.
Information To obtain useful notions to complete assignments	Demo	Access the demo of an advanced search.
	Texts	Access text documents that contain the course concepts.
	Video	Access the course introduction video.
	Archival utility	Access WinZip.
Production To help learners fulfill the course assignments	Screen freezes	Access Hypersnap software.
	Text editor	Access the word processor MS Word.
	"Prospector" Template	Access the template file to present the result of the activity "The Fruitful Prospector."
	"Communicator" Template	Access the template file to present the result of the activity "The Effective Communicator."
	Evaluation grid	Access the file used to evaluate the tools in the activity "The Informed Explorer."
	Presentation	Access the presentation software PowerPoint.
	Spreadsheet	Access Excel software.
	AV conference	Access NetMeeting software.
Collaboration To help the learner communicate and work with others	Chat	Access ICQ software.
	E-mail	Access electronic mail software.

Table 7-1. Explor@ Resources for the Project "Improve Your Efficiency with ICT," Cont'd.

Explor@ Spaces	Resources	Description
	Forums	Access the Coffee Shop and the Auditorium.
	Communication	Access Outlook software.
	Group profile	Observe the other participants' work, find collaborators, and communicate with them by chat.
Assistance	Tool box	Access the tool box and every course activity.
To obtain help	FAQ	Obtain technical help related to the technological environment of the course.
	Glossary	Clarify ICT terminology.
	Virtual exhibition hall	Obtain help with the Explor@ environment and the other course resources.
	Resources	E-mail trainers, technicians, administrators, and so forth

Development and Validation

Phase 5 consisted of producing the learning environment (Web site and Explor@ learner and trainer environments) on the basis of the media and delivery models, prior to learning system validation. Due to the approaching deadline, we decided to deliver the course, integrated in Explor@, in only one phase for validation in December 1999 and January 2000, during a pilot delivered at the LICEF Research Center. The end product was revised and delivered to each professional corporation in April 2000.

During this phase, a team meeting with the professional corporations made it possible to validate an outline of the generic contents of the interfaces, the graphic models, and the documents specific to each corporation. Then we proceeded, in parallel, to write and format the contents and to produce the graphics and digitized materials before we performed a functional validation of the documents produced. The validation was accomplished through the following three steps:

Prepare: recruit participants and trainers (carried out by the professional corporations); plan an information session for the course trainers and managers selected by each professional corporation; provide learning environment access codes; train the contributors appointed by each corporation; evaluate the training session; configure and deliver fifteen computers and cameras to the selected participants.

Test: perform the learning activities (carried out by the participants); supervise the professional corporation trainers; provide instructional, technical, and methodological assistance to the participants; gather progress traces and forum messages.

Evaluate: analyze trainers' and participants' course evaluations, forum messages, progress traces, and use of environment resources; write pilot report.

Each professional corporation was responsible for promoting the course to its members and ensuring sufficient and adequate participation in the pilot. It was decided that each corporation would recruit ten participants (learners) and at least one trainer and one manager. The data collection effort aimed to gather information about the learning environment (interface, tools), the course contents, the instructional approach, and the assistance offered. We planned to collect data from an evaluation questionnaire, from a suggestion box integrated into the site (Idearium), from learners' productions, trainers' comments, messages posted in the forums, progress traces in the activities (assessment), some interviews with the trainers and the professional corporations' coordinators, and a list of technical difficulties identified by the technicians and the users.

In spite of many difficulties, the test protocol was partly applied, and this led to major site interface revisions. Figure 7-6 presents the welcome page for LU-2, The Fruitful Prospector, and the instructions for Activity 3 of this module after revisions.

Figure 7-6. Revised LU-2 Interface and Activity Instructions.

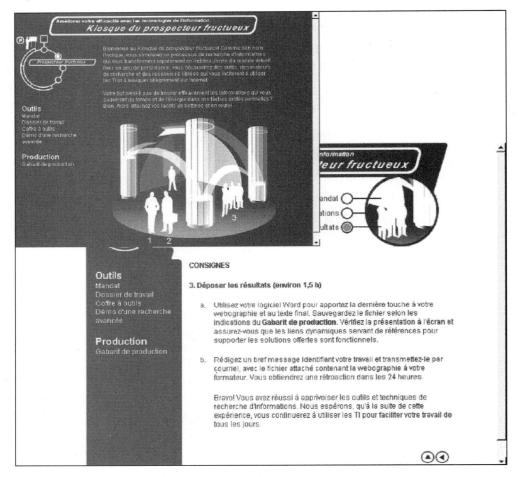

Delivery Planning

The last phase consisted of preparing the implementation of the learning system on the basis of the experience acquired during the test. The delivery plan was limited here to identifying the actors, their roles during the e-learning activities, and their training needs.

The course delivery was planned to require the intervention of a part-time distance trainer for each group of ten to fifteen learners. Having this instructional and organizational resource available was considered vital and required a training session. A support technician's presence was also planned, to oversee communication by e-mail (for personal or private messages) and by forum (for discussions or information useful to the whole group). We determined that supervision personnel should attempt to respond to every request within twenty-four hours.

The environment was to be accessible, from the Internet, to authorized participants only, that is to say, the members of the professional corporations who had registered for the course and the staff responsible for the instructional, technical, and administrative assistance. Each authorized participant received an access code and a password.

The registration and group composition processes and also the quality management of the system were not planned because of the lack of time left for the project and some staff unavailability.

Discussion

Almost the entirety of the instructional engineering method MISA 3.0 was applied to this project. Complete knowledge, instructional, and media models guided the construction of an Internet Web site providing the training activities and materials. The delivery model guided us in defining the actors and their roles, the series of materials, the services offered, and the telecom tools and services used or provided. This lead to the elaboration of two Explor@ environments: one for the learners, the other for the trainers.

Due to the modular structure of the knowledge, instructional, media, and delivery models, the contents can be updated frequently and rapidly, a critical feature in the ICT domain. Moreover, the course may be easily adapted so that other categories of professionals may participate in it.

The pilot run of this course with the three professional corporations made us realize how little the information technologies had been used before for the continuing education of professionals and the extent to which such an environment requires a well-planned management strategy. Thus the construction of an elaborated delivery model leading to the construction of a trainer environment constitutes a step in the right direction. However, the tasks accomplished in Phase 6, which were limited in this project, must be completed, especially in regard to the following elements: competency management; technical and instructional personnel training; creating and starting up learners' groups; course, materials, and resource management; and finally, quality control and periodic course revisions.

8

Engineering a Workplace E-Learning Environment

THE THIRD CASE I examine is a project in which my colleagues and I designed, produced, and implemented an Internet training program for certain employees of Hydro-Quebec to familiarize them with the company's operating code. The operating code is a communication protocol, involving both oral and written communication, that aims to ensure safe work practices among the employees who install and maintain electric power transmission lines. Written in 1993, the *Operating Code Handbook* contains a general presentation, fourteen maneuver orders with term definitions, and a table summarizing the maneuvers and their corresponding messages. The goal of the training program was to ensure that personnel can use the code and transmit suitable messages in each case. In the past this course had been given directly to employees in a traditional classroom.

This reengineering project provided well-defined content, but its pedagogy, the media and delivery approaches, would have to be built from scratch to allow Internet delivery of that content in a virtual learning center. Once implemented, this Internet training tool would also be used as a job aid, to help employees use and reference the operating code.

Due to the short duration of the training program, limited to a few hours of employee time, we decided to carry out only the main engineering tasks of MISA. The engineering tasks undertaken with MISA 3.0 in the fall of 1999 were completed in the fall of 2000 with ADISA and MISA 4.0, after an idle period due to the unavailability of the company's content expert. The course was produced and tested with the target audience in March 2001. The following sections present the results of each instructional engineering phase.

Definition of the Project

We determined that the learning objectives were threefold: to motivate the participants to use the operating code; to develop their capacity to locate the terminology required for a given maneuver in the operating code; and to improve their oral and written communication with peers through their efficient use of the operating code, that is to say, the use of the official terminology. The course was to be built to cover these main objectives in approximately four hours, and it would offer optional additional activities.

Initially, the course was designed for Hydro-Quebec employees of various trades, such as distributors, coordinators, operators, and support technicians. We foresaw approximately a hundred people accessing the course from eighty workstations spread throughout the various Hydro-Quebec facilities in the province of Quebec. The total number of people to be trained was estimated at approximately three thousand. Moreover, it was possible that the training session would be offered to Hydro-Quebec subcontractors.

We also found that the target audience communicated mainly orally and had little or no computer and information technology knowledge. Although most workers had already received an operating code training session, they used the code very little or not at all.

Preliminary Analysis

In Phase 2 we defined the basic orientations of the course; an initial knowledge model, drawn from the *Operating Code Handbook;* and the learning event network. The main knowledge model (ED 212) of the course is presented in Figure 8-1. This model represents the process "Use the operating code in the maneuvers," and was intended to produce peer communication that respects the operating code language and communication procedures. The general target competency consists of applying this process rigorously. The process is composed of the following procedures: notice the need to use the code, refer to the handbook, and create and communicate a message. These procedures are associated (A-link) with an appropriate skill: to notice, to find, to discriminate, or to apply. From this model we can list the target competencies (ED 214) the learner will need to grasp at the end of the course.

Figure 8-1. Knowledge Model for the Course "Operating Code."

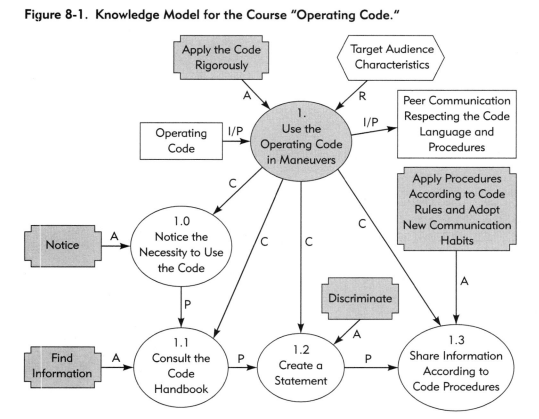

He or she needs the ability

- To notice the situations where the code should be used

- To locate the relevant information in the code

- To find, according to the situation, the relevant elements of the code necessary to build a statement

- To communicate that information according to the code procedures

Each of the procedures shown on the model is a main knowledge area for the course because it is associated with a skill to be grasped and a competency to be achieved. Each was developed further by deploying a submodel, such as the one displayed in Figure 8-2. This submodel breaks down the knowledge "Create a statement" into two procedures. The first consists of choosing the elements used to compose the statement and the second consists of assembling

Figure 8-2. Knowledge Submodel for the Course "Operating Code."

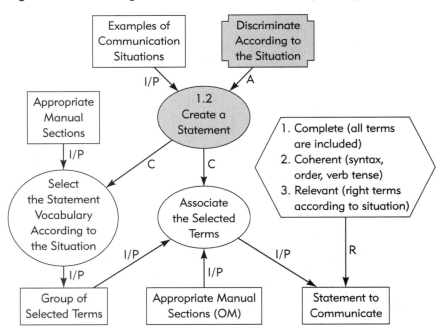

the elements of the statement while respecting certain quality standards: completeness, coherence, and relevance.

An analysis of the learning needs was conducted for two potential public audiences: code power users (that is, those with considerable ability in using the code) and code nonusers. Table 8-1 presents the estimated current and target competencies for a segment of the knowledge required. The numbers correspond to a competency performance scale ranging from 0 to 10: sensitization (0 to 2.5), familiarization (2.5 to 5.0), mastery (5.0 to 7.5), and expertise (7.5 to 10.0). The gap between the current and the target competency represents an estimate of the learning need for that competency. (A variation of 0 indicates there is no need for the knowledge at issue, as it is a prerequisite for taking the course.) We observed that the variations between the learning needs of the two groups of users were minimal and did not justify creating a different course for each target audience.

Table 8-1. Learning Needs Evaluation for Code Power Users and Nonusers.

Knowledge	Type	Code Power Users			Code Non-Users		
		Current	Target	Gap	Current	Target	Gap
The operating code	Concept	4	6	2	1	6	5
Apply the code correctly (written)	Procedure	1	6	5	1	6	5
Apply the code correctly (oral)	Procedure	1	6	5	1	6	5
Understand the importance of security	Principle	3	7	4	1	7	6
Basic PC knowledge	Skill	3	3	0	3	3	0
Web browsing	Skill	3	3	0	3	3	0

The course instructional orientations (ED 220) were established as follows:

- Instructional strategy: support simulation (case solving and games).

- Flexibility of the learning process: a nonrigid course with limited number and types of activities, continuous access to the course, variable lengths for each session, automatic return to the end point of the previous session.

- Self-assessment and individual progress scales.

- Advice provided by the system according to a learner's results.

- Respect of anonymity (demanded by the employees' union).

The learning event network (ED 222) was structured in four modules, according to these orientations:

Module 1. Introduction: familiarization with the technological environment and its resources, motivation through understanding the importance of the code, guided tour of the *Operating Code Handbook*, initial self-diagnostic and assistance in selecting activities

Module 2. Application of the code through problem solving: observation of problematic maneuvers, problem diagnosis, simulation of adequate communication, answer validation (fifteen maneuvers and one to three levels of difficulty)

Module 3. Improvement: choice of activities in the form of games (Minesweeper, sentences with blanks, puzzles)

Module 4. Individual evaluation: personal final assessment, advice, best results provided

The orientations for media and delivery were established as follows:

- Maximum use of sound and graphic elements to support vocal communication exercises with the operating code; minimal use of textual elements.

- Autonomous distance training accessible by Internet.

- Assistance available on request by electronic mail within twenty-four hours.

We also determined in this phase that the learning environment would be composed of a Web site and an Explor@ environment managing course access. The Web site would be simple, offering user-friendly browsing and tools that could be used by individuals who were not computer literate. And the system had to provide usage statistics to the training managers while preserving users' performance confidentiality.

The minimal hardware and software configuration we assumed to be necessary included PC Pentium 200 MHz; 32 MB RAM; sound and video cards; internal narrowband ISDN network; 600 x 800 monitor; Windows 95, 98, or NT; and Netscape version 4.0 or higher.

Architecture

The architecture phase marked the development of the instructional scenarios (ED 320) and the distribution of the knowledge model between the course modules, or learning units. Figure 8-3 presents the instructional scenario for Module 2. This instructional scenario takes the form of a simulation of an error to be repaired. The learner selects and observes an oral or written communication segment from a bank of exercises. The learner next seeks to identify the error inserted in the statement and then identifies the elements of a solution, that is, the terminology and the procedural elements. Using a keyboard or a microphone, the learner records his or her solution. The text or the voice recording produced is then used to validate the answer and evaluate the user's personal performance. The result of the exercise is recovered and anonymously compiled by the system.

Figure 8-3. Instructional Scenario for the Course "Operating Code."

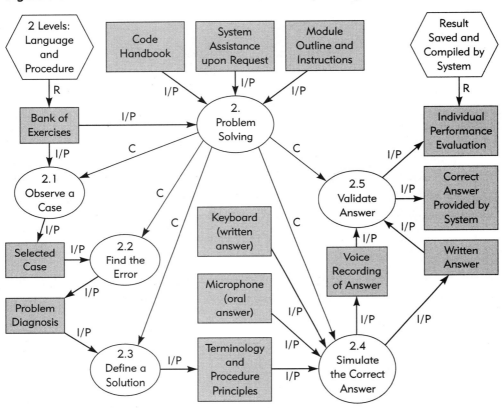

The knowledge models associated (ED 310) with each of the four learning units, or modules, are presented in Table 8-2.

Design of Learning Materials

The third phase focused mainly on the development of the Web site media model and the selection of the Explor@ resources to integrate into the delivery model.

Figure 8-4 presents the media model of the training Web site. At the top of this figure is the main model for accessing the course. At the bottom of the figure is a submodel showing the items immediately accessible from the course welcome page: for example, an introductory video clip, a course outline, and

Table 8-2. Knowledge Distribution for the Course "Operating Code."

Modules and Activities	Knowledge
LU-1 Familiarization: use of the learning environment, importance of the operating code, self-diagnosis of current competencies	Peripherals, interface navigation, finding and using available resources and tools
	General definition of the operating code, importance of the code, incident examples, consequences of code ignorance, theoretical notions specific to the operating code
	Understanding of the organization of the manual (structure and content available), efficient survey of the manual (nature and use of the sections)
	Statement creation rules
	Analysis of the course requirements, proposed scenario, schedule
	Evaluation of personal competencies (current domain knowledge, personal availability) and organizing of process: set goals, select activities, reserve workstation, organize personal schedule, identify strengths and weak points, motivation
LU-2 Problem solving: observe a case, present a diagnosis, identify a solution, simulate communication, validate answer	Types of problematic maneuvers
	Definitions and terminology, communication mode (written or oral), term association rules (syntax and verb tense), type of situation (context), identification of speakers, communication processes
	How to repair communication errors
LU-3 Improvement Minesweeper game	Associating devices and verbs to use
	Summary table of operating code
LU-4 Evaluation Update own profile	Learning supervision: content covered, performance, schedule, motivation, workstation functions
	Learning objectives: process progress and acquisition of target competencies

Figure 8-4. Media Model for the Course "Operating Code."

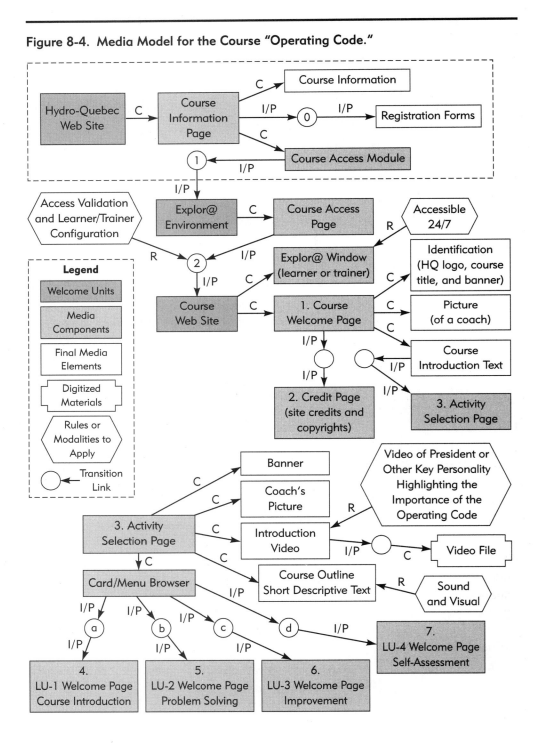

a browsing menu. This chart gives the user access to the initial pages of the four modules of the course, via the transition links a, b, c, and d.

The submodels of the preceding model present each course module. Figure 8-5 presents one of them, LU-2, which corresponds to the instructional

Figure 8-5. Media Submodel for LU-2.

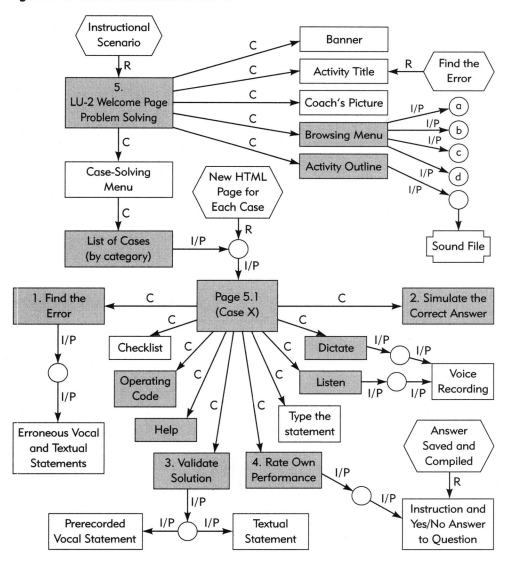

scenario presented in Figure 8-3. The initial page of this module gives the user access to a module outline and the browsing menu that allows transitions from one module to another. It also grants access to a list of cases to be resolved. For each case, a media component presents each activity of the instructional scenario: find the error, simulate the correct answer, validate the solution, and rate your performance.

In Activity 1 on this submodel, a listening and viewing activity is presented. An erroneous vocal or textual statement is presented to the learner, who must correct it. In Activity 2, learners listen to or read the erroneous statement again and respond by producing an error-free vocal or textual version. Activity 3 allows the user to validate his or her answer by listening to a correct statement or by reading a text. Activity 4 allows the recording of the case studied.

Completing the presentation of the media model, Figure 8-6 presents the resources to be integrated into the Explor@ resource center. This model is accessible from the main model (Figure 8-4). It structures the resources into five spaces: management, information, production, collaboration, and assistance. This is where we placed tools such as "progress assessment" and "group profile." From the self-assessment questionnaire, the environment provides the learner with an inventory of the initial and acquired competencies throughout the course. This interactive assistance appeared essential, insofar as the participants work individually. Also, a training environment was planned for the people responsible for supporting the learning process and motivating the participants.

Development and Validation

We followed our media model closely during the production phase, as indicated on the Web pages presented in Figure 8-7. The first Web page of the course, the welcome page corresponding to the model in Figure 8-4, gives the user access to the four modules of the course. The other two pages shown correspond to the submodel in Figure 8-5. The first of these two pages, the wel-

Figure 8-6. Explor@ Resources for the Course "Operating Code."

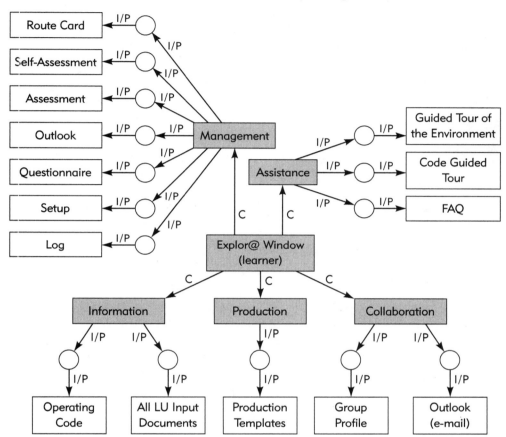

come page of Module 2, "Problem solving," presents the module activities. The second page corresponds to the first activity of Module 2, "Select a case." This page presents a list of all the communication cases, through which the user has access to the remaining module activities.

We carried out the first, experimental delivery of the course at the end of January and beginning of February 2001. Initially the course was tested during a half-day training session offered to a segment of the target audience.

Figure 8-7. Web Site for the Course "Operating Code."

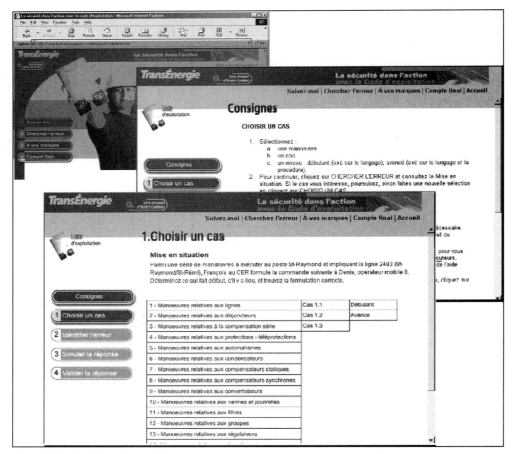

Delivery Planning

We proposed that a community of practice should be established as a means of collective communication. It would be supported by a forum or a FAQs list allowing users to express their opinions. Thus relevant questions and answers given to one learner would benefit other learners as well. Several individuals could share the important facilitator role for this community of practice. These recommendations have not yet been acted on by the company's training managers.

Discussion

This instructional engineering case displays another kind of MISA application for a typical corporate training session. The course lasts four hours and meets very specific objectives. It aims to develop practical competencies in a target population of technicians. It is closely related to an important aspect of their professional tasks.

Given the narrow scope of this course, it was possible to adapt the method so that we concentrated on its most essential elements. In Phase 1, the elements of documentation 102 (objectives), 104 (target audience), and 106 (context) were rapidly carried out to define the project. In Phase 2, the team relied on an existing major document (the *Operating Code Handbook*) to model the contents (212) so as to emphasize the target skills and the competencies (214) and evaluate the learning needs of both the code power users and nonusers. General orientations were stated early for the instructional (220), media (230), and delivery (240) design specifications. A LEN (222) comprising four modules was built. In Phase 3, instructional scenarios (320) were created for the four modules, and knowledge submodels (310) were associated with these modules. In Phase 4, an extensive media model was created (432), integrating the Web site and the delivery resources of the Explor@ virtual center. A table describing the instruments and the materials (430) was also created and integrated into the Explor@ Web site environment. Phase 5 concentrated on producing and validating the materials.

In total we created thirteen of the thirty-five elements of documentation available in the instructional engineering method and were able to skip some steps in certain cases.

Conclusion

THIS CLOSING SECTION offers some general comments on the instructional engineering methodology that is the subject of this book. The case studies presented in the previous chapters contain general information about the instructional engineering method MISA. They also illustrate the flexibility of such a method. The designer can select the elements of documentation to be built and can control the schedule for the engineering tasks. The following sections summarize the capabilities of the method and suggest ways such methods may be made even more practical and adaptable.

Adapting the Design Processes

The first and the third cases present two extremes in the scope of the system developed: one is a three-credit university course (forty-five hours plus assignments and studies) and the other is a short corporate training session (four hours), intended to support a specific task. The second case is intermediate in duration (fifteen hours) and, in contrast to the other two, deals with an engineering rather than a reengineering process, creating from scratch a course to improve the use of information communication technologies for three types of professionals. The first case is focused on conceptual knowledge, whereas the two others target procedural skills and knowledge.

The instructional structures of the three courses are similar in that the learning unit scenarios comprise a small number of interrelated activities. The scenarios for the first course follow a model centered on user consultation of information, followed by application exercises. The scenarios for the other two courses tend to be focused on processes corresponding to the target skills and competencies. The media models are also similar, as they exploit plurimedia materials, integrated into a hyperguide-type Web site supported by Explor@ environments.

The engineering method, therefore, is configured very differently from project to project, in the selection of the tasks to be carried out and in the manner by which they will be processed, depending on the type of system sought: Is the designer engineering a new learning system, reengineering an existing one, or making small revisions? Moreover, the designer's process will vary depending on whether he or she intends to engineer a simple activity, a custom vocational training course, a university course, a program comprising several predetermined courses or built dynamically by the learner, or a general training program for a certain organization. Finally, the method must be adapted to the contents and objectives of a project: Is the course intended to support initial general training, continuing education, recycling of people assigned to new functions, updating of tools and methods knowledge, or training centered on task support or preparation for professional accreditation, to name only a few possible orientations?

Overcoming Constraints

The practice of instructional engineering is not only demanding and subject to multiple constraints but also frequently misunderstood. It is misunderstood because most course or program designers tend to be content experts who have devoted most of their training, reflection, and energy to mastering the contents of their discipline. They are also likely to have received much of their own training in a classroom setting, which they then tend to reproduce when designing training. Through their experience, they have come to believe it is sufficient to present, repeat, and explain material for learning to take place. We all readily accept that constructing a bridge, making a medical diagnosis, or defining a computer solution can be a complex process, but we tend to be surprised by the complexity of the processes leading to the construction of a learning system. Nevertheless, surprising as it may be to many corporate trainers or academic educators, the engineering of a learning system is in fact a demanding process, and this book presents that reality and that complexity. The more situations one must plan for and the more general knowledge, instructional, media, and delivery concepts, procedures, and principles one must consider, the more difficult the venture gets.

In addition, instructional engineering is complicated by the many constraints designers must work with: time and budget constraints, information source limitations, the distance to be traversed between the conception and the use of the learning system. For example, corporations typically spend months or years developing new products, new methods, or new tools, yet designers are constantly asked to prepare the related required employee training in just a few days. In educational institutions, teachers at all levels are frequently asked to build courses using Internet and multimedia technologies with no financial resources and technical support. We underestimate the inherent difficulties in the distance between the design of a course and its repeated use over several years, while learners, contents, and tools evolve and change constantly.

These real problems invite all of us involved in instructional design to direct our future work by first recognizing the diversity of the engineering situations and the quality and productivity requirements to encounter. This recognition can lead us toward improving the assistance given to designers by computerized tools and toward offering better support to administrators who want to implement an instructional engineering method in their organizations.

Sustaining Diversity and Productivity

The constraints designers encounter in the exercise of instructional engineering have encouraged my colleagues and me to include more mechanisms in our instructional engineering method in order to make it adaptable to various needs and to provide the means to increase the productivity of the designers who use it. These two objectives are obviously closely interrelated.

In this regard, I have highlighted the generality of our method. It applies to various delivery models: distributed classroom, hypermedia self-training, on-line training, communities of practice, and electronic performance support systems. It also addresses various types of media: materials and learning event networks. It can be used to build entire training programs or simple activities lasting a few hours, with all kinds of contents, target competencies, and training objectives. The adaptability of an instructional engineering method could be further increased by integrating a series of adaptation principles into the method. At the end of the first phase, for example, once the training problems have been defined, the designer might be asked a number of questions regarding the characteristics of his or her learning system project. A computerized support system like ADISA could then suggest adaptation principles: prioritize some phases, some tasks, or some elements of a task; use some template or some predefined model from a model library.

Templates and model libraries can play a significant role in adapting a method to the needs of content experts and instructional designers. They can increase designers' productivity by reducing effort and design time without hindering product quality. In a method and a workbench like ADISA, for example, the existing elements of documentation templates facilitate the engineering tasks by propagating relevant data, posting useful data, and offering menus for selecting instructional objects.

In addition, we have undertaken the development of model libraries that can be imported into the workbench as a starting point for skill or knowledge models, instructional scenarios, or delivery models.

Finally, another way to sustain diversity and productivity is to facilitate modifications to the various components of the elements of documentation

(EDs). Decisions taken by others rarely satisfy any of us. And our own earlier decisions may not satisfy us later. Indeed, the members of the MISA development team changed their minds on several occasions regarding certain task and deliverables components. The ADISA workbench already offers options for making minor modifications to the selections it provides. In particular, designers may add choices and annotations to certain menus and import tables of attributes they have created themselves. This is only the tip of the iceberg, however; a more ambitious goal for an instructional engineering method or support is to be able to generate the ED templates themselves from a MOT model. It would then suffice for designers to modify the method model to create the templates of the corresponding EDs.

Providing Assistance to the Design Process

I have stressed some of the difficulties of instructional engineering, taking into account the great number of factors the designers must consider and the constraints they must work with. Beyond the improvements mentioned earlier, it will be important to develop various means of adaptive assistance for instructional engineering and to integrate them with the computerized tools.

This system assistance cannot rest only on providing templates and model libraries. In a previous version of ADISA, the AGD system, my colleagues and I integrated a contextual help feature for all the terms and operations, together with an adaptive adviser that provided heuristic advice to enhance the coherence and quality of the design specifications. A rule-based system then analyzed the designer's productions, signaled problems, and suggested possible improvements. Since then, as discussed in Chapter Two, we have developed tools that allow the integration of a computerized adviser for the various actors in a virtual learning center. We aim to extend this work and integrate such an adviser in the designer's environment to provide assistance with using MISA.

I have also emphasized the misunderstanding and underestimation that surrounds instructional engineering. It is not easy to implement any method in an organization, and implementation tends to be even more difficult in the case of an instructional engineering method. It suffices to consider the efforts required for a large data processing consultation firm to convince its customers to adopt software engineering methods. Information-processing systems, however, are becoming not only increasingly essential to organizational operations but increasingly complicated, and these realities provide strong arguments in favor of the adoption of such methods, making gradually anachronistic the individually and uniquely crafted programming exercises that marked the first decades of data processing. In the field of instructional engineering we haven't reached this point yet, although we can already see that in the coming years the same type of evolution will be increasingly necessary due to demands of the knowledge economy and society.

I am sometimes asked why a particular method is needed for designing instruction. After all, doesn't each trainer or teacher already have his or her own method that leads to acceptable results? Even when people are convinced of the theoretical value of employing a method, they may not easily accept that it is necessary to be trained in the processes of instructional engineering as one is trained in data processing or medicine. And even when they agree to make the effort to undergo such training, they tend to prefer retaining the option of exercising a large degree of freedom from the method. A method always appears at first (incorrectly) as a creativity constraint, an obstacle to freedom.

For this reason, promoting the extended use of instructional engineering must involve researching and developing implementation methods that support the knowledge management activities of the growing number of firms and organizations whose most important activities revolve around acquiring, using, and dispensing knowledge. The creation of these implementation methods can proceed in the same way as the future development of MISA and ADISA, which I outlined earlier in this chapter.

The arguments that it is time to do so are significant. This is understood by the managers of large organizations such as Hydro-Quebec and the Bank of Montreal, with whom my colleagues and I work. Instructional engineering seems essential to them if they are to have the level of training they require to improve the competencies of their personnel. The process of instructional engineering also develops common language and values within an organization. Particularly when it integrates a form of knowledge representation, it constitutes an essential element of the knowledge management processes. Finally, it offers a solution to the fundamental training issue faced by any modern organization: how to build and adapt network-based training environments more rapidly, more effectively, and with a better guarantee of quality of learning.

Actor. An agent or group of agents taking on one or several roles for which the agent or group of agents uses resources in a learning system. An actor may be a person or software.

Types

Learner.

Instructor.

Informer.

Manager.

Designer.

Analogical support. Support for printed (*scriptovisual*), audio, or audiovisual components of instructional materials, coded and stored in an analogical format.

Types and Examples

Audio analogical support. Audio track; record.

Audiovisual analogical support. Videocassette; videodisk; film.

Assistance activity. An instructional scenario component describing actions to be carried out by an instructor or other facilitator.

Examples

Actions for motivating learners.

Steps for forming learning teams.

Assistance scenario. An instructional scenario component that clusters the activities carried out by a tutor or any other type of facilitator, the resources to be used, and the productions to be created and also the rules and instructions for the types of interventions to be performed with learners.

Types and Examples

Lecturing assistance scenario. Learning through lectures followed by exercises. The role of the instructor is to present content and to supply exercises.

Tutorial assistance scenario. Learning through a branched tutorial: that is, a tutorial in which the sequence in which content is presented depends on the results obtained by the learner.

Case-based assistance scenario. Learning through case studies. The instructor presents a case and supplies the tools and techniques for learning a procedure.

Guided discovery assistance scenario. Learning through guided discovery. The role of the instructor is to present examples and exceptions; these are selected based on each learner's progress.

Methodological assistance scenario. Learning through problem solving. The role of the instructor is to give advice on methodology.

Asynchronous e-learning (distance learning; distance education). A type of learning system delivery in which learners and facilitators interact from different geographical locations and in which learners and facilitators are not both present at the same time during most of the learning events or activities.

Types and Examples

E-learning with nontelematic exchange. Distance education course in which the learners and facilitators exchange documents by mail or fax and leave messages through voice mail.

On-line learning. On-line distance course in which the learners exchange information and documents with a teacher or tutor, or peers by e-mail or electronic forums.

Competency The present or target capacity of a group or an individual to perform a cognitive, affective, social, or psychomotor skill with regard to a specific area of knowledge and in a specific context. This context is the situation or manner in which the skill attributed to the knowledge is performed: a guided or autonomous manner, a simple or complex situation, a familiar or new situation, a global or partial manner, a persistent or sporadic manner.

Examples

Target competency. Architecture students will know how to modify (cognitive skill "to repair") the plans for a triplex, working autonomously and taking into account complex constraints.

Present competency. Bob, Amy, and Clyde are capable of acting happy (affective skill "to apply") in an authentic manner in a play by Molière.

Concept. A type of knowledge describing natural objects in a domain ("what"). A concept describes a class of objects by the objects' common properties; every object representing the concept distinguishes itself from objects representing other concepts by the specific values of these properties.

Examples

Profession.

Animal.

Software.

Course outline.

Camera.

Conceptual model. A type of knowledge model consisting mainly of *concepts*.

Types and Examples

System with components. System consisting of a computer, its subsystems, and the subsystem components.

Typology and taxonomy. Set of classes and subclasses of mushrooms.

Hybrid system. System consisting of a mixture of geometrical figures and their components.

Delivery. A grouping of resources—for one or several actors—that will be produced, evaluated, and revised at different stages throughout the development of a learning system.

Examples

Delivery of the complete learning system.

Delivery of units 1, 2, and 3 is the first delivery, and units 4, 5, and 6 the second.

Delivery of the prototype is delivery 1, delivery of all the class modules is delivery 2, and the delivery of integrated modules with tools and communications services is the final delivery.

Delivery mode. The way actors use services, locations, tools, or means of communication and how they manage (send, receive, store) their own and other actors' productions.

Types and Examples

> *Self-paced learning or training.* Learners participate in learning events in an autonomous way, at their own pace, and possibly in a different location from the instructor and possibly without the instructor's assistance (see *EPSS*).

> *Classroom learning or training.* Learners use traditional or networked locations.

> *Synchronous e-learning or training.* Learners and instructors use mainly delivery modes that require them both to be present at the same time.

> *Asynchronous e-learning or training.* Learners and instructors use mainly delivery modes that do *not* require them both to be present at the same time.

Delivery model. A description of the roles of the actors during the delivery of a learning system and also the actors' interactions with the sets of materials, the tools, the means of communications, the services, and the locations that they either use themselves or supply to other actors.

Examples

> Learners follow a distance course using asynchronous conference calling. A tutor moderates the conference. The different technical and educational support services are specified.

> Learners receive a plurimedia kit (one containing material on a variety of media) or a multimedia CD. The modes of delivery and maintenance services are specified.

Electronic Performance Support System (EPSS). A learning system in the workplace that uses the same tools and the same means of communication that the work tasks use. Information is drawn partially from organizational databases. The system supports learning with several forms of assistance.

Facilitator. An actor who participates in the training by supplying direct assistance to the learner, by designing the learning system (designer, media producer, and so on), by supplying content elements (adviser, subject-matter expert, technical support staff, and so forth), by offering educational help (instructor, guide, lecturer, and the like), or by offering administrative support (administrator, program coordinator, and so forth).

Fact. A type of knowledge indicating a single, precise object defined by specifying the value of all its attributes. Facts may be derived from a concept (in which case the fact is called an *example*), from a procedure (*trace*), or from a principle (*statement, norm,* or *rule*).

Types and Examples

Example. Multiplication table.

Trace. Precise record of steps taken by an accountant to file his income statement.

Statement. List of attributes and characteristics that define a doctor as a health professional.

Factual model types. Knowledge models consisting mainly of facts.

Types

Examples. A multiplication table for the multiplication concept.

Traces. Cases of the process of filling out an income tax form.

Statements. Precise statement of the properties that describe a doctor as a health professional.

Formative evaluation. An evaluation mode that a learning system designer may adopt. A formative evaluation takes place during the learning and determines whether a given degree of the skill being taught was attained.

Example

Evaluation will be made during each learning activity, to ensure that the learner is keeping with the pace of the course.

Hypermedia. A network of electronic links (hyperlinks) enabling the user to navigate between different data sources and different types of media—text, digital, video image, audio (music, voice), and so forth—to gather information.

Types and Examples

Networked hypermedia (Internet). Web course including text, audio segments, and visual images.

Local hypermedia. Multimedia course on CD, forming a semantic network.

Instructional activity. An instructional scenario component consisting of a set of statements describing an activity. Instructional activities proposed for tutors or other facilitators are called *assistance activities* and those proposed for learners are called *learning activities.*

Types and Examples

Performance activity. Apply a methodology or follow the precise steps of a method.

Interaction activity. Discuss among peers.

Organizational activity. Plan teamwork.

Consultation activity. Read; query a data bank.

Collaborative activity. Working in a team, build an abstract model.

Recreational activity. Do yoga exercises between two instructional activities.

Meta-cognitive activity. Maintain an activities log.

Motivational activity. Conduct a spontaneous exchange with other participants using cooperative, or *ice-breaker,* techniques.

Perceptual activity. Compare colors.

Production activity. Produce a report.

Social activity. Participate in a community supper.

Instructional scenario. A learning unit (LU) component. An educational or instructional scenario consists of a learning scenario (proposed for the learner) and an assistance scenario (designed for tutors, teachers, or coaches, computerized or not). Modeling an educational scenario consists of specifying the activity or activities appropriate for the learner and the assistance, including all the resources required to complete these activities and all the productions that should result from these activities.

Types and Examples

Learning by reception and assistance by lecturing. Scenario consisting of a series of lectures.

Learning by reception and exercises and assistance from a tutor. Scenario consisting of an exercise-test-adjustment-exercise sequence (as in a traditional language class).

Learning through case studies and assistance by analogy. Scenario that has students analyzing a movement or a process through a case study and learning to apply this knowledge to other contexts.

Learning through guided discovery and assistance consisting of questioning techniques. Scenario that stresses assimilation of concepts through examples and exceptions.

Learning through construction, with methodological assistance. Scenario for a creativity workshop.

Instrument. An instructional resource generic description assigned to an instructional scenario, making knowledge or content available in the form of information to be consulted or used to produce knowledge in the learner. Instruments may be assembled and mediatized in materials.

Types and Examples

Lecture. Speech; briefing; report presentation.

List. Table; dictionary; glossary; index.

Form or template. Questionnaire; outline; evaluation grid.

Diagram. Organizational chart; network; graphic representation.

Situational presentation. Documentary; play; novel; poem; simulation; role playing; case study.

Representation of a physical object. Photo; drawing; scale model; animated drawing (of an animal, a plant, a house, and so forth).

Knowledge. Content structure that can be stored in the memory of a person or a computer and can be processed in various ways by other knowledge systems. Knowledge is anything that can be learned by the human mind, including facts (examples, traces, statements), abstract knowledge (concepts, procedures, principles), and cognitive, motor, and socioaffective skills.

Types and Examples

Factual knowledge (facts). Records of how to fill out a form.

Conceptual knowledge (concepts). A car, its subsystems and components.

Procedural knowledge (procedures). Income tax calculations.

Prescriptive knowledge (principles). Checklist for selecting a house fulfilling the buyer's needs.

Knowledge model. Knowledge units of various types—facts, concepts, procedures, principles, skills—in a structured relationship (various types of links reveal this relationship).

Types and Examples

Factual model. Traces of the processing procedure for a form.

Conceptual model. Taxonomy of the animal kingdom.

Procedural model. Income tax calculation procedure.

Prescriptive model. Laws of gravitation.

Process or method model. Project management process or method.

Learning activity. An instructional scenario component describing actions to be carried out by the learners.

Examples

Getting acquainted with the case being analyzed.

Meeting team members.

Learning event (LE). A learning event network (LEN) component that is part of the learning system. Learning units are the smallest events in a LEN. They can be grouped to define wider events that may in turn be grouped into even broader events.

Examples

Unit.

Module.

Course.

Program.

Learning event network (LEN). The instructional structure of a learning system consisting of several learning events. The links between events specify rules of advancement and suggest the most efficient way to progress through the learning system. LENs may be single level or multilevel.

Types and Examples

Linear single-level LEN. Series of three classes to be followed in a predefined order.

Branched single-level LEN. Drawing class followed by an oil or water-color painting class.

Modular single-level LEN. Series of three totally optional classes to be taken independently of each other.

Hierarchical multilevel LEN. Three-course training program with each course separated into five or six modules and each module subdivided into learning units.

Networked multilevel LEN. Modular course containing hyperlinked subjects, enabling learner navigation in all directions justified by the content.

Learning scenario. An instructional scenario component that specifies the learner's activities, the resources to be used, the productions to be created, and the rules and instructions for progressing through activities.

Types and Examples

Learning scenario using a reception approach. Series of language classes in which the instructor systematically presents terms and grammatical rules.

Learning scenario using a reception or exercise approach. Computerized tutorial (electronic tutoring) to learn how to use software. The learner is presented with an explanation followed by a set of multiple-choice questions and answers.

Learning scenario using a case study approach. Multimedia software accessed through the Internet that simulates certain real-life situations. The learner applies acquired knowledge to predict the result in new situations.

Learning scenario using a guided discovery approach. Set of activities during which the tutor regularly adjusts learners' paths to keep them on the right track.

Learning scenario using a knowledge construction approach. Set of activities with which learners build an electronic circuit.

Learning system. The set of all the design specifications, all the learning material, and the learning environments of all the actors involved in learning or in facilitating learning of a specific domain.

Learning unit (LU). A coherent organization, according to instructional principles, of activities proposed for learners and facilitators. It is described by an instructional scenario. The goal of an LU is to develop one or several of the skills included in a knowledge model. The learning unit is the basic element of a learning event network. It is a learning event that cannot be subdivided in other learning events.

Examples

Case study.

Computer programming project.

Tutorial presentation of a chapter of the material (subject).

Link. A knowledge model component that represents the relationship between two knowledge units (a source and a target). In a graphic model, arrows represent the link. Each arrow is marked with a letter indicating its link type.

Types and Examples

Instantiation (I). John's car is an instance of Renault cars.

Composition (C). The car is composed of a body, an engine, a brake system, and a set of wheels.

Specialization (S). Renaults are a sort of car.

Precedence (P). The procedure "make an outline" precedes the procedure "draft the text."

Input/product (I/P). The "outline" is the input to the procedure "draft a text"; the "text" is the product of the procedure.

Regulation (R). Page layout rules define the "plan." Air-traffic control rules govern "plane take off" procedure. Project management rules govern "project implementation."

Application (A). The skill that could be applied to the procedure. The procedure "name the capitals of the world" requires application of the skill "to memorize."

Location. Where the learning or training and the assistance activities take place. This resource is indicated during the design, production, or delivery of a learning system.

Examples

Class; place of residence or place chosen by the learner; library; workstation.

Scientific laboratory; computer lab; cutting and editing room; special training site; conference room in a company or at a hotel.

Welcoming organization; park.

Materials. Resources organized in such a way as to support, according to its content (instructional or organizational), information proposed for learning system actors.

Types and Examples

Instructional material. Material containing content information or describing learning strategies. There are three types of instructional materials.

Reference material. A combination of information materials proposed mainly for the use of learners and instructors. Instructional reference materials include one or several instruments from the learning system's instructional scenarios. Examples: texts, audio segments, and images used in a Web course; soundtrack for a course offered on cassette; printed document serving as a reference book.

Guides. Descriptions and instructions related to the activities and the instruments included in the learning system's instructional scenarios. Examples: course study guide; teaching guide; user's guide; guidelines on the use of a printed or audiovisual document.

Integrated material. A grouping of instructional reference materials and instructional guides, such as a multimedia CD containing both the content of instruments related to the course and the descriptions of pertinent activities. Example: a multimedia disk containing both the content manual and the study guide.

Organizational material. Material containing information not directly connected to the learning activities but serving to support the delivery of learning system services.

Reference material. Materials that contain support information for the services offered by one or several actors, other than learners or teachers, in the course of learning system delivery. Examples: course evaluation questionnaire; listing of evaluation results; reference documents for the management of a Web course.

Guides. Material that contains descriptions of services and instructions related to delivery of learning system services. Examples: management delivery guide; FAQs (frequently asked questions); file construction guide; student evaluation guide.

Promotional material. Material that contains program information, course listings, or general organizational activities proposed to motivate potential learning system users to participate. Examples: brochure or videotape describing a training program; informational Web site describing courses offered by an organization.

Media component. A subdivision (module, section, page, or sequence) within a material. A media component can be subdivided into media elements.

Media element. A media component subdivision that gives access to a specific piece of information. A media element cannot be subdivided and is normally associated with the source document supplying the element's content.

Examples

Real-life moving image; video sequence; animation.

Still picture; photo; drawing.

3D object (tridimensional); part of a scale model.

Audio; noise; musical sequence.

Text; letters of the alphabet; titles and subtitles of a Web site welcoming page.

Multimedia material. Instructional material containing digitized media elements (such as audio segments and dynamic and physical images) of two or more types. The information contained by multimedia material may be structured as a network accessed by hyperlinks (hypermedia), as a tree structure accessed through a system of menus (hierarchical multimedia), as a linear sequence (linear multimedia), or as a record of attributes (multimedia database).

Types and Examples

Hypermedia. Network of texts, audio segments, and images, accessed through hyperlinks.

Hierarchical multimedia. Two or more media contained on a menu-driven, interactive videodisk.

Linear multimedia. Two or more media, such as text and drawings, contained in a set of pages that are to be viewed in one specific order.

Multimedia database. Collection of texts with audio segments or images, or both, that can be accessed through attributes, keywords, or natural language queries.

Prescriptive model. A knowledge model in which the main knowledge units are principles.

Types and Examples

Decision tree. Set of rules that cover all the cases and sub-cases to consider, for example to select a house or a vehicle that meets the needs and budgets of a person.

Definition. Set of principles giving properties of an object, for example to describe the concept of cube.

Law and theory. Principle or set of principles stating relationships between quantities or qualitative concepts, for example, the laws of gravitation.

Iterative control structure. Set of principles to decide what procedure to apply, for example, when conducting a diagnostic check on a motor that has broken down.

Principle. A knowledge unit in the form of a statement describing object properties ("what"), establishing cause-and-effect relationships between objects ("why"), or determining under which conditions to apply a procedure ("when"). Often a principle can be generically expressed as follows: If condition X is true, then action Y will ensue.

Examples

Principles for managing staff grouped in buildings situated in several cities. ("If staff are in different buildings, then communicate by cordless phones.")

Principles leading to the choice of an educational strategy or certain media. ("If you choose a learning-by-knowledge construction scenario, then use a methodological assistance scenario.")

Procedural model. A knowledge model in which the main knowledge units are procedures.

Types and Examples

Serial procedures. Points and subpoints of a meeting agenda.

Iterative procedures. Thermostat feedback loop.

Parallel procedures. Tasks for writing a group assignment or for completing a group project that can be carried out simultaneously by different group members.

Procedure. A knowledge unit consisting of a set of descriptions of actions that are expected to lead to a certain type of result in certain cases. Each procedure differs from others in the objects to which the steps can apply and the intermediate or final product resulting from performing the procedure.

Examples

Agenda for a meeting.

Set of tasks for writing a group assignment or for completing a group project.

Process; Method. A knowledge model in which no one type of knowledge unit predominates. The model contains both procedures with their input concepts and resulting products and the principles governing the performance of the procedures or defining the concepts.

Examples

Procedures and principles for industrial steel production.

Procedures and principles for defining the roles in a multiagent system.

Procedures and principles for designing and developing software.

Production. A resource containing information produced by the learner or other actor during an instructional scenario activity or the delivery of a learning system.

Examples

Physical exercise.

Plan of a project implemented jointly by a group of learners and an instructor.

Completed assignments; exams corrected by a tutor.

Evaluation report on the conclusions drawn from the implementation of a pilot learning system.

Delivery manager's report to the design team.

Resource. An instructional scenario or a delivery model component that either serves to carry out one or more activities or is the product of an activity. Resources can be used or produced by a learner, an instructor, or other actors such as managers, administrators, or designers.

Types and Examples

Instructional resources. Instruments; guides; productions; tools; communications; services; locations.

Guide. Study guide; tutorial; guided tour of software.

Instrument. Report; table; organizational chart; case study; model.

Production. Physical exercise; plan of a project implemented jointly by a group of learners and an instructor; learner assignments.

Delivery resources. Package of material; productions; tools; communications; services and locations.

Package of materials. Web site giving access to a course's instructional materials; microbiology kit and a microscope.

Location. Laboratory; learner's residence; workstation; conference room in a company or at a hotel.

Tool. Scissors; microscope; e-mail; diary; word processor; computer; peripherals.

Means of communication. Mail, phone, or fax; radio or television; telematics (that is, applications such as videoconferencing or the Internet that involve both computers and telecommunication methods).

Production. Evaluation report produced during the implementation phase of a learning system.

Service. Support provided by a lab supervisor, tutor, field expert, or software.

Role. A process required upon delivery or during the engineering of a learning system and applied by an actor in order to ensure that all necessary elements of the system are present.

Examples

Using the bibliography (learner).

Correcting learners' assignments (tutor).

Forming groups (moderator).

Assigning the tutor (administrator).

Making course material available on a server (computer technician).

Rules. Principles guiding the completion of the learning events, learning units, or learning activities in an instructional scenario.

Types and Examples

Rules for customizing the learning scenario. Learners, on their own initiative, will be able to choose which learning events to attend, and to change the order in which they attend them.

Collaboration rules. The teams must consist of at least five learners.

Study rules. Learners will be able to carry out the LU or LE of their choice, depending on the results of a pretest.

Evaluation rules. Evaluation will take place after the learning session is completed to verify that it was successful.

Media rules. The titles of this page will be centered and set in a bold 14-point font.

Delivery rules. While using the multimedia laboratory, learners will work in pairs.

Service. A resource that involves an actor (supplier) giving assistance to other actors (users) during one or several activities in a learning scenario.

Examples

Assistance rendered by a laboratory supervisor or technician.

Support offered by a tutor.

Information given by an invited lecturer (subject-matter specialist).

Technical support supplied for software.

Skill. A generic process (meta-knowledge) that allows a person or a computer agent to process knowledge in various domains. Among essential skills are the abilities to pay attention, remember, clarify, translate, apply, analyze, repair, synthesize, and estimate.

Types and Examples

Reception. To perceive poor physical posture in someone sitting in front of a screen. (A specific skill of the reception type is *to pay attention;* psychomotor domain.)

Reproduction. To master a new situation by applying methods similar to those used with a previously experienced situation. (Specific skills of the reproduction type are *to transpose* and *to translate;* affective domain.)

Creation; production. To identify objectives, data, and constraints of a type of problem. (A specific skill of the creation type is *to analyze;* cognitive domain.)

Self-management. To regulate one's attitudes by frequent evaluation in order to improve quality of life.

Source document. A document or file associated with a media element that supplies its content. A source document is defined by one or by several objects in the instructional or delivery model. These objects may be instruments, guides, tools, services, communications, locations, graphs, directions, and so forth.

Summative evaluation. An evaluation mode that a learning system designer may adopt. A summative evaluation takes place after the learning events and determines the degree to which the skill was achieved.

Example

Evaluation will take place after the learning unit (LU) is completed and will measure whether the expected degree of the skill has been attained.

Support. A physical object making it possible to preserve and to retrieve information on demand. This information can then take the shape of a code or a tridimensional object (data carrier).

Types and Examples

> *Analogical support.* Long-playing record; videocassette.
>
> *Printed support.* Label; transparencies; exercise book.
>
> *Digital support.* Floppy disk; memory card; hard disk; RAM; ROM (computer's CPU memory).
>
> *Tridimensional object.* Model (such as a model of a molecule); building blocks.

Synchronous e-learning (distance learning). A delivery mode and type of e-learning in which learners and facilitator are present at the same time during most of the learning events or activities.

Types and Examples

> *Broadcast (radio or television) education.* Course broadcast via satellite or cable television, through a wired or wireless communication link.
>
> *Learning through audioconferencing or videoconferencing.* Course in which a tutor in one learning center and students in three or four other locations interact via audio or video links.
>
> *Teamwork facilitated by audioconferencing or videoconferencing.* Teamwork in which team members in various locations audioconference or videoconference using a workstation connected to a whiteboard (as in a Net meeting).

Tool. A resource enabling the perception or processing of materials or information necessary to perform one or more of the activities in the learning or assistance scenario.

Types and Examples

> *Noncomputer tools.* Mechanical tools (scissors); optical tools (microscope); electronic tools (radio or television).
>
> *Computer tools.* Computer; peripherals; operating systems; application software; specialized software (such as a word processor).

Videoconference. Real-time means of communication enabling users in different locations to both speak to and see each other.

Types and Examples

Without file sharing. Eight students in four different locations using videoconferencing to discuss a document that was faxed to them.

With file sharing. Participants in different locations using networked videoconferencing to discuss and annotate a text that they all can view and use on their computer screens.

Introduction

1. Whalen, T., and Wright, D. "Cost-Benefit Analysis of Web-Based Tele-Learning: Case Study of the Bell Online Institute Pilot Project." Faculty of Administration, University of Ottawa, 136 Jean Jacques Lussier St., Ottawa, Canada K1N 6N5, 1998.

2. Gustafson, K. L. "Instructional Transaction Fundamentals: Clouds on the Horizon." *Educational Technology*, Feb. 1993, pp. 27–32.

Chapter One

1. See, for example, Center for Educational Research and Innovation. *Information Technologies and Basic Learning*. Paris: OECD, 1987.

2. Québec Council for Higher Education, *Annual Report to the Government*, 1998. Translated by the author.

3. See Drucker, P. F., *Managing for the Future: The 1990s and Beyond.* New York: Truman Talley Books/Dutton, 1992.

4. Delphi Group. *Knowledge Management Special Report.* Boston, May 1998.

5. Deloitte Consulting. "From e-Learning to Enterprise Learning: Becoming a Strategic Learning Organization." 2001. [http://www.dc.com/obx/pages.php?Name=AllResearch].

6. W. R. Hambrecht. "Corporate E-Learning: Exploring a New Frontier." Mar. 2000. [http://www.wrhambrecht.com/research/coverage/elearning/fr/fr_explore.pdf].

7. Cushing Anderson. "E-Learning: The Definition, the Practice, and the Promise." *Corporate eLearning,* Oct. 2000. [http://worldsearch.idc.com/].

8. Information published in 2001 by the *New York Times,* http://www.nytimes.com/library/tech/00/01/cyber/education/12education.html

9. Tobin, D. R. *The Knowledge-Enabled Organization.* New York: AMACOM, 1998.

10. Wilson, J., and Mosher, D. "The Prototype of the Virtual Classroom." *Journal of Instructional Delivery Systems,* Summer 1994, pp. 28–33; Hiltz, R. "Evaluating the Virtual Classroom." In L. Harasim (ed.), *Online Education: Perspectives on a New Environment.* New York: Praeger, 1990.

11. Pea, R., and Gomez, L. "Distributed Multimedia Environments." *Interactive Learning Environments,* 1992, *2,* 73–109; Bourdeau, J., Frihida, A., Gecsei, J., Paquette, G., and De la Teja, I. "Accessing Distributed Multimedia Documents for Instructional Use." Paper presented at the ED-Media International Conference, Vancouver, Sept. 1994.

12. Harasim, L. "Online Education: An Environment for Collaboration and Intellectual Amplification." In L. Harasim (ed.), *Online Education: Perspectives on a New Environment.* New York: Praeger, 1990.

13. Wenger, E. *Communities of Practice. Learning, Meaning and Identity (Learning in Doing: Social, Cognitive, and Computational Perspectives).* Cambridge, England: Cambridge University Press, 1998.

14. Gery, G. "Granting Three Wishes Through Performance-Centered Design." *Communications of the ACM,* July 1997, *40*(7), 54–59.

15. This definition was adapted from *Étude comparative technique et pédagogique des plates-formes pour la formation ouverte et à distance* (*A Technical and Pedagogical Comparative Study of Platforms for Open and Distance Education*). Paris: Ministère de l'éducation nationale, de la recherche et de la technologie, Sept. 1999.

16. I have resisted the temptation to include platform descriptions in this book because the goal here is limited to helping the reader understand the concept of platforms. For an up-to-date summary of the systems available, the reader is advised to consult such specialized Web sites as www.ctt.bc.ca/landonline or www.101com.com.

17. Aska-Le Préau. *Choisir une solution de téléformation: 2000.* [http://www.preau.asso.fr/teleformation/default.htm].

18. Quoted in Aska-Le Préau, *Choisir une solution de téléformation.*

19. More information about this organization may be found at its Web site. [http://www.imsproject.org].

20. More information about this organization may be found at its Web site. [http://www.aicc.org].

Chapter Three

1. Lemoigne, J. L. *Les épistémologies constructivistes* (*Constructivist Epistemologies*). Paris: PUF, 1995. Simon, H. A. *The Sciences of the Artificial.* Cambridge, Mass.: MIT Press, 1981.

2. Newell, A., and Simon, H. *Human problem solving.* Upper Saddle River, N.J.: Prentice Hall, 1972.

3. Romiszowski, A. J. *Designing Instructional Systems.* New York: Nichols, 1981; Reigeluth, C. (ed.). *Instructional Theories in Action: Lessons Illustrating Selected Theories and Models.* Mahwah, N.J.: Erlbaum, 1983; Tennyson, R. D. "Cognitive Learning Theory Linked to Instructional Theory." *Journal of Structured Learning,* 1990, *10*(3),

249–258; Merrill, M. D. *Principles of Instructional Design.* Englewood Cliffs, N.J.: Educational Technology, 1994.

4. Polya, G. *How to Solve It: A New Aspect of Mathematical Method* (2nd ed.). Princeton, N.J.: Princeton University Press, 1957.

5. Polya, *How to Solve It.*

6. Goël, V., and Pirolli, P. "Design Within Information-Processing Theory: The Design Problem Space." *AI Magazine,* Spring 1989, pp. 19–36.

7. Reigeluth, *Instructional Theories in Action.*

8. Montessori, M. *The Montessori Method.* New York: Schocken Books, 1964.

9. Dewey, J. "Psychology and Social Practice." *Psychological Review,* 1900, *7,* 105–124.

10. Reigeluth, *Instructional Theories in Action.*

11. Skinner, B. F. "The Science of Learning and the Art of Teaching." *Harvard Educational Review,* 1954, *24*(2), 86–97.

12. Bruner, J. S. *Towards a Theory of Instruction.* Cambridge, Mass.: Harvard University Press, 1966.

13. Ausubel, D. P. *Educational Psychology: A Cognitive View.* Austin, Tex.: Holt, Rinehart and Winston, 1968.

14. Landa, L. *Instructional Regulation and Control: Cybernetics, Algorithmization, and Heuristics in Education* (trans. S. Desch, from Russian). Englewood Cliffs, N.J.: Educational Technology, 1976.

15. Gagné, R. M. *The Conditions of Learning* (2nd ed.). Austin, Tex.: Holt, Rinehart and Winston, 1970.

16. Scandura, J. M. *Structural Learning I: Theory and Research.* London: Gordon & Breach Science, 1973.

17. Collins, A., and Stevens, A. L. "A Cognitive Theory of Inquiry Teaching." In Reigeluth, *Instructional Theories in Action.*

18. Merrill, M. D. "Component Display Theory." In Reigeluth, *Instructional Theories in Action.*

19. Reigeluth, C. M., and Rodgers, C. A. "The Elaboration Theory of Instruction: Prescriptions for Task Analysis and Design." *NSPI Journal,* 1980, *19*(1), 16–26.

20. See, for example, Gustafson, K. L. "Instructional Transaction Fundamentals: Clouds on the Horizon." *Educational Technology,* Feb. 1993, pp. 27–32.

21. Firesmith, D. G. *Object-Oriented Requirements Analysis and Logical Design.* New York: Wiley, 1993, p. 1.

22. Bouchy, S. *L'ingénierie des systèmes d'information évolutif* (*The Engineering of Evolutive Information Systems*). Paris: Eyrolles, 1994, p. 27. Translated by the author.

23. Hayes-Roth, F., Waterman, D. A., and Lenat, D. B. *Building Expert Systems.* Reading, Mass.: Addison-Wesley, 1984; Waterman, D. A. *A Guide to Expert Systems.* Reading, Mass.: Addison-Wesley, 1986.

24. Wenger, E. *Artificial Intelligence and Tutoring Systems: Computational and Cognitive Approaches to the Communication of Knowledge.* San Mateo, Calif.: Morgan Kaufmann, 1987.

25. Merrill, *Principles of Instructional Design;* Spector, J. M., Polson, M. C., and Muraida, D. J. (eds.). *Automating Instructional Design, Concepts and Issues.* Englewood Cliffs, N.J.: Educational Technology, 1993.

26. Paquette, G., and Roy, L. *Systèmes à base de connaissances* (Knowledge-Based Systems). Montreal: Télé-université and Beauchemin, 1990.

27. See Romiszowski, *Designing Instructional Systems,* for an analogous definition (p. 254). He labels the first-level phases perception, memory recall, planning, and performance.

28. Pitrat, J. *Métaconnaissance, avenir de l'Intelligence Artificielle* (*Metaknowledge, the Future of Artificial Intelligence*). Paris: Hermès, 1991.

29. Wenger, E. *Artificial Intelligence and Tutoring Systems: Computational and Cognitive Approaches to the Communication of Knowledge.* San Mateo, Calif.: Morgan Kaufmann, 1987.

30. Bélisle and Linard classify the cognitive science work of authors such as Vygotsky, Leontiev, Piaget, Searle, Bruner, and Schank, to name only a few, under the term action theories. See Bélisle, C., and Linard, M. "Quelles nouvelles compétences des acteurs de la formation dans le contexte des TIC?" ("What New Actor Competencies Are Needed for ICT-Based Training?"). *Éducation permanente,* 1996, no. 127, pp. 19–47.

31. This profile relates to a single actor, although it results from a broad analysis of the field of multimedia that led to the identification of fourteen main actors and as many corresponding competency profiles. These competency profiles are available (in French) at http://www.technocompetences.qc.ca.

Chapter Four

1. Paquette, G., Aubin, C., and Crevier, F. "Design and Implementation of Interactive TeleLearning Scenarios." In *Proceedings of ICDE 1997 [International Council for Distance Education],* Pennsylvania State University, June 1997; Paquette, G., Aubin, C., and Crevier, F. "MISA: A Knowledge-Based Method for the Engineering of Learning Systems." *Journal of Courseware Engineering,* Aug. 1999.

Chapter Six

1. The three e-learning projects studied in Chapters Six, Seven, and Eight were carried out either by the LICEF Research Center of Télé-université or its associate company, Technologies Cogigraph. The author has directed and contributed to all of these projects. All three e-learning systems were built with MISA (discussed in Chapter Four), and have used two ADISA (discussed in Chapter Five), and were implemented and delivered with the Explor@ system presented in Chapter Three. For more details about the project presented in this chapter, see Paquette, G., De la Teja, I., and Dufresne, A. "Explor@: An Open Virtual Campus." In J. Bourdeau and R. Heller (eds.),

Proceedings of ED-MEDIA 2000: World Conference on Educational Multimedia, Hypermedia & Telecommunications, Montreal, QC. Charlottesville, Va.: Association for the Advancement of Computing in Education, 2000.

Chapter Seven

1. For more details on the project, see De la Teja, I., Longpré, A., and Paquette, G. "Designing Adaptable Learning Environments for the Web: A Case Study." In J. Bourdeau and R. Heller (eds.), *Proceedings of ED-MEDIA 2000: World Conference on Educational Multimedia, Hypermedia & Telecommunications, Montreal, QC.* Charlottesville, Va.: Association for the Advancement of Computing in Education, 2000.

BIBLIOGRAPHY

Anderson, J. R. *Cognitive Psychology and Its Implications.* New York: Freeman, 1985.

Ausubel, D. P. *Educational Psychology: A Cognitive View.* Austin, Tex.: Holt, Rinehart and Winston, 1968.

Bartlett, F. C. *Remembering.* Cambridge, England: Cambridge University Press, 1932.

Bélisle, C., and Linard, M. "Quelles nouvelles compétences des acteurs de la formation dans le contexte des TIC?" *Éducation permanente,* 1996, no. 127, pp. 19–47.

Bloom, B. S. (ed.). *Taxonomy of Educational Objectives: The Classification of Educational Goals. Handbook 1: Cognitive Domain.* White Plains, NY: Longman, 1956.

Booch, G., Jacobson, J., and Rumbaugh, I. *The Unified Modeling Language User Guide.* Reading, Mass.: Addison-Wesley, 1999.

Bouchy, S. *L'ingénierie des systèmes d'information évolutif* (*The Engineering of Evolutive Information Systems*). Paris: Eyrolles, 1994.

Bourdeau, J., Frihida, A., Gecsei, J., Paquette, G., and De la Teja, I. "Accessing Distributed Multimedia Documents for Instructional Use." In *Proceedings of the ED-Media International Conference*, Vancouver, Sept. 1994.

Breuker, J., and Van de Velde, W. *CommonKads Library for Expertise Modelling*. Amsterdam: IOS Press, 1994.

Brien, R. *Science cognitive et formation* (3rd ed.). Quebec: University of Quebec Press, 1997.

Bruner, J. S. *Towards a Theory of Instruction*. Cambridge, Mass.: Harvard University Press, 1966.

Bruner, J. S. *Going Beyond the Information Given*. New York: Norton, 1973.

Center for Educational Research and Innovation. *Information Technologies and Basic Learning*. Paris: OECD, 1987.

Chandrasekaran, B. "Towards a Functional Architecture for Intelligence Based on Generic Information Processing Tasks." In *Proceedings of the Tenth International Joint Conference on Artificial Intelligence (IJCAI 87)*. Milan: IJCAI, 1987.

Collins, A., and Stevens, A. L. "A Cognitive Theory of Inquiry Teaching." In C. Reigeluth (ed.), *Instructional Theories in Action: Lessons Illustrating Selected Theories and Models*. Mahwah, N.J.: Erlbaum, 1983.

Cranton, P. *Planning Instruction for Adult Learners*. Toronto: Wall & Thompson, 1989.

Dansereau, D. F. "The Development of a Learning Strategies Curriculum." In H. F. O'Neil Jr. (ed.), *Learning Strategies*. New York: Academic Press, 1978.

De la Teja, I., Longpré, A., and Paquette, G. "Designing Adaptable Learning Environments for the Web: A Case Study." In J. Bourdeau and R. Heller (eds.), *Proceedings of ED-MEDIA 2000: World Conference on Educational Multimedia, Hypermedia & Telecommunications, Montreal,*

QC. Charlottesville, Va.: Association for the Advancement of Computing in Education, 2000.

Dewey, J. "Psychology and Social Practice." *Psychological Review,* 1900, *7,* 105–124.

Drucker, P. F., *Managing for the Future: The 1990s and Beyond.* New York: Truman Talley Books/Dutton, 1992.

Firesmith, D. G. *Object-Oriented Requirements Analysis and Logical Design.* New York: Wiley, 1993.

Foshay, W. R. "An Alternative for Task Analysis in the Affective Domain." *Journal of Instructional Development,* 1978, *1*(2), 22–24.

Friedlander, P. "Competency-Driven, Component-Based Curriculum Architecture." *Performance Improvement,* Feb. 1996, pp. 355–362.

Gagné, R. M. *The Conditions of Learning* (2nd ed.). Austin, Tex.: Holt, Rinehart and Winston, 1970.

Gardner, H. *Multiple Intelligences: The Theory in Practice.* New York: Basic Books, 1993.

Gasser, L. "Social Conceptions of Knowledge and Action: DAI Foundations and Open Systems Semantics." *Artificial Intelligence,* 1991, *47,* 107–138.

Gery, G. "Granting Three Wishes Through Performance-Centered Design." *Communications of the ACM,* July 1997, *40*(7), 54–59.

Girard, J., Paquette, G., Miara, A., and Lundgren, K. "Intelligent Assistance for Web-based TeleLearning." In S. Lajoie and M. Vivet (eds.), *AI in Education: Open Learning Environments.* Amsterdam: IOS Press, 1999.

Goël, V., and Pirolli, P. "Design Within Information-Processing Theory: The Design Problem Space." *AI Magazine,* Spring 1989, pp. 19–36.

Goleman, D. *Emotional Intelligence.* New York: Bantam Books, 1995.

Gustafson, K. L. "Instructional Transaction Fundamentals: Clouds on the Horizon." *Educational Technology,* Feb. 1993, pp. 27–32.

Harasim, L. "Online Education: An Environment for Collaboration and Intellectual Amplification." In L. Harasim (ed.), *Online Education: Perspectives on a New Environment.* New York: Praeger, 1990.

Hayes-Roth, F., Waterman, D. A., and Lenat, D. B. *Building Expert Systems.* Reading, Mass.: Addison-Wesley, 1984.

Henri, F., and Ricciardi-Rigault, C. "Collaborative Learning and Computer Conferencing" (NATO Advanced Workshop, Grenoble, Sept. 1993). In T. T. Liao (ed.), *Advanced Educational Technology: Research Issues and Future Potential.* New York: Springer-Verlag, 1995.

Hiltz, R. "Evaluating the Virtual Classroom." In L. Harasim (ed.), *Online Education: Perspectives on a New Environment.* New York: Praeger, 1990.

Holley, C. D., and Dansereau, D. F. "Networking: The Technique and the Empirical Evidence." In C. D. Holley and D. F. Dansereau (eds.), *Spatial Learning Strategies: Techniques, Applications and Related Issues.* New York: Academic Press, 1984.

Inhelder, B., and Piaget, J. *The Growth of Logical Thinking from Childhood to Adolescence.* New York: Basic Books, 1958.

Jonassen, D. H., Beissner, K., and Yacci, M. *Structural Knowledge: Techniques for Representing, Conveying and Acquiring Structural Knowledge.* Mahwah, N.J.: Erlbaum, 1993.

Joyce, B., and Weil, M. *Models of Teaching* (2nd ed.). Upper Saddle River, N.J.: Prentice Hall, 1980.

Knowles, M. S., and Associates. *Andragogy in Action: Applying Modern Principles of Adult Learning.* San Francisco: Jossey-Bass, 1984.

Krathwohl, D. R., Bloom, B. S., and Masia, B. B. *Taxonomy of Educational Objectives: The Classification of Educational Goals. Handbook II: Affective Domain.* White Plains, NY: Longman, 1964.

Landa, L. *Instructional Regulation and Control: Cybernetics, Algorithmization, and Heuristics in Education* (trans. S. Desch, from Russian). Englewood Cliffs, N.J.: Educational Technology, 1976.

LeBoterf, G. *L'ingénierie des compétences* (2nd ed.). Paris: Éditions d'organisation, 1999.

Lemoigne, J. L. *Les épistémologies constructivistes* (*Constructivist Epistemologies*). Paris: PUF, 1995.

Leontiev, A. N. *Le développement du psychisme* (3rd ed.). Paris: Éditions Sociales, 1976.

Li, Z., and Merrill, D. "ID Expert 2.0: Design Theory and Process." *ET R&D Journal,* 1990, *39*(2), 53–69.

Li, Z., and Merrill, D. "Transaction Shells: A New Approach to Courseware Authoring." *Journal of Research on Computing in Education,* 1990, *23*(1), 72–86.

Martin, B. L., and Briggs, L. *The Affective and Cognitive Domains: Integration for Instruction and Research.* Englewood Cliffs, N.J.: Educational Technology, 1986.

McDermott, J. "Preliminary Steps Towards a Taxonomy of Problem-Solving Methods." In S. Marcus (ed.), *Automating Knowledge Acquisition for Expert Systems.* Boston: Kluwer Academic, 1988.

McGraw, K. L., and Harbisson-Briggs, K. *Knowledge Acquisition.* Upper Saddle River, N.J.: Prentice Hall, 1989.

Merrill, M. D. "Component Display Theory." In C. Reigeluth (ed.), *Instructional Theories in Action: Lessons Illustrating Selected Theories and Models.* Mahwah, N.J.: Erlbaum, 1983.

Merrill, M. D. *Principles of Instructional Design.* Englewood Cliffs, N.J.: Educational Technology, 1994.

Minski, M. "A Framework for Representing Knowledge." In P. H. Winston (ed.), *The Psychology of Computer Vision.* New York: McGraw-Hill, 1975.

Minski, M. *The Society of Mind.* New York: Simon & Schuster, 1985.

Montessori, M. *The Montessori Method.* New York: Schocken Books, 1964.

Newell, A., and Simon, H. *Human Problem Solving.* Upper Saddle River, N.J.: Prentice Hall, 1972.

Noël, B. *La métacognition.* Brussels: De Boeck-Wesmael, 1991.

Paquette, G. "Modeling the Virtual Campus." In B. Collis and G. Davies (eds.), *Innovating Adult Learning with Innovative Technologies.* Amsterdam: Elsevier Science, 1995.

Paquette, G. "La modélisation par objets typés: Une méthode de représentation pour les systèmes d'apprentissage et d'aide a la tâche." *Sciences et techniques éducatives,* Apr. 1996, pp. 9–42.

Paquette, G. "Virtual Learning Centres for XXIst Century Organisations." In F. Verdejo and G. Davies (eds.), *The Virtual Campus.* London: Chapman & Hall, 1997.

Paquette, G. "Designing Virtual Learning Centers." In H. Adelsberger, B. Collis, and J. Pawlowski (eds.), *Handbook on Information Technologies for Education & Training.* New York: Springer-Verlag, 2001.

Paquette, G. "TeleLearning Systems Engineering: Towards a New ISD Model." *Journal of Structural Learning,* 2001, *14,* 1–35.

Paquette, G., Aubin, C., and Crevier, F. "Design and Implementation of Interactive TeleLearning Scenarios." In *Proceedings of ICDE 1997 [International Council for Distance Education],* Pennsylvania State University, June 1997.

Paquette, G., Aubin, C., and Crevier, F. "MISA: A Knowledge-Based Method for the Engineering of Learning Systems." *Journal of Courseware Engineering,* Aug. 1999.

Paquette, G., Bergeron, G., and Bourdeau, J. "The Virtual Classroom Revisited." In G. Davies and B. Samways (eds.), *Teleteaching: Proceedings of the IFIP TC3 Third Teleteaching Conference,* teleteaching 93, Trondheim, Norway, 20–25 Aug, 1993. Amsterdam: North-Holland, 1993.

Paquette, G., Crevier, F., and Aubin, C. "ID Knowledge in a Course Design Workbench." *Educational Technology,* Nov. 1994, *34*(9), 50–57.

Paquette, G., De la Teja, I., and Dufresne, A. "Explor@: An Open Virtual Campus." In J. Bourdeau and R. Heller (eds.), *Proceedings of ED-MEDIA*

2000: World Conference on Educational Multimedia, Hypermedia & Telecommunications, Montreal, QC. Charlottesville, Va.: Association for the Advancement of Computing in Education, 2000.

Paquette, G., and Girard, J. "AGD: A Course Engineering Support System." In *Proceedings of ITS-96,* Montreal, June 1996.

Paquette, G., Ricciardi-Rigault, C., Bourdeau, J., Paquin, C., and Liégeois, S. "Modeling a Virtual Campus Environment for Interactive Distance Learning." Paper presented at the ED-Media International Conference, Graz, Austria, June 1995.

Paquette, G., Ricciardi-Rigault, C., Paquin, C., Liégeois, S., and Bleicher, E. "Developing the Virtual Campus Environment." Paper presented at the ED-Media International Conference, Boston, June 1996.

Paquette, G., and Roy, L. *Systèmes à base de connaissances* (Knowledge-Based Systems). Montreal: Télé-université and Beauchemin, 1990.

Paris, S., Lipson, M. Y., and Wixson, K. K. "Becoming a Strategic Reader." *Contemporary Educational Psychology,* 1983, *8,* 293–331.

Pea, R., and Gomez, L. "Distributed Multimedia Environments." *Interactive Learning Environments,* 1992, *2,* 73–109.

Piaget, J. *Logic and Psychology.* New York: Basic Books, 1957.

Pitrat, J. *Métaconnaissance, avenir de l'Intelligence Artificielle.* Paris: Hermès, 1991.

Pitrat, J. *Penser l'informatique autrement.* Paris: Hermès, 1993.

Polya, G. *How to Solve It: A New Aspect of Mathematical Method* (2nd ed.). Princeton, N.J.: Princeton University Press, 1957.

Popper, K. R. *The Logic of Scientific Discovery.* New York: Harper Torchbooks, 1967.

Reigeluth, C. (ed.). *Instructional Theories in Action: Lessons Illustrating Selected Theories and Models.* Mahwah, N.J.: Erlbaum, 1983.

Reigeluth, C. M., and Rodgers, C. A. "The Elaboration Theory of Instruction: Prescriptions for Task Analysis and Design." *NSPI Journal,* 1980, *19*(1), 16–26.

Ricciardi-Rigault, C., and Henri, F. "Developing Tools for Optimizing the Collaborative Learning Process." In *Proceedings of the International Distance Education Conference,* Pennsylvania State University, June 1994.

Romiszowski, A. J. *Designing Instructional Systems.* New York: Nichols, 1981.

Rumbaugh, J., Blaha, M., Premerlani, W., Eddy, F., and Lorensen, W. *Object-Oriented Modelling and Design.* Upper Saddle River, N.J.: Prentice Hall, 1991.

Rumelhart, D. E., and Ortony, A. "The Representation of Knowledge in Memory." In R. C. Anderson, R. J. Spiro, and W. E. Montague (eds.), *Schooling and the Acquisition of Knowledge.* Mahwah, N.J.: Erlbaum, 1977.

Scandura, J. M. *Structural Learning I: Theory and Research.* London: Gordon & Breach Science, 1973.

Schreiber, G., Wielinga, B., and Breuker, J. *KADS: A Principled Approach to Knowledge-based System Development.* New York: Academic Press, 1993.

Simon, H. A. *The Sciences of the Artificial.* Cambridge, Mass.: MIT Press, 1981.

Skinner, B. F. "The Science of Learning and the Art of Teaching." *Harvard Educational Review,* 1954, *24*(2), 86–97.

Spector, J. M., Polson, M. C., and Muraida, D. J. (eds.). *Automating Instructional Design, Concepts and Issues.* Englewood Cliffs, N.J.: Educational Technology, 1993.

Sycara, K. P. "The Many Faces of Agents." *AI Magazine,* Summer 1998.

Tardif, J. *Pour un enseignement stratégique, l'apport de la psychologie cognitive.* Montreal: Les Éditions, 1992.

Tennyson, R. D. "Cognitive Learning Theory Linked to Instructional Theory." *Journal of Structured Learning,* 1990, *10*(3), 249–258.

Tennyson, R., and Rasch, M. "Linking Cognitive Learning Theory to Instructional Prescriptions." *Instructional Science,* 1990, *17,* 369–385.

Thayse, A. *Approche logique de l'intelligence artificielle.* Paris: Dunod, 1988.

Vigotsky, L. S. *Mind in Society: The Development of Higher Psychological Functions.* Cambridge, Mass.: Harvard University Press, 1978.

Waterman, D. A. *A Guide to Expert Systems.* Reading, Mass.: Addison-Wesley, 1986.

Wenger, E. *Artificial Intelligence and Tutoring Systems: Computational and Cognitive Approaches to the Communication of Knowledge.* San Mateo, Calif.: Morgan Kaufmann, 1987.

Wenger, E. *Communities of Practice. Learning, Meaning and Identity (Learning in Doing: Social, Cognitive, and Computational Perspectives).* Cambridge, England: Cambridge University Press, 1998.

Wertheimer, M. *Productive Thinking.* New York: HarperCollins, 1945.

West, C. K., Farmer, J. A., and Wolff, P. M. *Instructional Design: Implications from Cognitive Science.* Needham Heights, Mass.: Allyn & Bacon, 1991.

Whalen, T., and Wright, D. "Cost-Benefit Analysis of Web-Based Tele-Learning: Case Study of the Bell Online Institute Pilot Project" (TL-NCE Research Report Series). Burnaby, B.C.: Simon Fraser University, July 1998.

Williams, R. G. "A Behavioural Typology of Educational Objectives for the Cognitive Domain." *Educational Technology,* 1977, *17*(6).

Wilson, J., and Mosher, D. "The Prototype of the Virtual Classroom." *Journal of Instructional Delivery Systems,* Summer 1994, pp. 28–33.

Winograd, T. "Beyond the Declarative/Procedural Controversy." In R. J. Brachman and H. J. Lévesque (eds.), *Readings in Knowledge Representation.* San Mateo, Calif.: Morgan Kaufmann, 1985.

Winston, P. *Artificial Intelligence* (4th ed.). New York: McGraw-Hill, 1984.

Yourdon, E. *Modern Structured Analysis.* Upper Saddle River, N.J.: Prentice Hall, 1989.

Gilbert Paquette is director of the Center for Interuniversity Research on Telelearning Applications, the holder of the Canada Research Chair for Cognitive Engineering of Tele-learning Systems, and a researcher at the LICEF Research Center (which he founded in 1992), at the Télé-université of Quebec. He has pioneered strategic projects in the field of knowledge-based systems, instructional engineering, and e-learning and is the author of three books and many scientific articles in this field. In addition, he is a practitioner of distance education and Web-based learning and has produced about twenty courses and many learning materials. He is the founder of the company Micro-Intel (1987 to 1991) and has served as Minister for Science and Technology in the Quebec government (1982–1984).

Rita C. Richey is professor and program coordinator of instructional technology at Wayne State University. She has been at Wayne State for over thirty years and is experienced in not only program development, but also in education and training research. She has published widely in the areas of instructional design theory, including such books as *The Theoretical and Conceptual Bases of Instructional Design, Designing Instruction for the Adult Learner,* and *The Legacy of Robert M. Gagne.* Rita is coauthor of the third edition of *Instructional Design Competencies: The Standards* and the third edition of *Training Manager Competencies: The Standards.* She is also coauthor of *Instructional Technology: The Definition and Domains of the Field,* a book that received the 1995 Outstanding Book Award and the 1996 Brown Publication Award, both from the Association of Educational Communications and Technology. She has also received four major awards from Wayne State University: the President's Award for Excellence in Teaching, the Outstanding Graduate Mentor's Award, a Distinguished Faculty Fellowship, and an award for Outstanding Scholarly Achievement by Women Faculty. In addition, she has been elected to the Wayne State University Academy of Scholars. In recognition of her career's work, she received the AECT Distinguished Service Award in 2000.

William J. Rothwell, Ph.D., SPHR certification, is professor in charge of the workforce education and development program in the Department of Learning and Performance Systems at Pennsylvania State University. He is also president of Rothwell and Associates, Inc., an independent consulting firm. He has been a training director in a government agency and a large insurance company, a consultant to many organizations, and a college professor.

William is the author and coauthor of many books. His most recent publications include *Mastering the Instructional Design Process: A Systematic Approach,* 3rd edition (with H.C. Kazanas, 2004), *The Strategic Development of Talent* (with H.C. Kazanas, 2003), *What CEOs Expect from Corporate Training: Building Workplace Learning and Performance Initiatives That Advance Organizational Goals* (with J. Lindholm and W. Wallick, 2003), *Planning and Managing Human Resources,* 2nd edition (with H.C. Kazanas, 2003), *Creating Sales Training and Development Programs: A Competency-Based Approach to Building Sales Ability* (with W. Donahue and J. Park, 2002), *The Workplace Learner: How to Align Training Initiatives with Individual Learning Competencies* (2002), and *Building Effective Technical Training: How to Develop Hard Skills Within Organizations* (with J. Benkowski, 2002).

In his consulting work, William specializes in human resources practices—particularly in competency modeling and succession planning and management.

Timothy W. Spannaus, Ph.D., is senior lecturer in instructional technology and research fellow with the Institute for Learning and Performance Improvement, at Wayne State University. He is also chief learning architect at The Emdicium Group, Inc., in Southfield, Michigan.

Tim is president of the International Board of Standards for Training, Performance, and Instruction and was previously president of the Association for Development of Computer-Based Instructional Systems. He is active in the International Society for Performance Improvement and the American Society for Training and Development.

His teaching, research, and development focus on interactive technologies for learning and performance improvement. Recent projects include the creation of a training vision for a major municipal utility, the design and development of web-based learning courses, and a knowledge management plan for a Fortune 500 manufacturer. Recent publications include *Training Manager Competencies: The Standards,* two chapters in the *ID Casebook*—a forthcoming book on development of web-based learning—and numerous papers and presentations.

Kent L. Gustafson, Ph.D., is professor emeritus of instructional technology at the University of Georgia, where he was chair of the department and taught courses in instructional design, research, and management of technology-based education programs. He has published three books and numerous articles, book chapters, and technical reports. Kent is a regular presenter at major educational conferences in the United States and has spoken in many other countries including Australia, Iran, Japan, Korea, the Netherlands, Malaysia, Mexico, Nicaragua, the Philippines, and Switzerland. He is also former president of the Association for Educational Communications and Technology. Kent's research interest includes design and evaluation of electronic performance support systems, management of technology design and delivery, and professional education of technologists.

M. David Merrill, Ph.D., is professor in the department of instructional technology at Utah State University. He is also the owner and president of Ascape, Tennsion & Sulphur Gulch RR. Recognized as a leader in instructional design,

David is listed among the most productive educational psychologists (*Educational Researcher,* 1984), the most frequently cited authors in the computer-based instruction literature (*Journal of Computer-Based Instruction,* 1987), and the most influential people in the field of instructional technology (*Performance & Instruction,* 1988.) As a major contributor in his field, David was the recipient of the Association for Educational Communications and Technology's 2001 Distinguished Service Award for advancing the field of instructional technology through scholarship, teaching, and leadership. His current work involves the identification of First Principles of Instruction.

Allison Rossett, Ed.D., is professor of educational technology at San Diego State University, with academic focus on workforce development, e-learning, and needs assessment. Allison received the American Society for Training and Development's award for Workplace Learning and Performance for 2002 and will join its International Board in January 2004. She is also a member of *Training* magazine's HRD Hall of Fame, the editor of the *ASTD E-Learning Handbook: Best Practices, Strategies, and Case Studies for an Emerging Field,* and co-author of *Beyond the Podium: Delivering Training and Performance to a Digital World.* Allison has worked with a who's who of international organizations, including IBM, Microsoft, MetLife, the Internal Revenue Service, Hewlett-Packard, SQL Star International, Ford Motor Company, SBC, and Fidelity Investments.

Pfeiffer Publications Guide

This guide is designed to familiarize you with the various types of Pfeiffer publications. The formats section describes the various types of products that we publish; the methodologies section describes the many different ways that content might be provided within a product. We also provide a list of the topic areas in which we publish.

FORMATS

In addition to its extensive book-publishing program, Pfeiffer offers content in an array of formats, from fieldbooks for the practitioner to complete, ready-to-use training packages that support group learning.

FIELDBOOK Designed to provide information and guidance to practitioners in the midst of action. Most fieldbooks are companions to another, sometimes earlier, work, from which its ideas are derived; the fieldbook makes practical what was theoretical in the original text. Fieldbooks can certainly be read from cover to cover. More likely, though, you'll find yourself bouncing around following a particular theme, or dipping in as the mood, and the situation, dictate.

HANDBOOK A contributed volume of work on a single topic, comprising an eclectic mix of ideas, case studies, and best practices sourced by practitioners and experts in the field.

An editor or team of editors usually is appointed to seek out contributors and to evaluate content for relevance to the topic. Think of a handbook not as a ready-to-eat meal, but as a cookbook of ingredients that enables you to create the most fitting experience for the occasion.

RESOURCE Materials designed to support group learning. They come in many forms: a complete, ready-to-use exercise (such as a game); a comprehensive resource on one topic (such as conflict management) containing a variety of methods and approaches; or a collection of like-minded activities (such as icebreakers) on multiple subjects and situations.

TRAINING PACKAGE An entire, ready-to-use learning program that focuses on a particular topic or skill. All packages comprise a guide for the facilitator/trainer and a workbook for the participants. Some packages are supported with additional media—such as video—or learning aids, instruments, or other devices to help participants understand concepts or practice and develop skills.

- *Facilitator/trainer's guide* Contains an introduction to the program, advice on how to organize and facilitate the learning event, and step-by-step instructor notes. The guide also contains copies of presentation materials—handouts, presentations, and overhead designs, for example—used in the program.

- *Participant's workbook* Contains exercises and reading materials that support the learning goal and serves as a valuable reference and support guide for participants in the weeks and months that follow the learning event. Typically, each participant will require his or her own workbook.

ELECTRONIC CD-ROMs and web-based products transform static Pfeiffer content into dynamic, interactive experiences. Designed to take advantage of the searchability, automation, and ease-of-use that technology provides, our e-products bring convenience and immediate accessibility to your workspace.

METHODOLOGIES

CASE STUDY A presentation, in narrative form, of an actual event that has occurred inside an organization. Case studies are not prescriptive, nor are they used to prove a point; they are designed to develop critical analysis and decision-making skills. A case study has a specific time frame, specifies a sequence of events, is narrative in structure, and contains a plot structure—an issue (what should be/have been done?). Use case studies when the goal is to enable participants to apply previously learned theories to the circumstances in the case, decide what is pertinent, identify the real issues, decide what should have been done, and develop a plan of action.

ENERGIZER A short activity that develops readiness for the next session or learning event. Energizers are most commonly used after a break or lunch to stimulate or refocus the group. Many involve some form of physical activity, so they are a useful way to counter post-lunch lethargy. Other uses include transitioning from one topic to another, where "mental" distancing is important.

EXPERIENTIAL LEARNING ACTIVITY (ELA) A facilitator-led intervention that moves participants through the learning cycle from experience to application (also known as a Structured Experience). ELAs are carefully thought-out designs in which there is a definite learning purpose and intended outcome. Each step—everything that participants do during the activity—facilitates the accomplishment of the stated goal. Each ELA includes complete instructions for facilitating the intervention and a clear statement of goals, suggested group size and timing, materials required, an explanation of the process, and, where appropriate, possible variations to the activity. (For more detail on Experiential Learning Activities, see the Introduction to the *Reference Guide to Handbooks and Annuals*, 1999 edition, Pfeiffer, San Francisco.)

GAME A group activity that has the purpose of fostering team spirit and togetherness in addition to the achievement of a pre-stated goal. Usually contrived—undertaking a desert expedition, for example—this type of learning method offers an engaging means for participants to demonstrate and practice business and interpersonal skills. Games are effective for team building and personal development mainly because the goal is subordinate to the process—the means through which participants reach decisions, collaborate, communicate, and generate trust and understanding. Games often engage teams in "friendly" competition.

ICEBREAKER A (usually) short activity designed to help participants overcome initial anxiety in a training session and/or to acquaint the participants with one another. An icebreaker can be a fun activity or can be tied to specific topics or training goals. While a useful tool in itself, the icebreaker comes into its own in situations where tension or resistance exists within a group.

INSTRUMENT A device used to assess, appraise, evaluate, describe, classify, and summarize various aspects of human behavior. The term used to describe an instrument depends primarily on its format and purpose. These terms include survey, questionnaire, inventory, diagnostic, survey, and poll. Some uses of instruments include providing instrumental feedback to group members, studying here-and-now processes or functioning within a group, manipulating group composition, and evaluating outcomes of training and other interventions.

Instruments are popular in the training and HR field because, in general, more growth can occur if an individual is provided with a method for focusing specifically on his or her own behavior. Instruments also are used to obtain information that will serve as a basis for change and to assist in workforce planning efforts.

Paper-and-pencil tests still dominate the instrument landscape with a typical package comprising a facilitator's guide, which offers advice on administering the instrument and interpreting the collected data, and an initial set of instruments. Additional instruments are available separately. Pfeiffer, though, is investing heavily in e-instruments. Electronic instrumentation provides effortless distribution and, for larger groups particularly, offers advantages over paper-and-pencil tests in the time it takes to analyze data and provide feedback.

LECTURETTE A short talk that provides an explanation of a principle, model, or process that is pertinent to the participants' current learning needs. A lecturette is intended to establish a common language bond between the trainer and the participants by providing a mutual frame of reference. Use a lecturette as an introduction to a group activity or event, as an interjection during an event, or as a handout.

MODEL A graphic depiction of a system or process and the relationship among its elements. Models provide a frame of reference and something more tangible, and more easily remembered, than a verbal explanation. They also give participants something to "go on," enabling them to track their own progress as they experience the dynamics, processes, and relationships being depicted in the model.

ROLE PLAY A technique in which people assume a role in a situation/scenario: a customer service rep in an angry-customer exchange, for example. The way in which the role is approached is then discussed and feedback is offered. The role play is often repeated using a different approach and/or incorporating changes made based on feedback received. In other words, role playing is a spontaneous interaction involving realistic behavior under artificial (and safe) conditions.

SIMULATION A methodology for understanding the interrelationships among components of a system or process. Simulations differ from games in that they test or use a model that depicts or mirrors some aspect of reality in form, if not necessarily in content. Learning occurs by studying the effects of change on one or more factors of the model. Simulations are commonly used to test hypotheses about what happens in a system—often referred to as "what if?" analysis—or to examine best-case/worst-case scenarios.

THEORY A presentation of an idea from a conjectural perspective. Theories are useful because they encourage us to examine behavior and phenomena through a different lens.

TOPICS

The twin goals of providing effective and practical solutions for workforce training and organization development and meeting the educational needs of training and human resource professionals shape Pfeiffer's publishing program. Core topics include the following:

Leadership & Management

Communication & Presentation

Coaching & Mentoring

Training & Development

E-Learning

Teams & Collaboration

OD & Strategic Planning

Human Resources

Consulting

What will you find on pfeiffer.com?

- The best in workplace performance solutions for training and HR professionals

- Downloadable training tools, exercises, and content

- Web-exclusive offers

- Training tips, articles, and news

- Seamless on-line ordering

- Author guidelines, information on becoming a Pfeiffer Affiliate, and much more

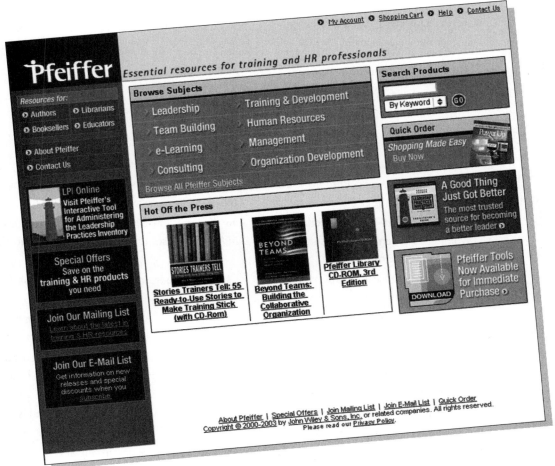

Discover more at www.pfeiffer.com

Customer Care

Have a question, comment, or suggestion? Contact us! We value your feedback and we want to hear from you.

For questions about this or other Pfeiffer products, you may contact us by:

E-mail: **customer@wiley.com**

Mail: **Customer Care Wiley/Pfeiffer**
10475 Crosspoint Blvd.
Indianapolis, IN 46256

Phone: **(US) 800-274-4434** (Outside the US: 317-572-3985)

Fax: **(US) 800-569-0443** (Outside the US: 317-572-4002)

To order additional copies of this title or to browse other Pfeiffer products, visit us online at **www.pfeiffer.com**.

For **Technical Support** questions, call **(800) 274-4434.**

For authors guidelines, log on to www.pfeiffer.com and click on "Resources for Authors."

If you are . . .

A **college bookstore, a professor, an instructor, or work in higher education** and you'd like to place an order or request an exam copy, please contact jbreview@wiley.com.

A **general retail bookseller** and you'd like to establish an account or speak to a local sales representative, contact Melissa Grecco at 201-748-6267 or mgrecco@wiley.com.

An **exclusively on-line bookseller**, contact Amy Blanchard at 530-756-9456 or ablanchard @wiley.com or Jennifer Johnson at 206-568-3883 or jjohnson@wiley.com, both of our Online Sales department.

A **librarian or library representative**, contact John Chambers in our Library Sales department at 201-748-6291 or jchamber@wiley.com.

A **reseller, training company/consultant, or corporate trainer**, contact Charles Regan in our Special Sales department at 201-748-6553 or cregan@wiley.com.

A **specialty retail distributor** (includes specialty gift stores, museum shops, and corporate bulk sales), contact Kim Hendrickson in our Special Sales department at 201-748-6037 or khendric@wiley.com.

Purchasing for the **Federal government**, contact Ron Cunningham in our Special Sales department at 317-572-3053 or rcunning@wiley.com.

Purchasing for a **State or Local government**, contact Charles Regan in our Special Sales department at 201-748-6553 or cregan@wiley.com.